ANCIENT IVORY

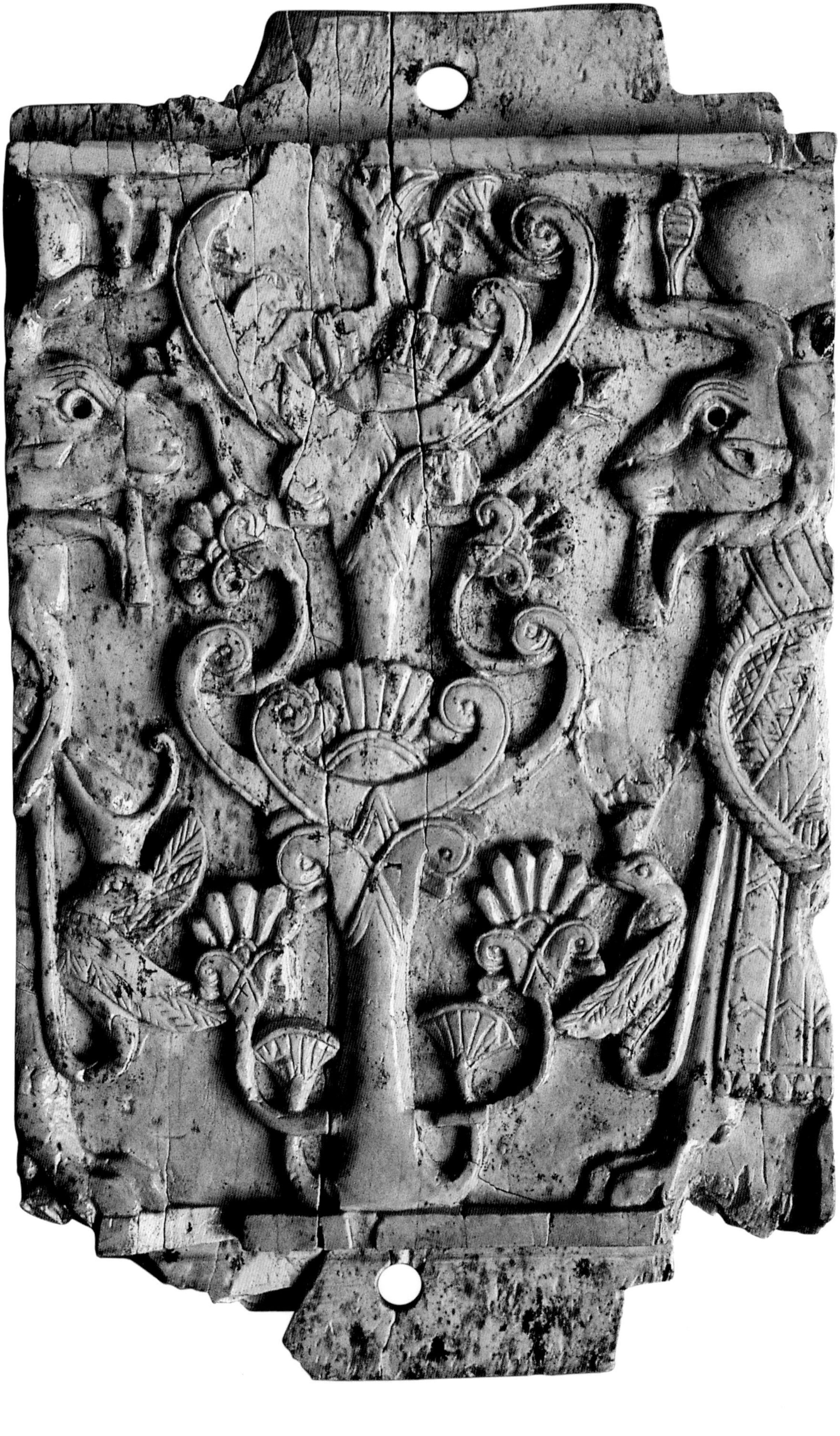

ANCIENT IVORY

Masterpieces
of the
Assyrian Empire

Georgina Herrmann

Thames & Hudson

For my late husband, Luke, who lovingly supported me for more than 52 years, and for Stuart Laidlaw, an invaluable colleague and friend.

FRONTISPIECE 1 A fine panel from Room SW37 in Fort Shalmaneser, showing a stylized tree flanked by a pair of ram-headed sphinxes, crowned with triple *atef* crowns and wearing Osiride beards; the form of the flowering tree is typically Phoenician (15 × 9 × 1.2 cm; 5 ⅞ × 3 ⁹⁄₁₆ × ½ in.). ND 9604, Cleveland Museum of Art.

First published in the United Kingdom in 2017 by Thames & Hudson Ltd, 181A High Holborn, London WC1V 7QX

Ancient Ivory: Masterpieces of the Assyrian Empire © 2017 Thames & Hudson Ltd, London

Photographs © 2017 Georgina Herrmann unless otherwise stated

Designed by Samuel Clark
www.bytheskydesign.com

All Rights Reserved. No part of this publication may be reproduced or transmitted in any form or by any means, electronic or mechanical, including photocopy, recording or any other information storage and retrieval system, without prior permission in writing from the publisher.

British Library Cataloguing-in-Publication Data
A catalogue record for this book is available from the British Library

ISBN 978-0-500-05191-7

Printed and bound in China by Reliance Printing (Shenzhen) Co. Ltd

To find out about all our publications, please visit www.thamesandhudson.com. There you can subscribe to our e-newsletter, browse or download our current catalogue, and buy any titles that are in print.

Contents

Preface   From Discovery to Destruction   6

Introduction   Masterpieces of Ancient Ivory   8

1 The City of Nimrud and its Discovery   18
2 Ah, Assyria!   40
3 The Phoenicians: Master Craftsmen   54
4 Syro-Phoenician Ivories   104
5 The Ivories of North Syria   118
6 The Influence of Regionalism on Furniture
     and the Minor Arts   152
7 The Age of Ivory   186

Map   196
Notes   198
Suggested Reading   201
Bibliography   202
Acknowledgments   205
Index   206

Preface

From Discovery to Destruction

From start to finish the omens were good.*

All archaeology is a form of destruction, but one that also reveals lost cities, their buildings and their contents. Among the many remarkable discoveries at the site of Nimrud in northern Iraq, with its palaces, temples and royal tombs, were thousands of superb ivories, the largest collection of ancient ivory ever found. The first ones were discovered in the mid-nineteenth century, but most were found in the second half of the twentieth century. The ivories were found in the ruins of buildings, either in rooms filled with broken mud brick or – in the case of the finest examples – better preserved in the sludge at the bottoms of wells.

In 1849 the first archaeologist of Nimrud, Austen Henry Layard, described the difficulty of raising them. He wrote: 'These ivories, when uncovered, adhered so firmly to the soil, and were in so forward a state of decomposition, that I had the greatest difficulty in extracting them, even in fragments.'[1] However, lifting the ivories is only the first step in a long process. They urgently need consolidation to enable them to survive the changes in their environment and the perils of transport. In the nineteenth century surviving examples were 'boil[ed] in Gelatine'.[2] As well as conservation, ivories need a stable environment, access to air and a reasonable level of humidity. Constant movement is a major risk, to which pieces are subjected as a result of the installation of new storage systems in museums, or because they are selected to be put on show, when they must be moved within the 'home' museum or sent away for a travelling exhibition. Fragments are often lost, like the hands of the beautiful kneeling pharaoh figure ND 7589 (**2**).[3]

However, this level of damage is minor compared to the results of political upheaval. In recent decades the ivories in Iraq and, more lately, Syria, have suffered major damage from the necessity to pack them away in haste, often with inadequate storage material, and move them to secure locations. In Iraq the ivories first had to be packed up as a result of the Gulf War fought by the United Nations coalition after the Iraqi invasion of Kuwait in 1990. Then, following the attack on New York on 11 September 2001, there was the even more disastrous American–British invasion of Iraq in 2003 and the 'Shock and Awe' campaign of widespread bombing. The results were appalling. A number of museums, including the National Museum of Iraq in Baghdad, were sacked and looted. Many of the finest ivories had been packed and stored in the vaults of the Central Bank in Baghdad, but they were seriously damaged when the site was flooded with sewage water. The vaults were drained and some basic conservation was applied to the objects, which were then returned to the vaults for security. If they are still there, their condition is unknown. Many objects were looted, both items that had remained on exhibition in museums and others from storage areas. One of the most famous looted ivories is the exquisite lioness mauling a youth (ND 2547, **103**, p. 90),[4] one of a pair, found in the sludge at the bottom of a well; fortunately, the other plaque survives in the British Museum (ND 2548, **104**, p. 91).[5] Since 2003 there has been widespread looting of sites.

In Syria the continuing horror of the Civil War, which began in 2011, has also resulted in massive looting and pillaging of sites and museums. However, a new level of destruction, the deliberate targeting of ancient sites and their destruction with bulldozers and explosives, has been initiated by the Islamic State of Iraq and the Levant (ISIL or IS). The group conquered much of northern and central Iraq

ABOVE **2** Kneeling pharaoh figure, in the Phoenician style, delicately inlaid (10.4 × 6.4 × 1 cm; 4⅛ × 2½ × ⅜ in.): (left) as it was when found at Nimrud in the 1960s, and (right) thirty years later. ND 7589, Baghdad, National Museum of Iraq. Photograph Mick Sharp. (See also **72**, p. 69.)

in a lightning invasion in 2014, their greatest coup being the capture of Mosul, the principal northern city of Iraq. Museums were ransacked, books in libraries were burnt, and the great Assyrian sites of Nineveh, Nimrud and Khorsabad were targeted, as well as Parthian Hatra and Christian monasteries. Videos, seen worldwide, show the great Throne Room of Ashurnasirpal II being blown up with drums of explosive, and bulldozers destroying the walls.

At the time of writing there is no sign of an end to the appalling destruction of life and heritage. This book tells the story of a few of the magnificent carved ivories found at Nimrud. Collected by the Assyrian kings from all over the Levant, these form an outstanding record of the minor arts of the early first millennium BC. Many of them may no longer exist.

From Discovery to Destruction 7

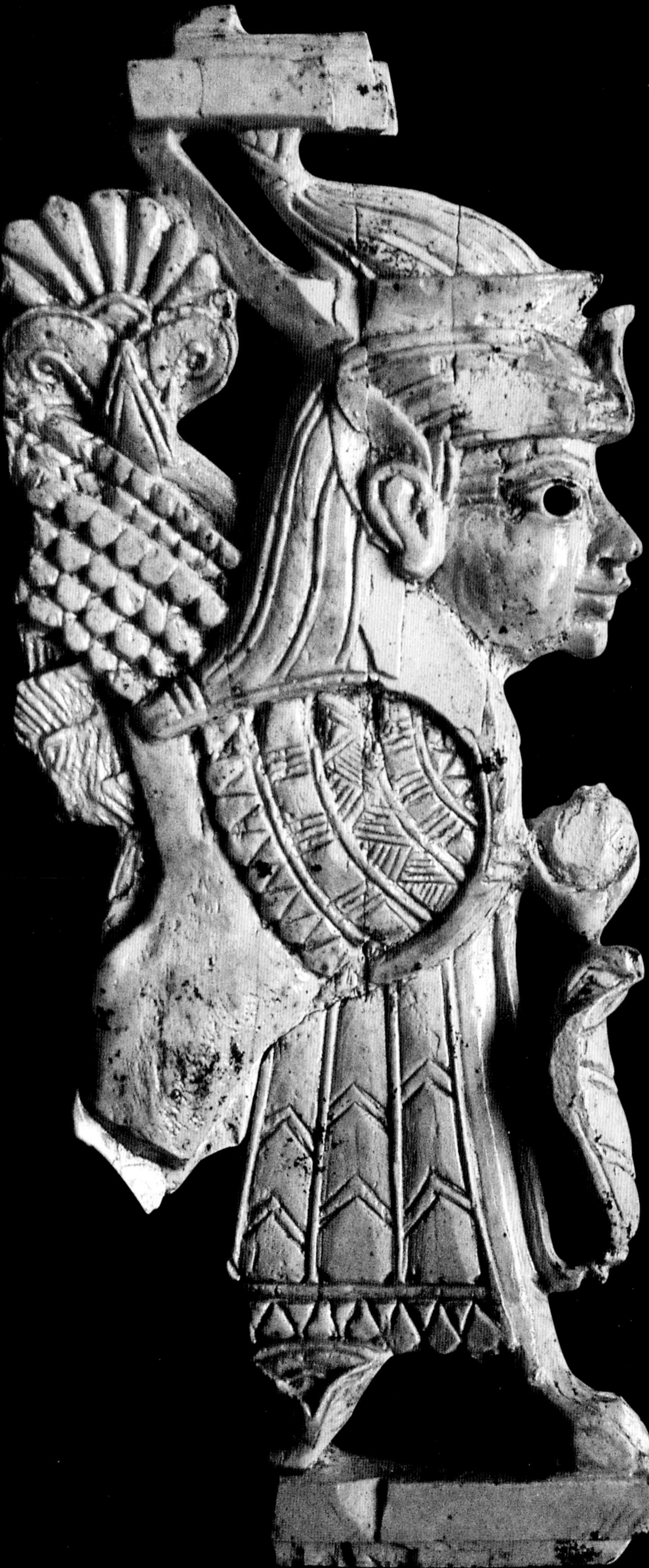

Introduction

Masterpieces of Ancient Ivory

A deep mystery hangs over Assyria, Babylonia, and Chaldaea. With these names are linked great nations and great cities dimly shadowed forth in history: mighty ruins, in the midst of deserts, defying by their very desolation and lack of definite form, the description of the traveller: the remnants of mighty races still roving over the land; the fulfilling and fulfilment of prophecies; the plains to which the Jew and the Gentile alike look as the cradle of their race.*

The ruins of one of these great cities can be found in northern Iraq at the site now known as Nimrud, so named by the Arabs after Nimrod, the mighty hunter. Nimrud is located in the heart of ancient Assyria, on the River Tigris, south of Mosul (see map, pp. 196–97). The remains are those of Kalhu, one of the Assyrian capital cities, which was founded by Ashurnasirpal II (r. 883–859 BC). Untold wealth has been found in its palaces and store-rooms, including more ancient ivory than has been discovered anywhere else in the world, as well as the richly endowed tombs of the Assyrian queens. Alas, the fame of Nimrud today arises not from its outstanding treasures, which should make it a household name, but from its destruction by Islamic State. Here, I intend to illustrate and describe a few of the thousands of superlative ivories found there.

Ivory

The tusk of an elephant (unfortunately for the elephant) provides one of the finest materials in the animal kingdom. It is strong and has a wonderful colour and shine. It works like a hard wood and can be used as a decorative inlay, but it is also strong enough to form a complete piece of furniture. It has always been highly valued and has been used continuously from Palaeolithic times right up to the present day. As a result, some elephant populations, such as the Syrian elephant, were hunted to extinction during the early first millennium BC, and many more have disappeared since. Once, herds of elephants roamed along the Nile (the city of Elephantine in Upper Egypt is named after them), through Sudan, Ethiopia and north Africa, as well as India. Present-day populations are restricted, and are under serious threat both because of loss of habitat and because of a continuing passion for ivory as a material from which to make luxury goods, such as trinkets and chopsticks. Despite the imposition of bans on the trade in ivory, its value is so high – and rising – that poaching is rife. Between 2010 and 2012 more than 100,000 elephants were killed; their tusks were mostly smuggled through east Africa to illegal markets in Asia. In 2015 it was reported that poachers were receiving as much as $2,015 per kilo for ivory. An undertaking by the Chinese authorities to ban the ivory trade by the end of 2017 is welcome, but there is still a real risk that this magnificent animal may become extinct because of the insatiable demand for the wonderful material furnished by its tusks.

3 One of a set of seven Phoenician panels, showing a human-headed sphinx, crowned with the Egyptian double crown on the *nemes* headcloth; an *uraeus* adorns the front of the crown and another is suspended from the sphinx's chest (10.9 × 4.4 × 1.2 cm; 4⁵⁄₁₆ × 1¾ × ½ in.). ND 9606, San Francisco, Fine Arts Museum.

with gold foil or coloured with paint or with inlays of glass or precious stones.

The same tools can be used for wood and ivory, and the two materials were frequently used together. As always, ancient Egypt provides a mass of material, both artefacts and images. Paintings from the Eighteenth Dynasty tomb of Rekhmire show carpenters at work, using a wide range of the same techniques as are still employed today (**6**). They show the use of the saw, the axe and the adze, and a range of hammers and chisels, as well as techniques for cutting angles, sharpening tools, applying glue with a brush and burnishing. Carpentry is a timeless profession, which continued unchanged until the twentieth century and the introduction of machine tools.

The finest ivory artefacts were carved from elephant tusks, but there were alternative materials, such as hippopotamus ivory and also bone. The lower canines of the hippopotamus are more curved than elephant tusks, forming almost a half-circle. The ivory is pure white and quite hard, with a protective outer layer of enamel. Hippo ivory was extensively used in the late second millennium BC, especially in the ivories found at Ras Shamra (ancient Ugarit) on the Syrian coast. A cheaper alternative was bone, used for more practical articles and for some carvings. Bone resembles ivory but lacks the grainy appearance, and the matter in the cavity is spongy. With the melting of some of the ice cover in Siberia in recent times, the bodies of mammoth elephants have been exposed; their tusks – larger than those of a modern elephant, a browny colour and often striated – are now widely exploited. They are nearly as valuable as those of the African elephant.

There has been dispute for many years about the source of the ivory used at Nimrud. Was it from the Syrian elephant, already extinct in the early first millennium BC, or from the African or Indian elephant? When the tusks are fresh, it is easy to differentiate between the latter two. African ivory is a pale blond colour, is harder and more brilliant and takes a finer polish than the Asian, which is denser, whiter and more opaque. Today, using DNA testing, it is possible to identify the exact game reserve from which ivory has been

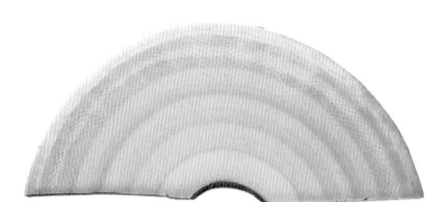

ABOVE **4** African savannah elephant. Photograph Tarquin Millington Drake.

LEFT **5** Horizontal section of a tusk, showing the growth rings and part of the central hollow.

The length of the tusks varies according to the species and sex of the animal. Tusks from African savannah elephants (**4**) are generally larger than those from African forest or Indian elephants: the tusks of male elephants may be up to 3 metres (10 ft) long and more than 20 cm (8 in.) wide at the base, and may weigh up to 68 kilos (150 lb). The tusk consists of a series of growth rings, which can be easily seen when the tusk is cut longitudinally or horizontally (**5**); a horizontal cut often shows a grainy 'herringbone' effect, and a longitudinal cut reveals vertical striations. Ancient ivory often breaks or striates on these fault-lines. All parts of the tusk can be used, from its hollow core where it joins the head to its curving tip. The hollow base was used to form cylindrical boxes, and the rest was cut either across or with the grain to form plaques of varying sizes. The principal limitation of working with ivory is the size of the pieces that can be obtained from a tusk, but the ancient craftsman made use of every fragment, joining pieces together with dowels and mortise joints, and patching imperfections where necessary. Ivory was worked both as solid panels and as openwork. Despite its inherent beauty, the material was rarely left plain. To emphasize its value it might be overlaid

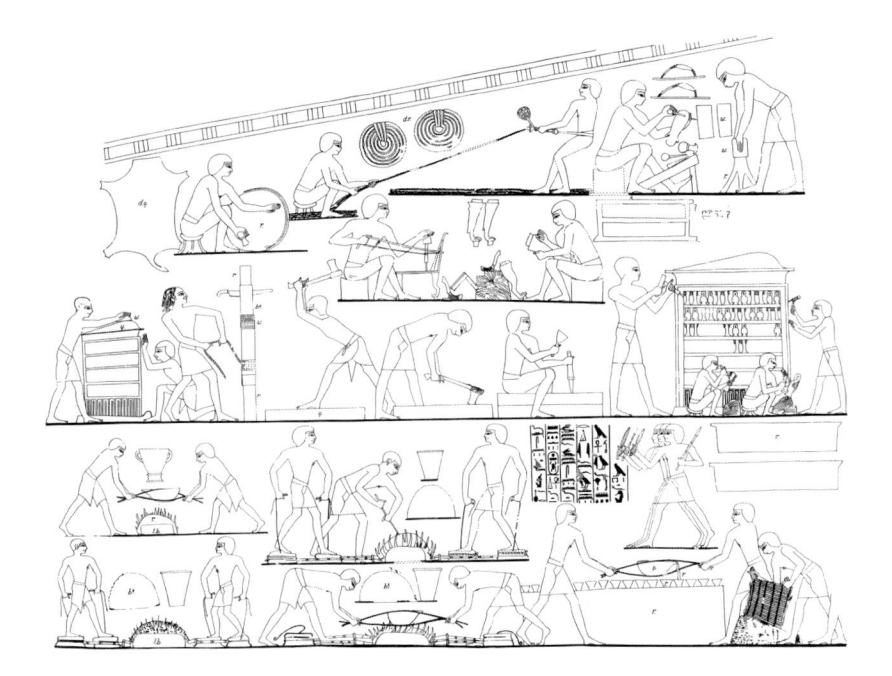

6 The whole range of carpentry skills, including splitting timber, drilling, checking for straightness, applying hot glue with a brush and burnishing, as illustrated on the wall of the Eighteenth Dynasty tomb of Rekhmire (Tomb 100) at Thebes. Killen 1980, 13, fig. 7. Metropolitan Museum of Art, New York.

poached, but, when ivory has been buried for thousands of years, all the collagen (the protein used in DNA analysis) has disappeared and no chemical differences are identifiable. However, the balance of probability must be that the principal source of the ivory used at Kalhu was the African elephant. This suggestion is based on two factors. One is the size of some ivories: for example, the head known as the 'Ugly Sister' (ND 2549; **177**, p. 123), which was cut from the longitudinal section of a large tusk, measures some 18 × 13.7 cm (7⅛ × 5⅜ in.) and weighs 332 grammes (c. 11¼ oz).[1] The other is that the majority of the ivories found at Nimrud were not made there but were imported from the Phoenician west. Phoenician traders were in frequent contact with Egypt, the Sudan and north Africa.

The importance of ivory

Ivory has always had a unique appeal by virtue of its rarity and the difficulty of acquiring it: hunting elephants in antiquity was fraught with danger. As a result, ivory has, since early times, been synonymous with status and luxury. Some ancient ivory was sourced in southern Egypt. A superb early example is a knife with an elaborately carved ivory handle and a flint blade, found in Gebel el Arak in Egypt and dating to about 3300 BC. Carved in low relief, the handle is decorated with a scene of Mesopotamian inspiration – a hero fighting lions, and processions of people – showing that even at this early date there was contact between widely separated cultures.

The late second millennium BC was a time of intense international diplomacy, long-distance trade and immense wealth: it is known today as 'the International Age'. The great rulers of the day, the pharaohs of Egypt, the Hittites in Anatolia, the Mitanni in Syria and the Kassites of Babylon, considered themselves to be 'brothers' and regularly sent one another good wishes and engaged in what was effectively a form of trade by means of carefully balanced gift exchange, including the giving of their daughters. This custom is recorded in a collection of cuneiform tablets known as the 'Amarna letters', which were found by a peasant woman in 1887.[2]

> I am told that in my brother's country there is everything and my brother is in want of nothing. In my country as well there is everything and I am in want for nothing. Nevertheless the custom of exchanging gifts, passed on from ancient times and early rulers, is a good thing….let this tradition remain firm between us.[3]

Egypt during the Eighteenth Dynasty entered a new world of splendour, luxury and artistic sophistication. Thanks to the Egyptians' belief in life after death, their tomb culture and the desert climate, many examples of their magnificent furniture, jewelry and small objects have survived. Egyptian furniture was a valued gift, and Amenhotep III (r. 1390–1352 BC) sent beds and chairs of ebony, gold and ivory to the king of Babylon: 'Behold I have sent thee as a present for the new house, by the hand of Sutti, one bed of ebony, overlaid with ivory and gold'.[4] Among the treasures found in the tomb of Tutankhamun is an exquisite headrest, supported on a kneeling male, flanked by a pair of lions, and carved out of two pieces of a huge tusk (7). Letters from the early second millennium site of Mari on the Euphrates make evident the high status of ivory, and of ivory furniture in particular, referring to thrones made for the gods,[5] while the Old Testament records that Solomon made 'a great throne of ivory, and overlaid it with pure gold' (2 Chronicles 9:17). Ivory thrones were so highly valued that they were probably reserved for deities and kings.

Such wealth is reflected in the Levant in the ivories found at the Late Bronze Age site of Ugarit, which illustrate the common artistic language of the time. The finest pieces include a superb head, a carved horn, a pedestal table inlaid with ivory, and a double-sided footboard of a bed decorated with panels of Egyptian inspiration.[6] Another Late Bronze Age collection was found in 1937 in the so-called 'treasury' at the Canaanite city of Megiddo. The ivories include boxes and caskets, fan handles and combs, cosmetics bowls, gaming boards and openwork furniture panels imported from a variety of sources: from Egypt itself, from Syria and Cyprus, and from Hittite Anatolia. The collection constitutes the first 'mixed assemblage' of ivories to be found in an excavation. This led the excavator to suggest that ivory collecting at Megiddo may have been the unusual hobby of a Canaanite prince.[7] However, since that time most collections that have been found are mixed assemblages, which suggests that ivory was not only an appropriate royal gift, but also (regardless of the form of the artefact) a source of wealth to be stored in treasuries. Gaming boxes, perhaps for playing the game of Twenty Squares, were a favourite luxury

ABOVE 7 The splendour and artistic sophistication of Eighteenth Dynasty Egypt is illustrated by discoveries from the Tomb of Tutankhamun, including this ivory headrest or pillow (H 17.5 cm; 6⅞ in.). Cairo, Museum of Egyptian Antiquities.

BELOW 8 A magnificent ivory gaming board, of box type, found in a tomb at Enkomi, Cyprus, showing a charioteering noblemen hunting bulls, goats and stags (6.3 × 29.1 × 8.1 cm; 2½ × 11⁷⁄₁₆ × 3³⁄₁₆ in.). London, British Museum.

item. A fine example, found in a tomb at Enkomi in Cyprus and dated to the late thirteenth or early twelfth century BC, was probably imported from Syria. The design on a long panel shows a dynamic bull hunt conducted from a chariot, in a mixture of western Asiatic and Mycenaean styles (**8**). What is of particular interest is that the image foreshadows a ninth-century depiction of a chariot hunt on a chair-back from Nimrud (**242**, p. 155), which suggests a continuity of design through several centuries.

While eclectic collecting and longevity of motif may be two factors affecting the study of ivory, another is the heirloom. One of the best examples of the long-term preservation of an object over many generations is an elephant tusk discovered in a treasury adjacent to the throne room at Tell Miqne (the site of the Philistine city of Ekron). Ekron was sacked by Nebuchadnezzar in 603 BC. The tusk, however, is dated to the thirteenth century BC by a cartouche of Pharaoh Mernephtah. As the excavator, Seymour Gitin, commented: 'The ivory appears to have been curated over a period of 600 years.'[8]

The importance of ivory has continued through the millennia and across the area to the present day. Its value, and the value also attached to the craftsmen who worked it, is illustrated by two superb caskets made in early Islamic Córdoba and now in the Ashmolean Museum, Oxford. These were made in the royal workshops, and both the patrons and the artists were named. One of the most famous surviving ivory thrones today is that of Maximian, Archbishop of Ravenna (r. 546–53), which is entirely covered with ivory panels depicting biblical themes (**9**); it has been suggested that it may have been made in Egypt or Syria. However, the largest quantity of worked ivory was recovered not from Egypt or Europe but from Nimrud. So many ivories, tens of thousands of pieces, have been found there that the period of their production in the first millennium BC can justifiably be called 'the Age of Ivory'. So great is the quantity that it represents a positive graveyard of elephants, and keeps scholars busy to this day.

BELOW **9** Thrones of ivory and gold were highly prestigious and were reserved for deities and kings. The throne of Solomon, mentioned in 1 Kings 10:18, is one of the most famous from antiquity, while that of Archbishop Maximian of Ravenna (shown here) is a rare survival from c. 546–53 AD. Ravenna, Archiepiscopal Museum.

Masterpieces of Ancient Ivory

The ivories from Nimrud

The first ivories were discovered at Nimrud in November 1845 by the young Victorian traveller and adventurer Austen Henry Layard. Many more were found in the following decades, principally by William Kennett Loftus, who unearthed a 'horse load' of burnt and broken ivories in the Burnt Palace. However, the majority was found a century later by an expedition of the British School of Archaeology in Iraq, directed by Max Mallowan, the husband of Agatha Christie. Since then, some of the finest and most complete ivories have been retrieved by the Iraqi State Board of Antiquities and Heritage from Well AJ of the North West Palace. The excavation of this well had been attempted by Mallowan but abandoned because of the danger that the structure would collapse.

It is remarkable that, although they were found in an Assyrian capital city, very few of the ivories were carved in the distinctive Assyrian style, well known from Assyrian sculptures. Most of the ivories were imported from other centres in the Levant, some as diplomatic gifts but most as tribute or booty after the conquest of their cities of origin, and were carved in a variety of different styles. Once they arrived at Kalhu, they were stripped of their gold overlays and were stored in huge magazines or repositories, though some may have been kept in treasuries. There is little evidence that the Assyrians actually used them – they preferred their own art. Art had a prophylactic purpose: magical figures were designed to keep evil spirits at bay.

The sheer volume of ivory recovered overwhelmed the small British team that worked at Nimrud from 1949 to 1963. For instance, one of the great halls, over 30 metres (100 ft) long, was filled to a depth of no less than 1.5 metres (5 ft) from the surface to the pavement with thousands of ivory fragments embedded in fallen mud brick. The task of gently raising these fragile fragments from their mud matrix, taking them back to the dig house, consolidating them, trying to find joins and recording them was only the beginning of a monumental task that is still continuing, and has resulted in the publication of many of them. No fewer than seven volumes of the *Ivories from Nimrud* series have appeared to date. The series is organized principally by the location of the finds, but other categories relate to function (notably the use of ivories to decorate the bridle harness of horses) and the easily recognizable Assyrian style.

Found smashed to pieces and out of context, the ivories still represent an enormous jigsaw puzzle, despite over a century of study. However, ongoing analysis is beginning to build a pattern of production. The fundamental division of the ivories into three regional groupings was made in the early twentieth century, based on only about 150 pieces, which had either been published in encyclopaedias or were exhibited in cases in the British Museum. The first group was the easy-to-recognize Assyrian style, well known from the Assyrian sculptures brought back to England by Layard. A fine example, found by the Iraqis in Well AJ, shows two registers of courtiers advancing to the left (IM 79537, **10**).[9] Of the upper register only the feet survive, but the two figures in the lower register are complete down to the knee; their lower legs would have been carved on the next panel, so originally there would have been three registers to the design. The nearer courtier has a fine moustache and is bearded; the curls of his shoulder-length hair and beard are similar to those of the king. The second courtier is clean-shaven. They have large eyes with strong eyebrows, and their noses are slightly curved, the mouths firm. They are wearing long garments, over which are wound fringed shawls with decorated borders. Similar courtiers are frequently represented both on the reliefs and on ivories.

The second group shows a strong debt to the art of Egypt and is called Phoenician. This is the largest group of ivories found at Nimrud and is the most aesthetically pleasing. It consists of slender figures, often deities or sphinxes, harmoniously displayed in the available space. Many examples are brilliantly coloured with gold overlays and glass inlays, and the panels are jewel-like. A typical fragment belonging to one of the groups of Phoenician ivories, known as the Ornate Group, one of the largest and most colourful groups, is a beautiful openwork winged deity from Fort Shalmaneser. He is wearing a short Egyptian-style wig, formed of raised pegs of ivory, once covered with gold

LEFT 10 A magnificently modelled Assyrian ivory, showing a pair of courtiers; part of a tall panel, which originally decorated a throne (13.7 × 5 × 0.6 cm; 5⅜ × 2 × ¼ in.). IM 79537, Baghdad, National Museum of Iraq.

ABOVE 11 A powerful image of a stocky sphinx with chubby cheeks, confronting the onlooker; carved at a North Syrian centre (6.6 × 10.3 cm; 2⅝ × 4¹/₁₆ in.). ND 10342, Baghdad, National Museum of Iraq. Photograph Mick Sharp.

overlays, which held blue glass cylinders set on a blue frit bedding. His eye and collar were inlaid with blue. Perched between his wings on a papyrus bud is a hawk, holding a flail over his back (ND 8068, **130**, p. 100).[10]

The third group is very different. It generally lacks Egyptian elements but is related to a series of sculptures found at sites along the Syro-Turkish border, and therefore became known as North Syrian. A typical example from one of these series of North Syrian ivories shows a round-faced sphinx that completely fills the surface of the panel (ND 10342): it boldly stares out at the onlooker – all grace and elegance abandoned, to be replaced by raw power (**11**).[11]

The three divisions still hold good, though they have been refined and subdivided, and another group, Syro-Phoenician ivories, has been added. These are based on Phoenician originals but are carved in an un-Phoenician way, with squatter figures filling the panels.

Masterpieces of Ancient Ivory 15

The published archive today includes both the ivories found in the nineteenth century by Layard and Loftus and many of those found in the twentieth century; it consists of thousands of pieces, some fairly complete, some fragmentary. Relatively little help with the analysis of this huge corpus is provided by the locations in which the ivories were found. All the information the context offers is that imported ivories must have reached Nimrud before the sacks of the city by an alliance of Babylonians and Medes in 614 and 612 BC. It supplies no clue to where or when they were made, or even to when they arrived at Nimrud.

The first step, once this mass of material was recorded, was to look for similar pieces from a particular room. Despite the comprehensive sacking of Nimrud, the archaeological context, though disturbed, remains important. It provides a sensible starting point – one recognized as early as the 1840s by Layard, who carefully recorded where he found his ivories. Fortunately, many items were used in sets of matching panels or plaques, which would have been mounted on wooden frames; they share the same shape, size, style, framing and method of fixing, and are often decorated with the same subject. Sets form the foundation of the study of the Nimrud ivories: they make it possible to begin to assemble coherent groups of ivories from the vast quantity of material. The next step is to arrange sets into larger groups called 'style-groups'. This is more subjective because there are fewer points of direct comparison. Layard found most of his ivories in the doorway of Room V/W of the North West Palace. These form an excellent illustration not only of the importance of context but also of the possibility of uniting sets by subject. He found two sets of panels, one showing young males and the other the 'woman at the window' motif. Because they were found in the same place, are similar in height, framing and tenoning, and share similar carving of faces, ears and eyes, Layard suggested that they formed parts of the same piece of furniture (see further chapter 1, p. 39). Matching these to similar pieces from elsewhere in the site makes it possible to expand the group, gathering related pieces into larger assemblages or traditions.

An outline of the book

The first chapter discusses the discovery of Nimrud, one of the iconic sites of ancient Mesopotamia, and describes some of those who worked there in the nineteenth and twentieth centuries. While the best-preserved ivories were found in the wells of the North West Palace, the majority were found in store-rooms in an outlying palace–arsenal known as Fort Shalmaneser. The second covers the rise of Assyria in the ninth century BC, and the building of his capital, Kalhu (biblical Calah), by Ashurnasirpal II (r. 883–859 BC). His building programme was complemented by the development of an artistic one. The walls of his new palace were lined with carved marble slabs, decorated with magical figures and with dynamic scenes showing the victorious king as a divine intermediary, as a hunter and as a warrior. His distinctive style was applied across the media, from stone sculptures to bronze bands decorating doors and furniture and to ivory, ceramics and painting, the narrative scenes complementing but not copying those on the reliefs, thus creating an integrated decorative programme. However, the Assyrians were master metal-smiths rather than carpenters: there was no wood-working tradition in Assyria and relatively little ivory carved in the Assyrian style has been found. Furthermore, the distribution of ivory within the site is significant. Ivories decorated with narrative scenes cluster around areas close to throne daises, clearly because they were reserved for the decoration of the royal throne. None was found in the great store-rooms filled with booty, and there was a similar absence, not only of Assyrian ivories but of any ivories, in the richly equipped tombs of the Assyrian queens. This raises the question whether these luxury items were reserved for kings and priests.

Chapters 3–5 discuss the imported Levantine ivories – the Phoenician, Syro-Phoenician and North Syrian ivories. The ongoing programme of the publication of the Nimrud ivories has made possible numerous revisions and refinements to the three regional traditions originally identified. Using context, style and technical features, ivories can be attributed not only to these traditions but to specific style-groups within them. On the basis of this analysis, it is clear that Phoenician examples make up the majority of the ivories found at Nimrud. Indeed, there are more Phoenician ivories than all the others put together.

The Phoenician ivories at last provide a proper record of the art of this little-known people, who were famed in antiquity for their skill as mariners, traders, and craftsmen. Nevertheless, the Phoenicians themselves suffered a bad press in classical literature, where they are characterized as thieves and kidnappers, and in modern times their ivories have been considered 'repetitious and largely mass-produced', the 'product of commercial minds',[12] a criticism based on minimal evidence. Much of the book is, therefore, dedicated to the Phoenician ivories, which are the finest, both aesthetically and technically, of the ivories found at Nimrud.

The majority of the thousand-odd pieces attributed to the Phoenician tradition consist of a number of style-groups that are closely linked in character and technique. The use of colour is very much a feature of these groups, though some examples are simply gilded. These ivories share so many features that it is probable they were carved in a single, extremely wealthy and powerful centre. The rest, while still typically Phoenician, are slightly less well designed and competently executed, and lack inlays. They probably originated in one or more of the many Phoenician city-states located along the Levant coast.

While Phoenician ivories reflect the Egyptian influence long evident in the coastal cities, North Syrian ivories are fundamentally different in character, style and technique. Their message is compelling and often confrontational, with a characteristic range of subjects and types of object. There are a number of different style-groups, some of which can be linked to the varied sculptural traditions of the newly independent minor kingdoms of the area. With the ivories of this tradition it is possible to suggest a number of different centres where they might have been made, and to propose possible dates for their manufacture.

In the 1970s the three regional traditions – Assyrian, North Syrian and Phoenician – began to be questioned, not only owing to the recognition of individual style-groups, but also because it emerged that there was probably a fourth tradition, perhaps located in south or central Syria. This Syro-Phoenician tradition, again made up of a number of style-groups, consists of ivories that combine traditional Phoenician iconography with squat, 'un-Phoenician' proportions. Interestingly, the subjects of these ivories all prove to be versions of Phoenician motifs, perhaps reflecting borrowing by the recently founded Aramaean states, who were striving to establish their independent identities and adapting ideas used by their well-established neighbours.

Within the limitations imposed by the size of the elephant's tusk, ivory was used both to decorate furniture and to make a range of small objects, such as boxes, bowls and fan handles. The varied regional traditions are reflected in the range of production of the different types of object. For instance, furniture influenced by Egypt and used in Phoenicia is very different from that current in northern Syria or Assyria. Chapter 6, therefore, discusses the various types of furniture and small objects recovered from Nimrud.

While identifying the regional traditions is important, another key task is to try to suggest where and when the ivories might have been made, and to consider the possible organization of workshops and the ivory trade. This relies on various strands of evidence, such as the few ivories that have been excavated outside Assyria, which have been found in contexts from western Iran to Italy. Equally, it is also usually accepted that 'minor art', such as the ivories and the beautiful engraved bowls of gold, silver and bronze, reflects 'major art' – that is, the sculptures found along the Syro-Turkish border, as well as a few in the Levant

Finally, there is historical and literary evidence; references in the Old Testament, in Assyrian records of tribute and booty and in classical texts. The last chapter discusses some of these issues. However, with so little 'hard' evidence, especially from the probable areas of production, suggestions may be made but proof must await new discoveries. Little archaeological work can be undertaken while conflict and political turmoil in the region persist. In the meantime these small masterpieces are a testament to the skill and virtuosity of the ancient craftsmen and their patrons.

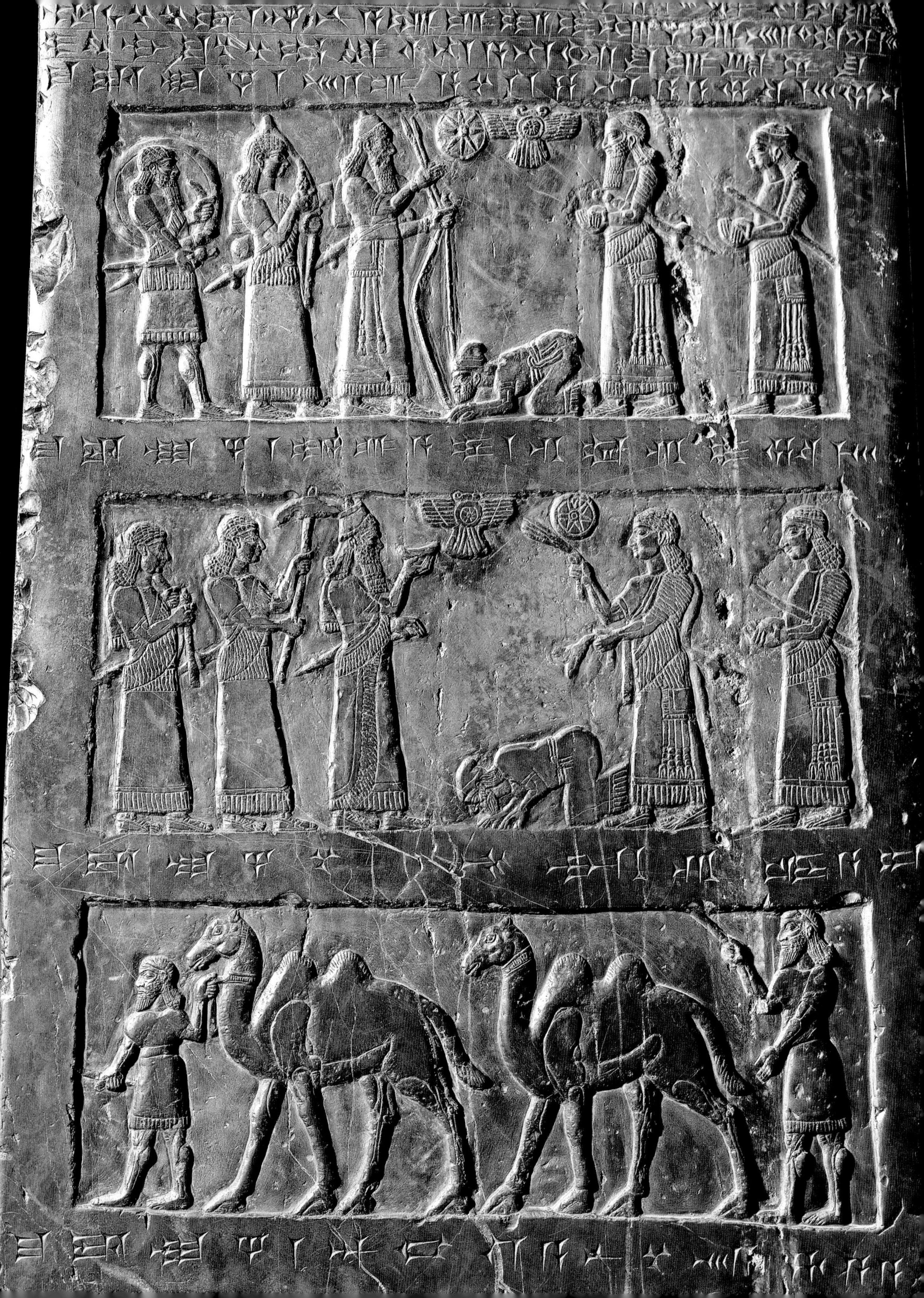

Chapter 1

The City of Nimrud and its Discovery

It was at the site of Nimrud that [Mallowan] decided he had found the perfect mound, redolent as it was with history of the sort of archaeological endeavours he wished to emulate, and ringing with the names of archaeologists in whose tradition Mallowan was beginning to see himself: Layard, Rassam, Loftus and George Smith.*

Nimrud is one of the most beautiful archaeological sites in Iraq, and it is also one of the most generous to those who have worked there. With its magnificent bas-reliefs lining the walls of palaces and temples and its untold wealth – the greatest quantity of superbly carved ivories found at any site and the treasures from the tombs of named queens of Assyria – the site should be as famous as the tomb of Tutankhamun in the Valley of the Kings. Although the tombs were mentioned in press reports at the time of their discovery in 1988 and 1989, they did not receive the international coverage and attention they deserved. Today, Iraq is better known for military disasters during the ill-fated reign of Saddam Husain, with his invasion first of Iran in September 1980 and then of Kuwait in August 1990, and the subsequent attacks by the UN coalition in 1991 and by American and British forces in 2003. These have been followed by years of continuing political chaos, culminating with the invasion of northern Iraq by Islamic State in 2014 and the capture of Mosul. In 2015 the ruins of the North West Palace, with its fine bas-reliefs, were deliberately smashed and destroyed by so-called Islamic State. The outstanding wealth of this iconic site is today largely forgotten: the focus is on the appalling recent events rather than the glory of the past.

Nimrud is situated between the dynastic capital of Ashur and the other major Assyrian city, Nineveh, across the River Tigris from Mosul. The period of relative Assyrian decline, caused by disruptions at the end of the second millennium BC, was reversed in the early first millennium by a series of strong kings. Ashurnasirpal II (r. 883–859 BC) dramatically expanded their programme of conquest, successfully campaigning to north, east and south, but above all to the west, reaching the Mediterranean in 877. For some three centuries, albeit with periods of decline, the Assyrian kings created an empire, which at its greatest stretched from Iran to Egypt, from the Mediterranean to the Gulf, and they brought vast quantities of tribute and booty back to their capital cities. Ashurnasirpal II moved his capital from Ashur to Kalhu, known as Calah in the Bible and now as Nimrud. It consists of an acropolis or walled citadel, on which were built palaces and temples, and a large walled outer or lower

12 The Black Obelisk, discovered at Nimrud by Austen Henry Layard in the mid-19th century, limestone, 825 BC (H 197.48 cm; 77¾ in.). London, British Museum, inv. no. 118885. The obelisk records the campaigns of Shalmaneser III. This detail shows Shalmaneser, accompanied by his officials, receiving the submission of the king of Gilzanu (top register) and of Jehu of Israel (middle register); the two-humped camels (bottom register) are listed as tribute from the land of Musri (Egypt).

THE NORTH WEST PALACE

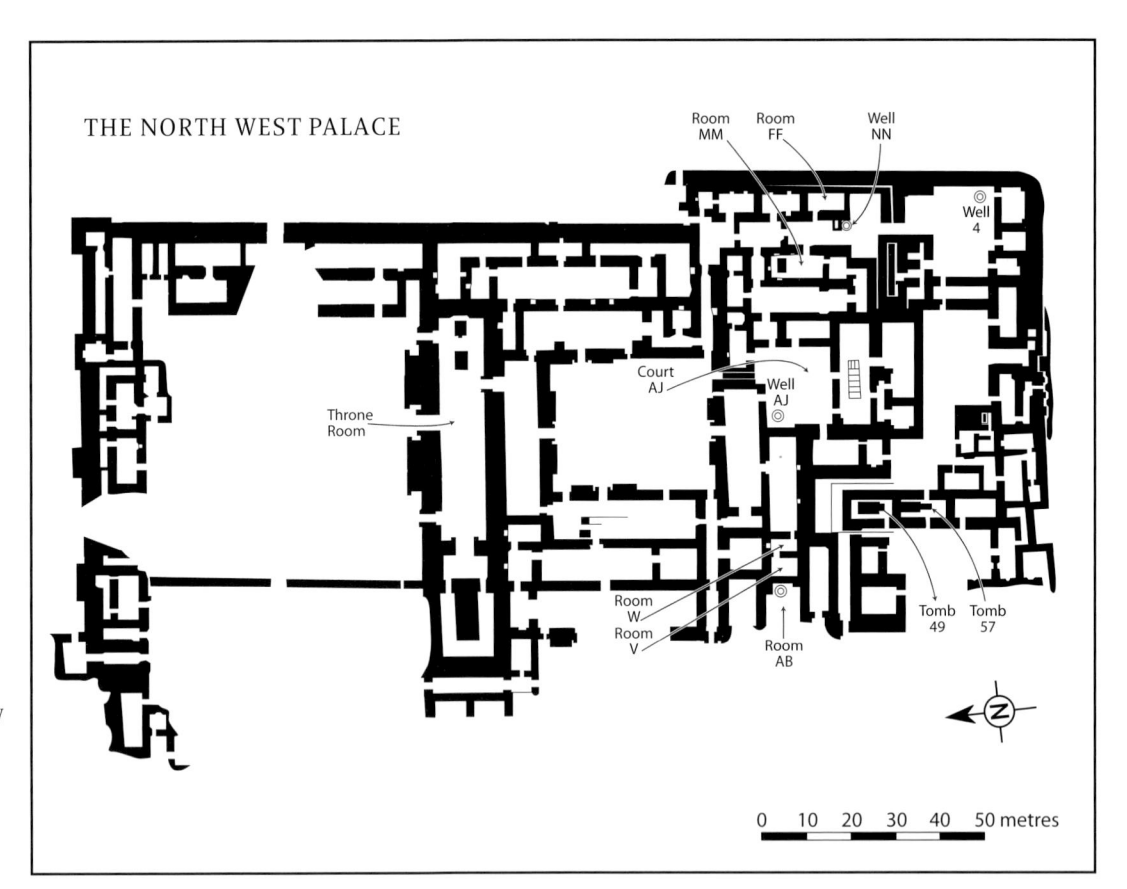

13 Plan of the North West Palace, as revealed by the excavations of Austen Henry Layard in the 1840s, Max Mallowan from 1949 to 1953, and the Iraqi State Board of Antiquities and Heritage from 1956 to the 1990s.

town of some 360 hectares (nearly 900 acres) with a palace-arsenal, built by Ashurnasirpal's son, Shalmaneser III (r. 858–824 BC), in the south-east corner of the lower town, called Fort Shalmaneser by its excavators.

The discovery of the first ivories

The first ivories were found at the dawn of Assyrian archaeology in the mid-nineteenth century by the remarkable Austen Henry Layard (1817–1894); hundreds more were found a decade later by William Kennett Loftus (c. 1821–1858). The great mass of ivories, however, was not discovered until the mid-twentieth century by Max Mallowan (1904–1978), the husband of Agatha Christie. As director of the British School of Archaeology in Iraq, he began excavations in 1949, which continued to 1963, finding major buildings and thousands of artefacts. However, while Mallowan discovered many outstanding pieces, the finest ivories were found by the Iraqi State Board of Antiquities and Heritage in the 1970s, in the sludge of a well in the North West Palace (**13**), a well that Mallowan had

tried to empty but had abandoned because the work was too dangerous. The Iraqis also found the immensely rich tombs of the Assyrian queens.

AUSTEN HENRY LAYARD

Layard was one of the giants of the Victorian age, a traveller, an adventurer, a linguist, a brilliant and pioneering archaeologist, a politician and a diplomat (**14**). His childhood was unusual. Brought up in relative poverty in Florence, he met a wide range of people – poets, painters, writers, antiquaries and travellers. His father, a connoisseur of Italian painting, taught his son about the great masters and how to distinguish one from another, and he learned to draw, all of which were to prove to be of fundamental importance in his work at Nimrud. He read widely – the Elizabethan poets, history and Walter Scott's novels, though *The Arabian Nights* was his favourite. As he wrote in his *Autobiography*.

my admiration for *The Arabian Nights* has never left me. I can read them even now [1885] with almost as much

14 Amadeo Preziosi, portrait of Austen Henry Layard in tribal dress, watercolour drawing, 1843. London, British Museum, inv. no. PD 1976-9-25,9, presented to the museum by Miss Phyllis Layard. A. H. Layard, *Early Adventures in Persia, Susiana and Babylonia*, London, 1887.

delight as I read them when a boy. They have had no little influence upon my life and career; for to them I attribute that love of travel and adventure, which took me to the East, and led me to the discovery of the ruins of Nineveh.[1]

At this time, before the decipherment of cuneiform, the Assyrian cities were known by their local (modern) names. Layard erroneously thought that Nimrud was the Nineveh of the Bible and his books, notably his two-volume account of the site, *Nineveh and its Remains*, used that name.

At the age of sixteen, Layard was articled as a clerk in his uncle's solicitors' office in Gray's Inn, which he hated. In an attempt to help him earn his living in a more congenial manner, his family sent him, with a young companion, Edward Mitford, to Ceylon to practise as a barrister. The two set off in summer 1839 and travelled across Europe and Anatolia, as the crusader knights had done, on horseback, following the old Roman routes:[2]

> I was accompanied by one no less curious and enthusiastic than myself. We were both equally careless of comfort and unmindful of danger. We rode alone; our arms were our only protection; a valise behind our saddles was our wardrobe, and we tended our own horses, except when relieved from the duty

The City of Nimrud and its Discovery

by the hospitable inhabitants of a Turcoman village or an Arab tent. Thus, unembarrassed by needless luxuries, and uninfluenced by the opinions and prejudices of others, we mixed amongst the people, acquired without effort their manners and enjoyed without alloy those emotions which scenes so novel, and spots so rich in association, cannot fail to produce.[3]

They left Aleppo for Mosul on 18 March 1840, setting off to traverse 'some of the most unfrequented roads of Turkish Arabia',[4] and reached Mosul on 10 April. They spent a fortnight there, visiting the three Assyrian capital cities, Nineveh, Ashur and Nimrud. In his later account of the site, Layard memorably described his first sight of Nimrud:

> From the summit of an artificial eminence we looked down upon a broad plain, separated from us by the river. A line of lofty mounds bounded it to the east, and one of a pyramidal form rose high above the rest. Beyond it could be faintly traced the waters of the Zab. Its position rendered its identification easy. This was the pyramid which Xenophon had described, and near which the ten thousand had encamped: the ruins were those which the Greek general saw twenty-two centuries before, and which even then were the ruins of an *ancient* city.[5]

Leaving Mosul en route to Baghdad on 18 April 1840, the two men floated down the Tigris on a raft supported on fifty inflated sheepskins, exactly as the Assyrians had crossed rivers two millennia earlier. Layard saw Nimrud again as they passed it on their journey:

> It was evening as we approached the spot. The spring rains had clothed the mound with the richest verdure, and the fertile meadows, which stretched around it, were covered with flowers of every hue. Amidst this luxuriant vegetation were partly concealed a few fragments of brick, pottery, and alabaster, upon which might be traced the well-defined wedges of the cuneiform character. Did not these remains mark the nature of the ruin, it might have been confounded with a natural eminence. A long line of consecutive narrow mounds still retaining the appearance of walls or ramparts, stretched from its base, and formed a vast quadrangle....My curiosity had been greatly excited, and from that time I formed the design of thoroughly examining, whenever it might be in my power, these singular ruins.[6]

Although he was not to start work there for five more adventurous years, the story of Nimrud and its ivories begins with him.

Interest in Mesopotamia had been aroused by the brilliant Orientalist Claudius James Rich (1786/7–1821), who served for many years as the political resident of the East India Company in Baghdad. He travelled widely in Iraq, visiting ruins and collecting antiquities, and surveyed the ruins of both Nineveh and Nimrud in 1820–21. He died young, but his studies, published posthumously in 1836, and his collections of antiquities on display in the British Museum were to inspire the French to initiate Assyrian studies. In 1841 the French government appointed Paul Émile Botta to be the new consul in Mosul and promised him support in any archaeological work that he began. Starting at the huge mound of Nineveh, he found little, but was advised by a workman to try the mound at his local village of Khorsabad. He immediately discovered what proved to be the ruins of the palace of Sargon II (r. 722–705 BC), built by that king in the new Assyrian capital city of Dur Sharrukin, which he founded.[7]

In August 1840 Layard and Mitford parted company, as Layard had abandoned plans to travel to Ceylon. Instead, he spent time adventuring with the Bakhtiari tribe in western Iran, and then moved to Constantinople, where he was employed as an assistant by the British ambassador to the Sublime Porte, Sir Stratford Canning. After seeing drawings of the superb sculptures found by Botta at Khorsabad, Layard became desperate to return to Mosul, and tried to interest Canning in financing an expedition to Nimrud.

Asked for an estimate of the costs of a preliminary survey, he reported that he would need 'a small tent, a horse and a guard and the total cost would be about sixty pounds for the journey and two thousand five hundred piastres a month (twenty pounds) in expenses'.[8] By 1845, with Canning's support, he was back in Mosul.

There, Layard enlisted the help of the Rassam brothers: the elder, Christian, was British vice-consul in Mosul, and his younger brother, Hormuzd, was to become Layard's assistant and successor. Henry Ross, an English merchant and Christian Rassam's partner, was a much needed friend and companion. They hired a raft and left Mosul on 8 November. The countryside was in a desperate state: most of the villages were deserted, the local tribe having been crushed by the pasha. Staying overnight in a hovel, they found the local sheikh, Awad, whom Layard persuaded to recruit some workmen to assist in the explorations. After a sleepless and dream-filled night, Layard later recalled:

> The day had already dawned; he [Awad] had returned with six Arabs, who agreed for a small sum to work under my direction. The lofty cone and broad mound of Nimrud rose like a distant mountain in the morning sky.[9]

As they walked around on the surface of the mound, Awad led Layard

> to a piece of alabaster, which appeared above the soil. We could not remove it, and on digging downward, it proved to be the upper part of a large slab. I ordered all the men to work around it, and they shortly uncovered a second slab to which it had been united. Continuing in the same line, we came upon a third; and, in the course of the morning, laid bare ten more, the whole forming a square, with one stone missing at the N.W. corner.[10]

On his very first morning Layard had discovered a room in what proved to be the North West Palace of Ashurnasirpal II,

15 Layard found his first ivories on only his second day of excavations at Nimrud, in what proved to be the North West Palace; in rubbish at the bottom of the first room, he discovered this figure of a bearded male in a pleated robe holding an *ankh* (6.6 cm × 2.1 × 0.7 cm; 2⅝ × ¹³⁄₁₆ × ¼ in.). London, British Museum, inv. no. 118274.

though Layard was not to know the name of the builder for many years; this was engraved on the slabs he discovered, but cuneiform was as yet undeciphered. On his second day Layard found the very first ivories:

> In the rubbish near the bottom of the chamber, I found several ivory ornaments upon which were traces of gilding; amongst them was the figure of a man in long robes, carrying in one hand the Egyptian *crux ansata*, part of a crouching sphinx and flowers designed with great taste and elegance [BM 118274, **15**].[11]

Having begun with only six workmen, Layard increased his workforce to eleven and finally to thirty-one. He worked at Nimrud from the autumn of 1845 to 1847 and again from 1849 to May 1851, when he left Mosul never to return. He was only thirty-four, but his health had been seriously undermined. He discovered the North West and South West palaces, two of the principal buildings on the citadel. He excavated the state apartments of the North West Palace, trenching round the walls, where he found bas-reliefs, as well as uncovering colossal gateway figures.

16 Layard directing the transport of one of the great human-headed bulls from the mound of Nimrud to a raft to be floated down the river to Basra and eventually to the British Museum. Frontispiece to Layard 1849, ii.

Layard was remarkable in many ways. With only Hormuzd Rassam to help him, he had 'to superintend the excavations; to draw all the bas-reliefs discovered; to copy and compare the innumerable inscriptions; to take casts of them; and to preside over the moving and packing of the sculptures'.[12] The frontispiece of volume ii of *Nineveh and its Remains* shows him directing the removal of one of the great gateway figures from the mound to the river, whence it was floated down and eventually transported to London and the British Museum (**16**). He also had the challenging task of coping with the local authorities and people, and organizing the workmen. He felt 'far from qualified to undertake these multifarious occupations'.[13]

Layard was far ahead of his time in many ways, and particularly in the care he took to record provenance. He drew and listed the locations of the bas-reliefs he found, as well as many of the small antiquities. Of the ivories he found in the king's suite in the residential wing of the North West Palace he wrote:

> The chamber V is remarkable for the discovery, near the entrance a, of a number of ivory ornaments of considerable beauty and interest. These ivories, when uncovered, adhered so firmly to the soil, and were in so forward a state of decomposition, that I had the greatest difficulty in extracting them, even in fragments. I spent hours lying on the ground, separating them, with a penknife, from the rubbish by which they were surrounded. Those who saw them when they first reached this country, will be aware of the difficulty of releasing them from the hardened mass in which they were embedded. The ivory separated itself in flakes. Even the falling away of the earth was sufficient to reduce it almost to powder.[14]

RAWLINSON AND LOFTUS

Many of the sculptures that Layard unearthed carried cuneiform inscriptions. There was considerable European interest in its decipherment, particularly because of any light it could shed on the Bible. One of the leading scholars attempting to read inscriptions was Henry Creswicke Rawlinson (1810–1895), from 1844 political resident in Baghdad. He had succeeded in copying the trilingual inscription carved on the cliff at Bisitun, which would eventually provide the key to cuneiform. Rawlinson was greatly excited by Layard's discovery of new texts at Nimrud, and Layard was desperate to know the names of the kings on the inscriptions. When Layard found the famous Black Obelisk of Shalmaneser III, he recognized that it was extremely important. It was covered with sculptures and inscriptions, but he could not know that it described Shalmaneser's campaigns, and showed Jehu of Israel, kneeling before the king in submission (**12**, p. 19). When at last cuneiform was deciphered, the text and sculptures on the obelisk proved direct links between Assyria and events described in the Old Testament.

The principal preoccupation at this time was with the written word rather than the pictorial representations on the sculptures, and this neglect and total lack of understanding of the value of Assyrian art continued throughout the nineteenth century. When Rawlinson received Layard's first cases of sculptures from Nimrud he wrote:

> We have been regaling our antiquarian appetites on the contents ever since. The dying lion and the two Gods (winged and Eagle headed) are my favorites. The battle pieces, Seiges [*sic*] etc. are curious, but I do not think they rank very highly as art.[15]

Understandably, Layard was in despair. Rawlinson's focus was determined by the perspective of history, not the history of art, and classical Greek art was the standard of the time. After the arrival of the sculptures in London, the famous sculptor Richard Westmacott considered that the Assyrian reliefs were entirely devoid of artistic qualities and might, indeed, have a damaging influence on artists: 'The less people, in their capacity as artists, view objects of this kind, the better.'[16] Fortunately, however, there were alternative views.

Work continued at Nimrud after Layard's departure, first under Hormuzd Rassam, and then under the supervision of Rawlinson, who himself did some excavating. The standard of recording was abysmal. The next major find was made by William Kennett Loftus and the artist William Boutcher, who were employed by the Assyrian Excavation Fund and the British Museum. Working in what is now known as the Burnt Palace, but was initially called the South East Building, Loftus found:

> an immense collection of ivories, apparently the relics of a throne or furniture broken up for the sake of the gold or jewels with which they were adorned…they were strewed together at the bottom of the chamber among the black ash of the wood from which cause they are nearly all burnt black. They appear to have generally escaped the fire but to have lain among the smouldering ashes.[17]

In a letter published in *The Athenaeum* on 24 March 1855, Loftus wrote 'I have got up a horse load of objects and am fitting them together as fast as possible, preparatory to boiling them in Gelatine'.[18] He also found a series of incised, Assyrian-style ivories, probably in the Central Palace. After returning to England, he published two articles, in the *Illustrated London News* and the *Literary Gazette* in April 1856, but there was no other publication. There being no further funds to pursue the work at Nimrud, Loftus's employment in Assyria ended. The Loftus ivories were essentially forgotten, and in 1867 Layard wrote, in *Nineveh and Babylon*, that Loftus had found nothing of importance. A few ivories found by Layard and Loftus were displayed in cases in the British Museum. Some were mentioned in various dictionaries and encyclopaedias. And some were illustrated in *The Mansell Collection of Photographs*[19] and the British Museum *Guide to the Babylonian and Assyrian Antiquities* of 1908.[20] The ivories were essentially forgotten.

The twentieth century

The first serious study of the ivories was made by the scholar Frederik Poulsen in *Der Orient und die frühgriechische Kunst* (1912), who based his studies on fifty published pieces and about a hundred exhibited in the galleries of the British Museum. He recognized that the ivories were carved in a variety of styles, some similar to the art of Assyria, as seen on the Assyrian reliefs, some with strong links to Egypt (called Phoenician), and some with links to sculptures found along the Syro-Turkish border (known as North Syrian). Poulsen was a perceptive critic and his basic division is still valid.

Richard Barnett joined the British Museum in 1932 and was assigned the task of publishing the Nimrud ivories, both those found by Layard and the 'horse load' of burnt and broken ivories found by Loftus. The latter were still in the state as excavated – 'a vast pile of unsorted fragments, calcined and often barely recognizable, which had clearly intimidated all my predecessors'.[21] The first edition of Barnett's magisterial *Catalogue of the Nimrud Ivories in the British Museum* appeared in 1957, and a revised edition in 1975. It is salutary to compare the nine pages of plates of Layard's ivories (pls I–IX) with the 105 of Loftus (pls XVI–CX) in that volume, disproving Layard's disparaging comment on Loftus's finds.

MAX MALLOWAN

While Barnett was labouring on his mammoth task, which could not have been carried out by anyone other than a museum employee with the facilities of conservation and photography in house, Max Mallowan was following in the footsteps of Layard at Nimrud, starting work there a century after Layard had left. Mallowan began his archaeological career as an assistant to Leonard Woolley at the iconic site of Ur of the Chaldees. Woolley was a brilliant and highly disciplined archaeologist, a formidable organizer, a considerable linguist, an inspiring lecturer and a brilliant publicist. Mallowan was to develop many of these qualities himself, including the ability to inspire the public. He first visited northern Iraq in March 1926 at the end of the season at Ur. It was on that drive to the north that he had his first glimpse of a country that seemed like an archaeologist's paradise, and he visited the great Assyrian capital cities of Nineveh, Nimrud and Ashur.

While at Ur, he had met Agatha Christie, who later became his wife. She had travelled to Iraq to recover from the end of her marriage to Archibald Christie. Bored with the social round in Baghdad in 1928, she had asked to visit Ur and fell in love with the site. Returning the following year, she met Max, who was given the task of taking her round the nearby sites. Despite the disparity in their ages (Mallowan was fourteen years Christie's junior), they shared a love of adventure and a sense of fun. Theirs was a supremely happy marriage. Christie accompanied Mallowan on all his excavations, working as site photographer, registrar, repairer of pottery and medical adviser, her own work being frequently interrupted.

On his return to England after the Second World War, Mallowan was keen to resume his archaeological career and visited Iraq, seeking for a suitable site. In 1947 he was appointed the first Professor of Western Asiatic Archaeology at the Institute of Archaeology in London. In 1949 he was made the first director of the British School of Archaeology in Iraq, and charged with starting a major excavation. After inspecting many sites, Mallowan decided, with the encouragement of the Iraqi State Board of Antiquities and Heritage, to mount an expedition to Nimrud, despite (as has always been the case with British expeditions from the time of Layard to the present day) having no certainty of adequate funding. As he himself wrote, 'I had a feeling that things yet unknown, of great quality and worthy of long contemplation, would emerge from the soil'.[22] He began work there on 18 March 1949, with only four British staff (including his wife), his Iraqi representative, Dr Mahmud el Amin, and his highly trained Sherqati foremen (**17–18**). The Sherqati had been trained by the great German archaeologist Walther Andrae in his long-running excavations (1903–12) at the dynastic Assyrian capital, Ashur.

The surface of the site consisted of a bewildering mass of pits and ancient dumps, but after only a day and a half Mallowan and his surveyor, Robert Hamilton, succeeded in

ABOVE **17** Max Mallowan and Agatha Christie (centre), supervising the excavations on the citadel at Nimrud in the early 1950s.

RIGHT **18** The Sherqati workman Saleh Mohammad al-Muslah exposing an ivory plaque in the fill of Room SW11/12 in Fort Shalmaneser, 1963. Photograph Dr Vaughn Crawford.

finding the room where Layard had discovered most of his ivories. They even found an ivory, left on a raised patch of mud (ND 362, **19**).[23] It was the last of a set of cows and calves, the rest of which had been found by Layard. While the cow may have been Mallowan's favourite piece, being both the first one he discovered and the one directly linked to his famous predecessor, his finest ivories were to be found in the wells of the North West Palace, specifically in Well NN.

Excavating an Assyrian well is difficult and dangerous and requires specialized equipment. Well NN, located in the domestic wing of the North West Palace, was discovered in April 1951 and cleared in March 1952, with the help of the Iraq Petroleum Company. It was built of burnt bricks, often inscribed with the name of Ashurnasirpal II. The internal diameter of the well was 1.7 metres (5 ft 7 in.), wide enough to enable two workmen to be winched up and down simultaneously. The top of the well was filled with mud and rubbish to a depth of 15.5 metres (50 ft 10 in.) below the well-head, where the first water appeared. Working continuously, day and night, and bucketing out the water as it flowed in (no pumps were available), the workmen reached the bottom at a depth of 25.4 metres (83 ft 4 in.) from the top of the well. Treasures were found in the sludge, including superb ivories, which had been miraculously preserved in the mud. Perhaps the most famous piece is the front of a magnificent head or mask (ND 2550, **20**),[24] carved from a massive tusk. As Agatha Christie evocatively wrote:

> How thrilling it was; the patience, the care that was needed; the delicacy of touch. And the most exciting day of all – one of the most exciting days of my life – when the workmen came rushing into the house from their work clearing out an Assyrian well, and cried: 'We have found a woman in the well! There is a woman in the well!' And they brought in on a piece of sacking, a great mass of mud. I had the pleasure of gently washing the mud off in a large wash-basin. Little by little the head emerged, preserved by the sludge for about 2,500 years. There it was – the biggest ivory head ever found: a soft, pale brownish colour, the hair black, the faintly coloured lips with the enigmatic smile of one of the maidens of the Acropolis. The Lady of the Well – the Mona Lisa, as the Iraqi Director of Antiquities insisted on calling her – one of the most exciting things ever to be found.[25]

It was the discoveries in Well NN that inspired Mallowan to return to two other wells in the residential wing of the North West Palace, Wells AB and AJ. Well AB was sited in a corner of Room AB (**21**), Layard's 'Treasure Chamber', where he had found a superb collection of 150 bronze bowls, elaborately decorated with human and animal figures, as well as elephants' tusks, horse-trappings, bronze bells, beads, an alabaster vase and the remains of a royal throne made of wood and ivory and decorated with winged figures in bronze, which disintegrated as he revealed it. His workmen had dug the well to a depth of 18.3 metres (60 ft), the level of brackish water, but had failed to go lower into the ivory-bearing sludge. With the aid of a winch and a pump operated by a diesel engine, Mallowan reached water level at 20.5 metres (67 ft 3 in.). In the grey sludge below they found a mass of ivory and wooden fragments, a huge jumble of an unknown quantity of pieces. The fragments ceased to appear at a depth of some 22.3–22.9 metres (73–75 ft), though the bottom was

19 Mallowan's first find in spring 1949, and his favourite piece – a cow, left behind by Layard, who had removed the remainder of the set to which it belonged (3 × 7.5 cm; 1 1/16 × 2 15/16 in.). ND 362, Baghdad, National Museum of Iraq.

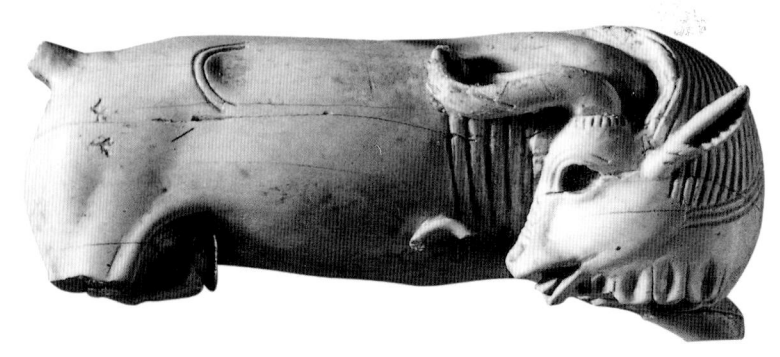

28 Ancient Ivory

20 The most famous piece found at Nimrud, known as the 'Mona Lisa'; the front of a head or a mask carved from a massive tusk, in the state in which it was found in Well NN in the North West Palace, in spring 1952 (16 × 13.2 × 5.6 cm; 6⅝ × 5³⁄₁₆ × 2³⁄₁₆ in.). ND 2550, Baghdad, National Museum of Iraq.

probably a few feet lower. But work came to a hurried end when an old well-digger realized that the walls were about to collapse. He pulled on the rope, collected his lamp and tools and reached the surface just as the bottom of the well caved in with a mighty roar – a disaster narrowly averted.[26]

Agatha Christie, who loved puzzles of all kinds, spent hours reassembling the ivory fragments, which turned out to be the pieces of sixteen writing-boards, measuring some 33 × 15.25 cm (13 × 6 inches). These were hinged and had once folded, like the leaves of a screen, to form a book (**22**). On all of them the sunken section was covered with criss-cross scratching. The slightly larger wooden boards showed the remains of beeswax, marked with traces of cuneiform; this is the earliest known use of beeswax as a writing medium The front cover of one of the ivory 'books' carried a four-line cuneiform inscription, which read:

Palace of Sargon, king of the world
king of Assyria. The series Enuma Anu Enlil
he had written on an ivory board and
placed in his palace at Dur Sharrukin

thus not only naming the owner but also describing the contents (**23**). *Enuma Anu Enlil* is the opening phrase of a long astrological text, based on observations taken from the sun, moon and stars.[27] Omens were of immense importance in antiquity.

The third well, in Court AJ, was built by Ashurnasirpal II but repaired by his son Shalmaneser III (r. 858–824 BC), with whose bricks the courtyard was paved. To keep the water clean from the animals tethered in the courtyard (stone tethering blocks were found), the well stood on a raised platform, accessed by steps, and was sealed with a great cap-

The City of Nimrud and its Discovery

ABOVE **21** F. C. Cooper, watercolour drawing, 1850, showing part of Layard's 'Room of the Bronzes' and Well AB in the North West Palace; Mallowan and his workmen later recovered from the well a hoard of ivory fragments that were reassembled into a collection of writing-boards. London, British Museum.

LEFT **22** Three leaves of a hinged, ivory writing-board, the central panels of which were originally filled with wax (each leaf: 33.5 × 15.6 cm; 13¹³⁄₁₆ × 6⅛ in.). ND 3559–3561, Baghdad, National Museum of Iraq.

BELOW **23** The cover of the writing-board (**22** above), inscribed with the name of its owner, Sargon II, king of Assyria, and the title of the astrological text written on the rest of the board. ND 3557, Baghdad, National Museum of Iraq.

stone (**24**).²⁸ Since it had been covered, the well was empty of debris. However, the brick lining of the walls was badly worn, and work was stopped at a depth of 16.5 metres (54 ft) because the walls were undercut. Local experts were called in, and one old man – 'a veritable Noah, thick-set, bow-legged and blessed with a massive, hennaed, patriarchal beard'²⁹ – spent an hour in the well, tapping the sides with his hammer, before coming up, saying 'Danger, great danger!' As he had enjoyed a long life and the bottom of the well was an honourable place to die, he was prepared to continue the exploration, but work was abandoned.

Some idea of the pandemonium that probably occurred during the sack of Nimrud in 612 BC is given in Mallowan's account of the work in Court AJ: 'Beneath the level of the latest well-head, in a belt of ash 25 cm [9⅞ in.] thick, there were fragments of ivories, gold foil overlay, faience beads and glass; this was all debris from the destruction.'³⁰ The fragments included Assyrian-style ivories, as well as assorted fragments of Levantine pieces. One of these, the remains of a pyxis, had a cuneiform inscription on the rim, which read that it had been given to Shalmaneser III by Shamshi-ilu, the governor of many western provinces.³¹ Alas, no photograph survives of the pyxis, though there is one of the inscription. Another fragment (ND 893)³² must have been dropped on its way to Well AJ, as it was found in a passageway between the two wells; this Syrian-style piece, showing a man in a cutaway coat saluting a stylized tree and holding an *ankh* (the sign of 'life'), can be exactly matched to parts of a long openwork panel from the well.³³

Little did Mallowan know, but the most astonishing assemblage of ivories yet to be found at Nimrud was lying in the sludge at the bottom of Well AJ. While he tried and failed with Well AJ, he also stopped work in Room MM, a large room in the domestic wing, despite having found a burial in a ceramic 'bathtub' coffin under the floor of the nearby Room DD. This might have suggested to him that there could be more such under-floor burials, though there was no reason to expect to find royal burials at Kalhu. It was assumed that the Assyrian royal burial ground was at Ashur, where the Assyrian kings had been buried; their great stone sarcophagi had long been plundered. Mallowan thus failed to find the royal tombs of the Assyrian queens, and moved on to other buildings on the citadel, where he stopped work in 1957 before initiating the massive task of excavating the huge palace–arsenal known as Fort Shalmaneser.

THE ROYAL TOMBS
Four richly equipped royal tombs were found thirty years after the British had left Nimrud, during a programme to restore the North West Palace undertaken by the Iraqi State

24 A view of Well AJ, dug by Ashurbanipal II (d. 859 BC) in the North West Palace, with the steps and pavement laid by his son Shalmaneser III. The finest ivories found at Nimrud were recovered by Mallowan and his team from the sludge at the bottom of this well.

Board of Antiquities and Heritage. This was begun as early as 1956, with the aim of making the site available to the public. By the 1980s it was possible to stroll through the state apartments and domestic quarters of the great palace, now destroyed by so-called Islamic State.

The first of the royal burials was found in Room MM, which, because it was relatively empty, Mallowan had not excavated to floor level. This was left to the director of the Iraqi State Board of Antiquities and Heritage, Muzahim Mahmoud Hussein, who noticed that the original bricks of the floor had been replaced. Investigating further, he found the crown of a vault of an underground room, entered via a shaft, with steps leading into an entrance chamber. Against the west wall of the main chamber he found a sealed terracotta sarcophagus containing the skeleton of a woman of some fifty to fifty-five years. A silver bowl had been placed under her head, and she had been provided with superb jewelry, gold earrings and necklaces, armlets and finger rings, as well as vessels of copper and bronze.

This discovery led to the intensive investigation of the floors of new rooms as they were excavated, leading to the discovery in 1989 of a second tomb in Room 49, with the bodies of two queens, Yaba, the wife of Tiglath-pileser III (r. 745–727 BC), and Ataliya, the queen of Sargon II (r. 722–705 BC), while the name of a third queen, Banitu, the wife of Shalmaneser V (r. 726–722 BC), was inscribed on a gold bowl. The tomb therefore contained the bodies of two queens but the treasures of three. There was an astonishing number of grave goods, exceptional both for their quantity and superb workmanship.

Indeed the objects found in the sarcophagus alone, a total of 157, made this tomb one of the most remarkable ever found in the Near East. Among these were a gold crown, a gold mesh diadem with a tasselled gold fringe and 'tiger-eye' agate rosettes, 79 gold earrings, 6 gold necklaces, 30 finger rings, 14 armlets, 4 gold anklets, 15 gold vessels, gold chain, etc. Among the most beautiful objects recovered were a group of rock crystal vessels. Of the gold anklets one weighed almost a kilo [2 lb 3 oz], another over 1100 g. [2 lb 6 oz], while the multi-coloured glass and stone inlays on some of the gold armlets was of a level of craftsmanship not previously attested. There was also a very large number of necklaces, perhaps as many as 90, of semi-precious stones.[34]

Of these incredible treasures, two may be singled out: a magnificent gold bowl, probably of Phoenician workmanship, showing a complicated series of scenes set in boats afloat in the papyrus marshes (**113**, p. 94), and a hinged component of a necklace decorated with a palm tree (**111**, p. 94). The workmanship of both is of the highest quality. The designs on the gold bowl are gently hammered up, while the work on the palm tree element is astonishing: the fine gold chains and pomegranates that hang from the rectangular fragment are superbly worked, as also are the delicate glass inlays making up the tiny palm tree in its blue ground, set in a gold, hinged frame.

A third tomb was found under the floor of Room 57, immediately to the south of Room 49. The tomb chamber contained a massive stone sarcophagus, with an inscription on the lid, saying that it belonged to Mullissu-mukannishat-Ninua – the queen of the founder of Nimrud, Ashurnasirpal II, and mother of Shalmaneser III. Although the sarcophagus had been looted, the doors into the tomb had been re-sealed, and no fewer than three bronze coffins, containing the bones of at least thirteen individuals and even more treasure than in Tomb II, were found in the antechamber (**109**, p. 94). Among the grave goods were a magnificent crown with a delicate canopy of vine leaves and bunches of blue grapes, set above a series of winged deities (**110**, p. 94), and a superb gold-spouted ewer. Inscribed objects included the seal of a courtier of Adad-nirari III (r. 810–783 BC), a gold bowl belonging to Shamshi-ilu, commander-in-chief in Syria from 782 to 745 BC, and a duck weight of the time of Tiglath-pileser III. These are, of course, all considerably later than the time of Ashurnasirpal's queen, but the contents probably pre-date those in Tomb II. The total number of separate items was 449, and the gold and silver alone weighed some 23 kg (more than 50 lb).

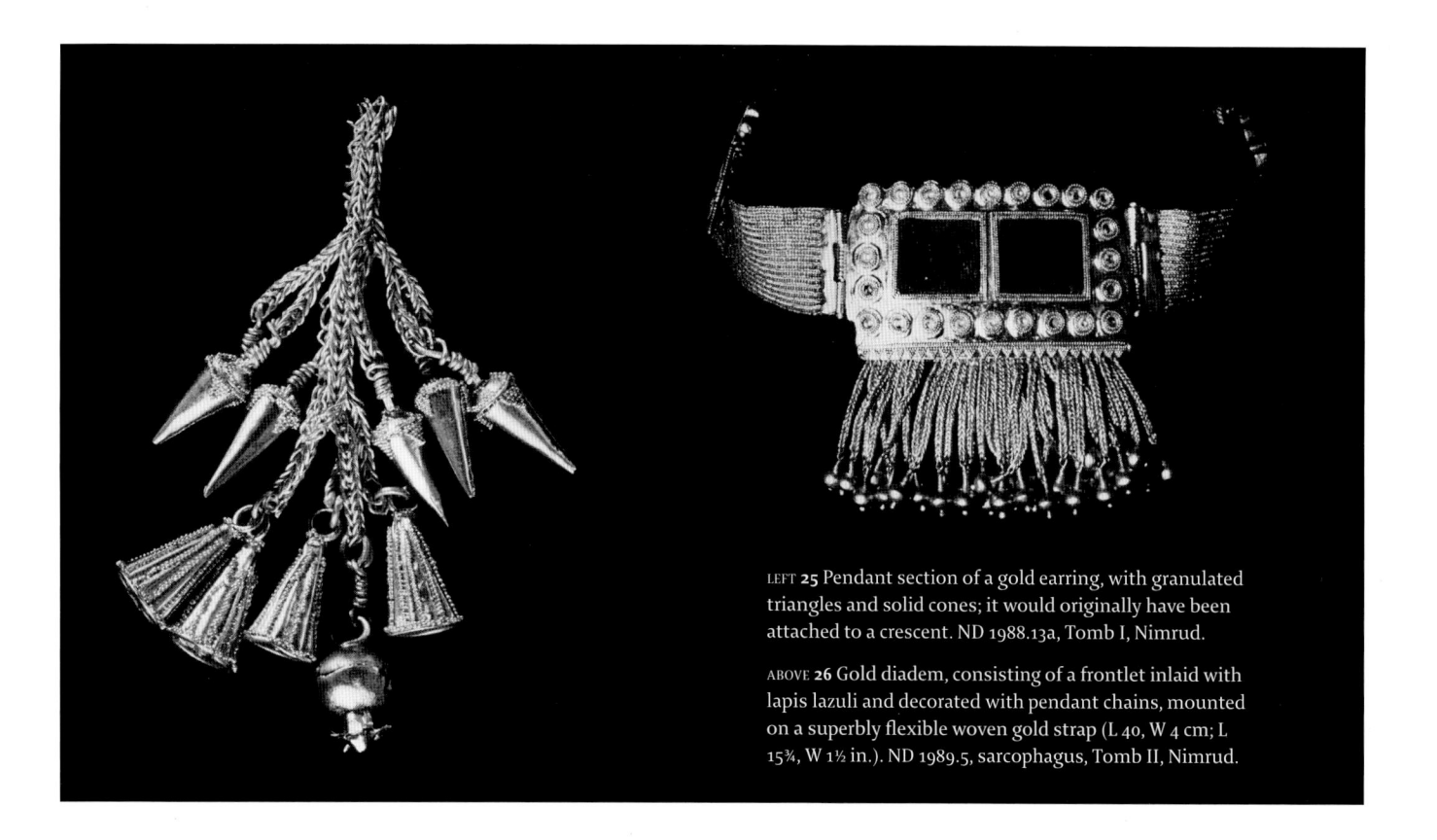

LEFT **25** Pendant section of a gold earring, with granulated triangles and solid cones; it would originally have been attached to a crescent. ND 1988.13a, Tomb I, Nimrud.

ABOVE **26** Gold diadem, consisting of a frontlet inlaid with lapis lazuli and decorated with pendant chains, mounted on a superbly flexible woven gold strap (L 40, W 4 cm; L 15¾, W 1½ in.). ND 1989.5, sarcophagus, Tomb II, Nimrud.

While the discovery of such magnificent, unplundered royal graves is, in itself, of international importance, so also is the information on burial practices that the tombs present, and the workmanship of the contents provides new material on the history of technology, especially of metal-working. The queens were endowed with immense wealth, but it is also of interest to see what they lacked: they had no furniture – no beds, chairs, tables, or trays on which to serve food – and although they were endowed with wonderful gold and silver bowls and vessels of rock crystal, they had none of the ivory boxes and fan handles so familiar from other contexts at Nimrud. This absence is particularly significant since two of the queens were probably of Levantine origin: their names, Yaba and Ataliya, may be West Semitic. This raises a fascinating and important question. When the queens were furnished with such a wide range of grave goods, the absence of ivory in all three royal tombs must have been deliberate. Is it possible that objects of ivory were reserved for masculine or ceremonial use?

IVORIES FROM WELL AJ AND WELL 4

In 1974–75 the Iraqi State Board of Antiquities and Heritage successfully emptied Well AJ, the well that had defeated Mallowan. They reached the bottom at a depth of 25.9 metres (85 ft) and recovered numerous superb ivories in the local Assyrian style, as well as examples from all the Levantine traditions. Many of the pieces are unique and relatively complete. They include parts of a statuette of an Assyrian courtier, as well as pyxides and flasks, still with their lids and bases. Of the many thousands of magnificent pieces found at Nimrud, those from Well AJ are outstanding. The nervous stag (IM 79526, **27**) is just one of these pieces.[35] Before it was discovered it was not possible to guess in what way the various broken bodies of stags, found elsewhere in the site, might have been set. The stag is standing in the mountains and browsing in a forest of fronds that grow in a curve. Just how the piece was used remains uncertain.

An interesting idea, which unfortunately cannot be proved, was proposed by a member of the Iraqi team of excavators: he suggested that many of the ivories may have been lowered to the bottom of the well in wicker baskets. If this were so, it would be of fundamental importance, since it would imply an attempt to preserve the ivories rather than their simply being thrown down during the sack of the building.

In June 1992 the last of the wells, Well 4, was found in the south-east corner of the North West Palace. It was emptied by Muzahim Mahmoud Hussein and Junaid al Fakhri over a period of four and a half months. The well was sealed by a mass of clay and a stone lid, and the first 6 metres (20 ft) were filled with ash and broken bricks. This layer was followed by metres filled with human bones, some with hands or legs shackled; altogether, some 400 skeletons were recovered, all belonging to young men, eighteen to twenty years old – presumably prisoners, thrown into the well at the time of the sack. In addition to many small antiquities, seals, jewelry, pottery and bottles accompanying the human remains, of interest here was a collection of cylindrical kohl tubes, mostly made of bone, as well as a few of ivory.

FORT SHALMANESER

As early as 1852, an English naval officer, Felix Jones, had recognized the outlines of a large building in the south-east corner of the site (**28**). A walk round the outer town by Max Mallowan, accompanied by the Danish archaeologist and epigraphist Jorgen Laessoe provided the impetus to start work there, for they found a brick inscribed with the name of Shalmaneser III, which gave the building its name. It was in the Fort that Mallowan achieved

the climax to a decade of work at Nimrud: the rich bounty of treasure which suddenly appeared within our grasp; the unique character of the architecture; the historical sequences revealed by its inscriptions, and finally, the fact that it had been almost untouched by any diggers before our time since its abandonment at the end of the Assyrian empire, combined to make every day's labour a thrilling experience.[36]

27 Openwork panel showing an alert stag, disturbed while browsing in a forest of entwined branches (9.8 × 11.8 × 1.6 cm; 3⅞ × 4 5/16 × ⅝ in.); the scene is set in the mountains, as represented by the scale pattern along the bottom of the panel. IM 79526, Baghdad, National Museum of Iraq.

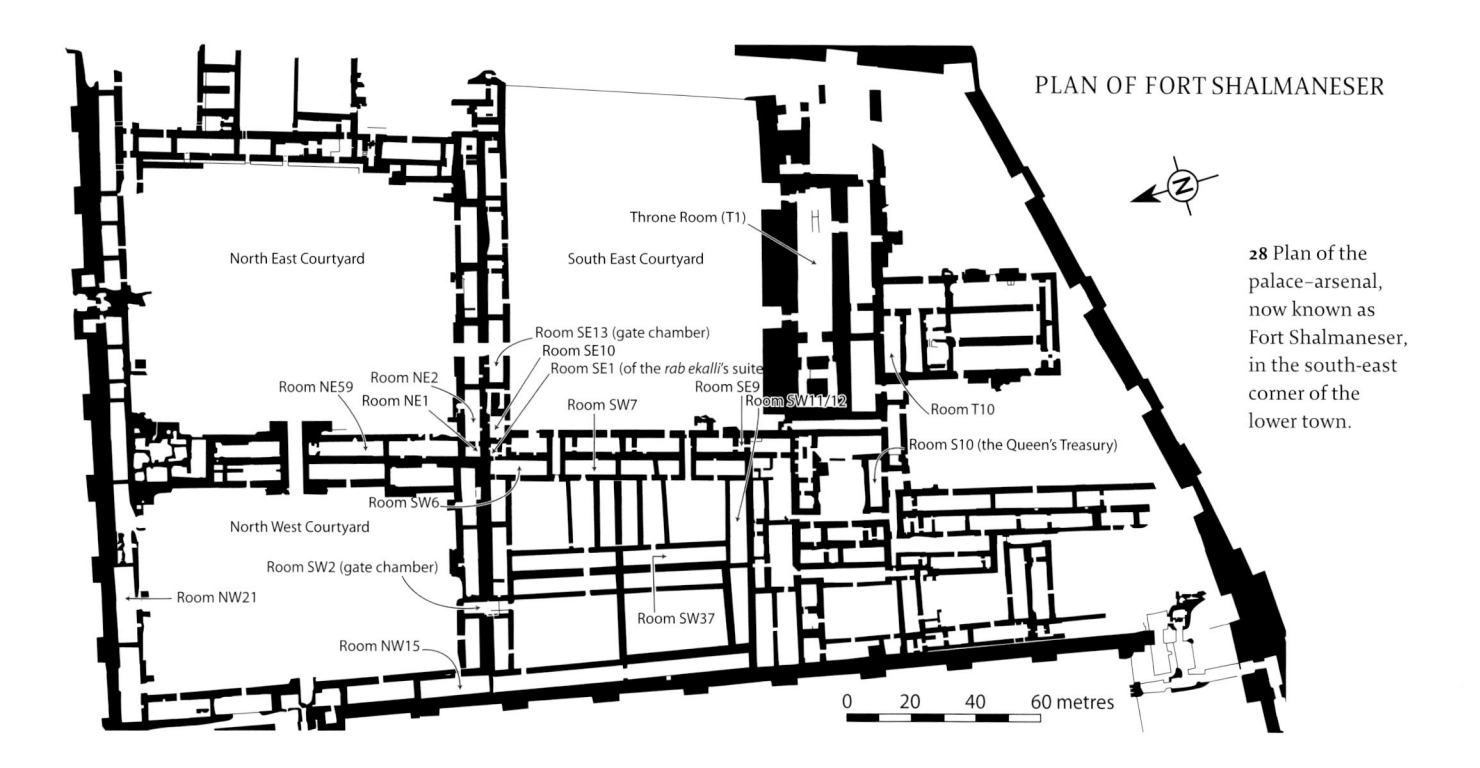

PLAN OF FORT SHALMANESER

28 Plan of the palace–arsenal, now known as Fort Shalmaneser, in the south-east corner of the lower town.

In 1957, as Agatha's health was not robust, Mallowan appointed David Oates to be the field director of the Fort Shalmaneser excavations. Oates had gone to Iraq to study Roman remains but was soon invited to join the team at Nimrud. He was an outstanding mud-brick archaeologist and a superb planner – skills that he put to good use at the Fort. The expedition had two principal aims: one to recover the plan of this enormous building, the other to retrieve ivories, for which Mallowan had a passion. Both aims were brilliantly achieved. The scale of the building meant that only the main outlines of the plan could be recovered, principally by surface scraping. The Fort consists of an enclosure, measuring some 200 × 300 metres (655 × 985 ft), with four large quadrangles and a residential palace. The purpose of the building, known as an *ekal masharti*, was described on a cylinder belonging to Esarhaddon (r. 680–669 BC):

> The preparation of the camp (equipment), the mustering of the stallions, chariots, harness, equipment of war and the spoil of the foe of every kind. ...May I – every year without interruption – take stock during the New Year's Festival, the first month, of all stallions, mules, donkeys and camels, of the harness and battle gear of all my troops and of the booty taken from the enemy.[37]

The inscription proved to be literally correct: the excavators identified a palace and a palatial area for reviewing the troops, areas for the maintenance of kit, the storing of armour and horse harness, and large magazines for booty. The Fort, with its combination of uses, is unique. So also is the quantity of ivories recovered there.

Three quadrangles consist of central courtyards lined with halls; the South East Courtyard gives access to the Throne Room, while the fourth, that to the south-west, is divided into smaller courtyards. Although ivories were found throughout the Fort, thousands were found in just three rooms in the South West Courtyard – Rooms SW7, SW11/12 and SW37; most were broken and scattered through the mud-brick matrix, but those from SW7 were relatively complete and seem to have been deliberately stacked there. Oates described their discovery:

> the whole north end of the room including the doorway was covered by a rusty mass of scale armour, lying in layers up to 35 cm. [14 in.] thick interspersed

The City of Nimrud and its Discovery

with broken brickwork....The south end of the room served for the storage of objects of an entirely different nature. From the surface of the ground to the floor, a depth of over two metres [6½ ft], fragments and plaques of ivory carved in relief were tightly packed among the debris of the fallen walls and roof, and their removal and treatment occupied us for a period of more than two months....

During the 1957 season we succeeded in removing only the upper layers of this rich deposit, but in the lower part of the room in 1958 we uncovered many more pieces in position, as they had been left at the abandonment of the building, and were able to reconstruct their original arrangement. The plaques had been attached in rows of four or five to the concave surface of a curved screen, between two side posts which projected some distance above and below the screen and were also veneered with sheets of ivory, some carved with the same figure motifs.[38]

These 'screens' were initially identified as bed-heads, but thrones found in a royal tomb at Salamis in Cyprus, as well as illustrations on sculptures, have since suggested that they formed the backs of chairs (see chapter 6).

The ivories found in the 'ivory rooms' SW37 and SW11/12 were not so well preserved as those in SW7 and apparently lacked any sort of order. Many were broken, and all had had their gold overlays deliberately removed before deposition. The fill consisted entirely of

broken mud brick, compressed and baked by the sun to a rocklike hardness....Distributed throughout this fill are a great many pieces of carved ivory, some forming complete plaques or segments of some larger decorative pattern, others obviously shattered in antiquity.[39]

Nearly 1,600 pieces are listed in the publication of the ivories from SW37 but, because of problems of access to museum store-rooms and lack of time and resources, it was not possible to record all the ivories, and there may well have been more than 3,000 pieces from SW37 alone. Equally, it was possible to record only some 850 ivories from Room SW11/12: many more – again, literally thousands – were found. Not one of these ivories was carved in the characteristic Assyrian style: all originated in the west and must have formed part of the vast quantities of booty seized from captured cities. Like the panels from SW7, many of these had once formed parts of furniture. In addition there were some small decorative plaques, which formed parts of small boxes or cup-stands, as well as sets of ceremonial bridle harness.

Ivories were also found in a number of residential contexts in the Fort, particularly in the queen's residence, and in the suite of the *rab ekalli*, the palace manager. The assortment of burnt and broken Levantine ivories in the Queen's Treasury, Room S10, included a number of versions of the popular 'woman at the window' motif. One of these (ND 7739; **154**, p. 107),[40] is of particular interest as it can be exactly matched to a set found in the Nabu Temple built by Sargon II in his city of Dur Sharrukin (modern Khorsabad). The Nabu Temple ivories must have formed part of a donation by the king to his new temple. The presence of identical ivories at the two sites is important, both for showing the distribution of sets between the Fort and the Nabu Temple and because it suggests that these ivories had reached Kalhu by the end of the eighth century BC. The pieces in the *rab ekalli*'s suite consisted of a range of high-quality Levantine ivories, as well as a few in Assyrian style. This is one of the few contexts where Assyrian ivories were found alongside Levantine pieces.

Another location with a mixture of Levantine and Assyrian ivories was Room T10, a store-room sited conveniently close to the Throne Room, and heavily burnt in the sack of the city. A few hundred ivories were found there, as well as bronze furniture fittings and wooden furniture parts, armour scales and the long bones of an elephant. Unfortunately, because of lack of time and access, it has not yet proved possible to record more than a few of these ivories. This is a disaster, for, while the ivories from Rooms SW37 and 11/12 are typically Levantine, those from T10

29 North Syrian plaque depicting a god wearing a flattened version of the Egyptian double crown and framed by four wings; the eye is outlined in black (8.4 × 4.4 × 1.3 cm; 3⁵⁄₁₆ × 4³⁄₄ × ¹⁄₄ in.). ND 14566, Baghdad, National Museum of Iraq.

include, as well as standard examples, some very different and unique pieces. For instance, the fine sphinx, facing forwards (ND 14500), is typically Phoenician and belongs to an exceptionally finely carved group (**201**, p. 138).⁴¹ A totally different set of small plaques shows provincial-looking deities with kohl-rimmed eyes (ND 14566, **29**).⁴² Other pieces from the set show gods, warriors, women and musicians. Many ivories from T10 await preliminary recording, but the range found there forms a salutary reminder that many centres, not just those in the Levant, were producing ivories.

Starting to bring order out of chaos

The Nimrud ivories form an enormous jigsaw puzzle, but one with many missing pieces and few clues. Relatively few ivories have been found elsewhere to help provide a chronological framework, and internal evidence is limited. Nimrud itself was sacked by the combined forces of the Babylonians and Medes in 614 and 612 BC, so the ivories must pre-date those years. Kalhu ceased to be the principal Assyrian capital at the end of the eighth century, by which time Assyria had conquered many of the Levantine sites. So this may suggest that the majority of the booty was deposited before then. But this is simply the possible time of deposition, not of production.

The find places of the ivories within the site are helpful. There is, for instance, a marked difference between the locations of Assyrian-style and Levantine ivories. The finest Assyrian ivories cluster in important reception areas near throne daises, suggesting that they were used to decorate royal thrones. Most belong to the ninth century BC, as they can be dated by comparing them to dated Assyrian reliefs, but there are some eighth-century examples. Levantine ivories, on the other hand, were stripped of their gold and stored in large magazines, where no Assyrian ivories were found. They were, in Esarhaddon's words, 'the booty taken from the enemy'.⁴³

Many ivories were used in sets of matching panels or plaques, often found in the same rooms. Once the sets are reassembled, they can be united into groups according to their different subjects. Layard found two sets of ivories in the doorway of Room V/W of the North West Palace, one decorated with young males and the other with the motif of the 'woman at the window'. The panels are all the same size and fixed in the same way, and Layard immediately considered that they 'formed the panelling of a throne or chest'.⁴⁴ Six show pharaoh figures, three facing to the right and three to the left; they have close-fitting wigs, with residual *uraei* (sacred cobras) at the front, and necklaces, and they wear short, belted tunics with open overskirts of a pleated material. Two of the six are almost identical (BM 118148 and 118152, **30–31**),⁴⁵ sharing numerous details, such as their facial features, the form of their ears, the long fingers of their raised hands, the double ribbons that fall over their shoulders, the 'tails' that hang from their belts at the back, the decoration of the necklaces, the voluted belts and the narrow lotus flowers that they hold. However, though they are generally similar to another pharoah figure, facing in the other direction (BM 118147, **32**), there are differences of detail. Compare the faces, ears and necklaces, the absence of the double ribbon and tail, the placing of the hands, the garments and belts and the lotus flowers. BM 118147 may have been carved by a different craftsman in the workshop, a suggestion reinforced in this (exceptional) case by the fitters' or makers' marks (letters in the Aramaic alphabet occasionally incised on the backs or tenons of panels): the pair of right-facing youths have a form of the letter *gimel* incised on their backs, while the third youth has a different mark, a *beth*, this time placed on the front of the tenon. The marks may identify the craftsmen, and they reinforce the differences observed between the panels.

Although there are fewer points of direct comparison between the four 'woman at the window' panels and the pharaoh figures, the carving of eyes and eyebrows is similar, and two of the panels also have *gimel* marks on their backs (BM 118159, **33**).[46] It is a good working hypothesis that the youths and 'women at the window' with the same marks were carved by the same craftsman. This suggests, unsurprisingly, that not only were there a number of craftsmen working together in a workshop to produce sets of similar panels but also that they were able to carve different subjects.

While it is possible tentatively to identify specific craftsmen who worked on these carvings, this is a rare example, though an important one. Many sets of panels exhibit minor differences of style within an overall similarity, suggesting that they were worked by different hands. Indeed, such a practice was common and has been recognized in the carving of the bas-reliefs decorating the walls of the North West Palace. Julian Reade, formerly at the British Museum, commented:

> the work of different artists may be plainly traced in the Assyrian edifices. Frequently where the outline is spirited and correct, and the ornament designed with considerable taste, the execution is defective or coarse, evidently showing that, whilst a master drew the subject, the carving of the stone had been entrusted to an inferior workman. . . .It is rare to find an entire bas-relief equally well executed in all its parts.[47]

Similarly, at Persepolis, Michael Roaf of the University of Munich was able to demonstrate that teams of sculptors worked on those reliefs, with craftsmen assigned different parts of the figures.[48] In both these cases, Reade and Roaf were helped by having, at the start, fixed locations and dates for their material; in the case of the ivories, neither their places of origin nor their dates are known. Nevertheless, the pattern of a team of craftsmen at work either on bas-reliefs or ivories is common. The ancient workshop, like those illustrated in the superb wall paintings preserved in the tomb of Rekhmire (**6**, p. 11), will have been a busy place, employing a number of artisans.

In 879 BC Ashurnasirpal II gave an enormous party to celebrate the completion of his palace and his new city. He built his palace and temples in the walled citadel, located on an ancient tell (or mound), but the lower town, with its walls, gardens and zoos, stretched out to occupy a large area below. Occupation in a more limited way continued at Nimrud after the fall of the Assyrian empire, and the Greek soldier Xenophon marched by, presumably because the city was of little importance. Thereafter, much of it may have been deserted – the lower town turned over to agriculture – for more than 1,800 years, until Layard began work there in 1845. He and his successors in the nineteenth century worked mainly on the citadel.

A century later, in 1949, Max Mallowan started a major programme of excavation, both in the citadel and in the lower town, where he discovered the great palace–arsenal as well as thousands of ivories. At the same time, work on restoration was undertaken by the Iraqi State Board of Antiquities and Heritage, who were to discover both the finest ivories and the outstanding tombs of the Assyrian queens, filled with treasure. In the late 1980s an Italian expedition began to map the entire city, as well as finding some more ivories.

The majority of the ivories have been published in the *Ivories from Nimrud* series,[49] while the treasures from the tombs were published rapidly in Arabic and have now appeared in English, published by the Oriental Institute of Chicago. Study of all this remarkable material will rewrite our understanding of the art of the time and the history of technology.

ABOVE 30–32 A set of Syro-Phoenician panels, found by Layard in Room V/W in the North West Palace, showing youths wearing corrupted versions of the Egyptian 'blue crown' and saluting lotus flowers; variations in the design between 30–31 and 32 suggest that two different craftsmen were at work, an impression supported by the makers' marks (10.9 × 5.1 × 1 cm; 4⁵⁄₁₆ × 2 × ⅜ in.). London, British Museum, inv. nos 118148, 118152, 118147.

RIGHT 33 An example of the 'woman at the window' motif, one of a set of panels found with the young pharaoh figures in Room V/W in the North West Palace and made by the same craftsmen; the woman's hair is dressed in the Egyptian style and the parapet is supported by palm columns (10.9 × 8.8 × 1.1 cm; 4⁵⁄₁₆ × 3½ × ⁷⁄₁₆ in.). London, British Museum, inv. no. 118159.

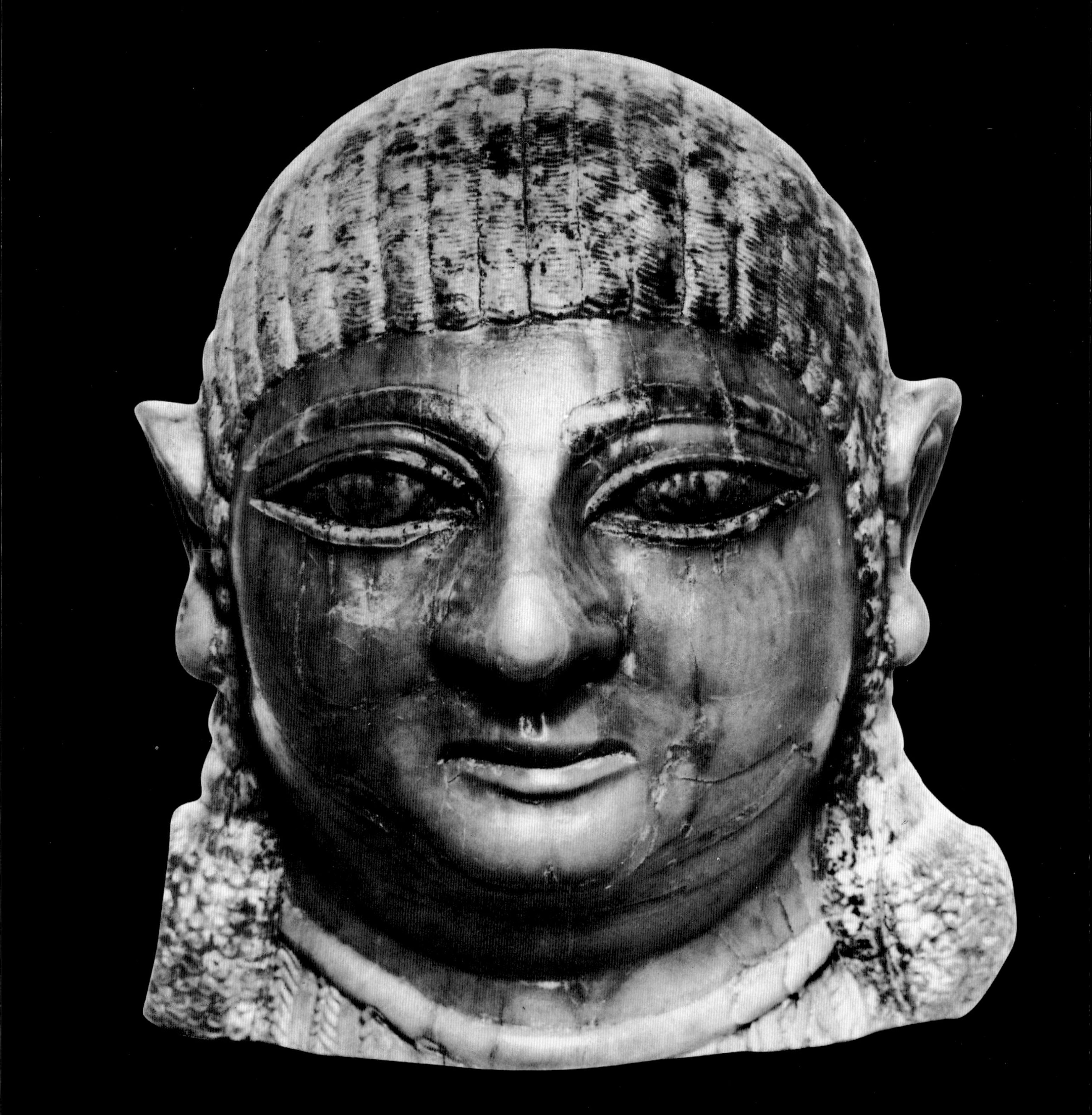

Chapter 2

Ah, Assyria!

Ah, Assyria, the rod of my anger, the staff of my fury! Against a godless nation I send him, and against the people of my wrath I command him, to take spoil and seize plunder[.]*

The land of Assyria is quite small. It consists of a triangle, occupying an area of some 500 square miles (c. 130,000 hectares) from the dynastic capital, Ashur, to Nineveh in the north and Erbil in the east. It is a land of limited resources, good for growing corn, but lacking minerals and quality timber.

Assyria first entered the international stage in the fourteenth century BC, when it was ruled by Ashur-uballit (r. 1363–1328 BC). He claimed equality with the great kings of the day, the pharaoh of Egypt, and the kings of the Hittites and Mitanni: they regarded themselves as members of a single royal family, whose relationships were maintained by exchanging a finely judged array of gifts, including their daughters in marriage. Assyria continued to expand under a series of effective kings in the thirteenth century, before entering a period of decline. Assyrian fortunes began to recover at the end of the tenth century during the reign of Adad-nirari II (r. 911–891 BC). Like most Assyrian kings, he boasted of his hunting exploits, claiming to have killed six elephants and captured four more; these would have been Syrian elephants, which were hunted to extinction in the following century. His grandson, Ashurnasirpal II (r. 883–859 BC), built on his successes, carrying out campaigns in every direction, most notably to the west in Syria and the Levant. The small city-states that had developed there after the collapse of the Hittite empire and the Egyptian withdrawal from the area proved no match for resurgent Assyria.

In 877 BC Ashurnasirpal reached Mount Lebanon and the Mediterranean. He wrote:

I cleansed my weapons in the Great Sea (and) made sacrifices to the gods. I received tribute from the kings of the sea coast, from the lands of the people of Tyre, Sidon, Byblos, Mahallatu, Maizu, Kaizu, Amurru, and the city Arvad, which is (on an island) in the sea – silver, gold, tin, bronze, a bronze casserole, linen garments with multi-coloured trim, a large female monkey, a small female monkey, ebony, boxwood, ivory of *nahiru* (which are) sea creatures.[1]

34 The head of a magnificent statuette of a beardless Assyrian, formed of many pieces, probably fitted together on a wooden core; carved fully in the round from a single tusk, the massive head measures 18.2 cm (7⁷⁄₁₆ in.). between the ears. IM 79520, Baghdad, National Museum of Iraq. Photograph Mick Sharp. (See also **53**, p. 51.)

Ashurnasirpal's new capital

Ashurnasirpal II celebrated his conquests by building himself a new capital city, Kalhu (Nimrud), near the junction of the Tigris and the River Zab. Work took some fifteen years to complete, during which he built city walls enclosing an area of 360 hectares (nearly 900 acres) and constructed palaces and temples on the remains of an old city. His new palace, the North West Palace, followed the typical Assyrian plan, with a huge outer courtyard, state apartments around an inner courtyard, and a domestic wing. The doorways into the great Throne Room, which measured 47 × 10 metres (154 × 33 ft), were marked by human-headed lion or bull colossi (**35**), while the façade and the walls of the room itself were lined with carved stone panels or bas-reliefs. The themes were either religious or royal, showing the king in the traditional roles of Mesopotamian monarchs, as high priest, warrior and hunter. Almost all the carvings were essentially paintings in stone, two-dimensional drawings, either incised or only lightly modelled. The hunting and battle scenes, narrative scenes with a mass of detail, were a new development. Originally, the sculptures looked very different from how they appear in museums today, for the stone, a Mosul marble, was a creamy colour rather than dark grey and was painted. The walls and ceilings above the reliefs were also brightly painted. Equipped with rich rugs and hangings, these great halls must have been full of colour.

Mallowan made one of his most significant discoveries in a recess next to the great Throne Room. This recess probably served as a shrine, for in it was found an outstandingly important Assyrian stela. The great sandstone block, some 1.3 metres (4 ft 3 in.) high, has a carving of the king at the top and 134 lines of cuneiform inscribed on the front and back. It had been erected to commemorate the founding of Ashurnasirpal's new capital and the building of his palace, which is described in detail, as are the festivities that celebrated its consecration in 879 BC. The inscription begins 'Palace of the man Ashurnasirpal, priest of Ashur, beloved of the God Enlil and of the God Ninurta',[2] and gives the king's titles and ancestry, before listing his conquests. With the help of the gods, he has taken tribute and hostages in many lands. He affirms his faith in the god Ashur, who is often shown as a man wearing the horned crown of divinity within a winged disc (ND 1715h, **36**).[3] He describes his palace, his 'heart's delight', his garden, his zoo and his city, and concludes with the festivities:

BELOW **35** The fallen and broken figure of a *lamassu* or bull-man from Gate D of the North West Palace, excavated in 1952.

BELOW RIGHT **36** An incised Assyrian-style fragment, showing the god Ashur wearing the horned cap of divinity and set within a winged disc (3.6 × 2.5 × 0.3 cm; 1⁷⁄₁₆ × 1 × ⅛ in.). ND 1715h, Baghdad, National Museum of Iraq.

42 Ancient Ivory

Vast quantities of food were brought in to feed, over the ten days of the celebrations, the 16,000 citizens of Kalhu, 5,000 visiting dignitaries from as far away as Tyre and Sidon, 1,500 officials and the 47,074 workmen and women 'summoned from all the districts of my land'.[4]

The carving at the top of the stela shows the king holding a long sceptre in his right hand and a mace in his left (**37**). He is wearing the high royal crown with a knob at the top, tied with a long diadem, and full ceremonial robes, consisting of a richly decorated, short-sleeved robe, belted at the waist with a shawl crossing over his shoulder. Suspended from his jewelled collar are the symbols of the gods, which are repeated on the top of the monument: Sin, the moon god; Ashur, the patron god of Assyria; Shamash, the sun god; Enlil, Anu or Ea, probably representing kingship; Adad, the storm god; and, finally, the Sibitti or Pleiades.

In the debris at the foot of the stela, Mallowan found two ivories, one of which shows the Assyrian king, dressed similarly to the image on the stela (ND 1082, **38**).[5] He is balancing a shallow bowl on the fingertips of his right hand and holding the eagle-headed sickle of Ninurta in his left. As Mallowan wrote, 'there can be little doubt that

LEFT **37** The panel at the top of the great sandstone stela of Ashurnasirpal II, found next to the Throne Room in the North West Palace, showing the king with the symbols of the gods (H, panel 127 cm; 50 in.); fifty-four lines of inscription celebrate the completion of the king's new capital city and describe the great banquet given to mark the occasion in 879 BC. Formerly Mosul Museum of History.

RIGHT **38** Ivory panel found near the stela of Ashurnasirpal II, showing the king wearing a crown and elaborate garments, holding a bowl in his right hand and the sickle of the god Ninurta in his left (27.2 × 7.5 × 0.5 cm; 10¹¹⁄₁₆ × 2¹⁵⁄₁₆ × ³⁄₁₆ in.). ND 1082, Baghdad, National Museum of Iraq.

Ah, Assyria! 43

ABOVE LEFT 39 Assyrian-style modelled panel from Well AJ in the North West Palace, showing (above), a four-winged, eagle-headed genie, kneeling, and (below) the heads of two courtiers (14.1 × 6.1 × 0.6 cm; 5 9/16 × 2 1/8 × 1/4 in.). IM 79589, Baghdad, National Museum of Iraq.

ABOVE RIGHT 40 Assyrian-style incised panel from Well AJ, in three registers; the central scene shows a winged, human-headed genie, holding a bucket and cone, perhaps for fertilizing, with the remains of winged sphinxes in the registers above and below (16.2 × 5.8 × 0.2 cm; 6 3/8 × 2 1/4 × 1/16 in.). IM 79553, Baghdad, National Museum of Iraq.

BELOW 41 Assyrian-style incised panel, part of a frieze of spotted deer kneeling between stylized pomegranate bushes, from the Queen's Treasury in Fort Shalmaneser (2.3 × 10.3 × 0.4 cm; 15/16 × 4 1/16 × 1/8 in.). ND 7742, London, British Museum.

the ivory plaque...represents no less a person than King Ashurnasirpal II himself'.[6] The panel is a relatively rare example of a modelled ivory, worked on a thin piece of material only some 5 mm (3/16 in.) thick. It is remarkable that it survived so well, in spite of being covered with so much fallen mud brick.

Another superb modelled ivory, found in Well AJ, shows a magical figure (IM 79589). Magical figures, such as the great *lamassu* that guard doorways, or the genies holding bucket and cone shown on many reliefs, played an important part in the protection of the king. The ivory shows a four-winged, eagle-headed genie, kneeling and facing to the right, holding a cone in his right hand and a bucket in his left (**39**).[7] Genies are regularly equipped with bucket and cone, one interpretation of which is that they represent the fertilization of the date palm, which has to be done by hand. The genie has a feathered crest, long hair and curls below his beak. Only the upper parts survive of the two Assyrians shown in the lower register. The bearded one on the left wears a diadem with a central rosette and a curl, and probably represented the crown prince. He is accompanied by a clean-shaven courtier.

Assyrian ivories are easy to recognize because of their distinctive style, designs and technique. Most were lightly incised on thin panels, often only 0.2 cm (1/16 in.) thick, while modelled examples were worked on slighter thicker panels. The backs of the panels were lightly scratched to aid adhesion to their wooden forms. Characteristic is their relatively rough fixing to the form by means of ivory dowels or bronze nails set into recessed hollows, which take no account of the image. Parts of three registers survive on an incised example from Well AJ of a genie (IM 79553, **40**).[8] The top and bottom registers once showed pairs of winged sphinxes, to either side of central rosettes that frame the winged, human-headed genie in the central register. The genie is wearing the horned cap of divinity, surmounted by a disc with a rosette, and has shoulder-length hair and a long spade-shaped beard. He wears a knee-length kilted tunic with a long open overskirt. A fringed shawl passes over his shoulder and down his chest. As usual he carries a cone in his raised right hand and probably held a bucket in his left.

Although Assyrian artists drew lively representations of animals and birds, including various types of caprid (such as the spotted deer kneeling beside stylized pomegranate bushes in ND 7742, **41**),[9] it is the narrative scenes that are typically Assyrian. They depict the king in his roles as high priest, warrior and hunter, and record his battles and victories. These scenes are illustrated on the bas-reliefs that line the principal rooms, on the bronze bands of great doors, on furniture and on ivory panels. Narrative art was an indigenous Assyrian development, beginning in the late second millennium BC, but it was not one followed by any of the neighbouring powers. The other area with a much longer and richer tradition was, of course, Egypt, but that is very different.

Ivories from the Throne Room of the North West Palace

One of the most important rooms on the citadel, and perhaps in the whole of Kalhu, was the Throne Room of the North West Palace. As far as we know, Layard did not find any ivory there, but his focus was to recover sculptures by digging tunnels around the walls. When Mallowan cleared the area to the south of the throne base, which Layard had revealed a century earlier, he found a few fragments of ivory. Although he was aware of their significance, he did not clear the centre of the room, despite commenting that ' the centre of this great Hall may be worth digging again'.[10] The clearing of the Throne Room was finally undertaken by the Iraqi State Board of Antiquities and Heritage, who, indeed, found more fragments of ivory, which have not yet been published.[11]

Mallowan's fragments are exceptionally important, for they probably decorated the actual throne of Ashurnasirpal II. They are the only ivories that can be dated, both by context and by style, to his reign.[12] They were found lying on a hard mud pavement, overlaid with bitumen and flush with the foot of the plinth on which the throne rested, and were covered by a 10 cm (4 in.) layer of clay. That they survived at all is remarkable. As Mallowan noted:

LEFT 42 Fragment of a deeply incised panel showing a bearded, bare-chested Assyrian felling a tree with a spike-butted axe (6.4 × 3.8 cm; 2½ × 1½ in.). ND 1715a, Baghdad, National Museum of Iraq.

RIGHT 43 A lively battle scene, the remains of which show parts of three chariots; an enemy wearing a feather-crested helmet (lower right) is trapped between the second and third chariots (2.9 × 7.7 × 0.3 cm; 1⅛ × 3 × ⅛ in.). The panel is so lightly incised that it must always have been barely legible. ND 1715, New York, Metropolitan Museum.

They are executed in a peculiar style and exquisitely engraved with Assyrian scenes, some of which have never appeared before. The most remarkable of these are two strips illustrating a ritual which is taking place on a hill-top or in the mountains, shown by the scale pattern running along the bottom of the panel. In one of them a bearded hero stripped to the waist is felling a tree with a heavy, three-pronged axe. The deliberate cutting down of trees was very much part of an Assyrian 'scorched earth' policy after conquering a rebellious state [ND 1715a, 42].[13]

Other fragments illustrate subjects similar to those on the contemporary bas-reliefs, such as ritual scenes, sieges and battles, the bringing of tribute and the hunting of bulls and lions. The scenes on the ivories do not copy the reliefs but complement them. This suggests that the decorative programme for the Throne Room, the focus of power, was designed as a unit and would have included the royal throne on the great throne dais.

Since these ivories probably formed parts of the king's throne, they should have been of a uniformly high quality. However, the immediate impression is of varying standards of craftsmanship, in both the drawing and the technical execution. Interestingly, the same variation in quality applies to the reliefs on the walls.[14] The drawing of the tree-cutting sequence is, for instance, easy to make out, while that of soldiers shooting from a chariot (ND 1715, 43),[15] is so lightly incised that it is difficult to see, even in a low raking light. The designs would, of course, have been painted, which would have helped visibility, but even so the drawing is slight. Such variation raises interesting questions about what was considered important. Presumably, it was the actual design and its content rather than how well it was drawn. The relative unimportance of the image is also suggested by the Assyrian practice, in the reign of Ashurnasirpal II, of writing cuneiform inscriptions across sculptures, even of the king himself.

Other Assyrian ivories

The largest number of Assyrian ivories was found in the private throne room of the Nabu Temple on the east of the citadel mound. Nabu was the god of writing, whose cult centre was at Borsippa, near Babylon. He was believed to be the son of Marduk, the city god of Babylon, and became popular in Assyria in the first millennium BC. The temple was built by Ashurnasirpal II and remained in use until the final sack of Kalhu in 612 BC. It consisted of two large courtyards to the east of the site, one of which included the scribal library. Two great shrines faced onto the inner court and were dedicated to the god and to his wife, Tashmetum. In the north-west corner were two smaller courtyards containing smaller shrines to the god and his wife, and a reception suite that served as the private throne room of the temple. It was in this area that the *akitu* (or sacred marriage) ceremony took place. The throne room contained the usual stepped dais and the tramlines for a brazier in front. The area had been fiercely burnt, leaving a bed of ash, in places up to 80 cm (c. 2½ ft) thick, covering the floor, particularly around the dais. Amid the ashes, Mallowan and his team 'found the charred fragments of the king's throne overlaid with carved ivory burnt black and grey',[16] as well as the smashed remains of cuneiform tablets. When reconstructed, these proved to be treaties imposed on vassal states by Esarhaddon (r. 680–669 BC), which had probably been deliberately sought out and destroyed during the sack of Kalhu.

The burnt and broken ivories, found on top of the dais and against the front and sides, were lightly incised. The principal panel, reconstructed from numerous fragments, some 68 cm (27 in.) long (ND 4193, **44**), shows Ashurnasirpal receiving processions of tribute bearers. As Mallowan described him, the king,

> wearing the high crown of Assyria, has emerged fully armed from the royal tent after descending from his chariot which is drawn by a pair of fully caparisoned horses led by the charioteer. The umbrella bearer and squire with fly whisk are in attendance whilst the king balances a ceremonial bowl on the tips of his fingers. Into the presence of the king an Assyrian warrior armed with a long sword ushers in the procession of foreign tributaries who are distinguished from the Assyrians by their dress.[17]

ABOVE **44** Part of a long panel from the Nabu Temple, with an incised Assyrian design showing the king, having descended from his chariot and attended by his courtiers, about to receive foreign tributaries bringing gifts (H 8 cm; 3⅛ in.). Reproduced from Mallowan, 1966, i, p. 248, fig. 209.

RIGHT **45** An 8th-century panel with decorated frame from the Central Palace, showing the Assyrian kind and the crown prince (15.2 × 9.3 × 0.3 cm; 6 × 3⅝ × ⅛ in.). London, British Museum, inv. no. 127065.

The Assyrian reliefs found at Nimrud, Khorsabad and Nineveh are dated from the reign of Ashurnasirpal II (r. 883–859 BC) to that of Ashurbanipal (r. 668–627? BC). Thanks to this dated sequence of reliefs, it is possible to identify changes in style and composition, dress and equipment during that period. For instance, the relatively small, six-spoked, ninth-century chariot becomes in the seventh century a massive vehicle with large, studded wheels – an ancient tank. The ivories from the Nabu Temple and the North West Palace can safely be assigned to the ninth century, while some found by William Kennett Loftus in the 1850s would have been carved in the eighth century.

Loftus, accompanied by his artist, William Boutcher, was probably working in an area known today as the Central

46 Drawing in black ink on tracing paper (27.8 × 38 cm; 10 15/16 × 14 15/16 in.) by William Boutcher of an 8th-century Assyrian panel from the Central Palace, showing a procession of tributaries bearing gifts, including wine skins, jewelry and horses (H 8 cm; 3 1/8 in.). London, British Museum, inv. no. 118099 (panel), 2007,6024. 18 (drawing).

Palace. He found some incised rectangular panels, one of which, showing the king and the crown prince facing each other (BM 127065, **45**),[18] can be compared to sculptures of Tiglath-pileser III (r. 745–727 BC). Features such as the taller form of the king's crown, his hairstyle and the garment of the crown prince, decorated with rectangles, are typical of the eighth century. There are also technical differences between ninth- and eighth-century panels. The ivory of the later panels is slightly thicker and the incision clearer. The backs are roughened with chisel marks, rather than striations, and they were more subtly fixed to the wooden form by means of simple dowels the holes for which avoid the images, rather than dowel holes with recessed heads driven through the designs.[19]

One of the fragments found by Loftus, drawn by Boutcher, shows a lively scene of tributaries bringing gifts (BM 118099, **46**).[20] One man has a wineskin slung over his shoulder, a second carries a tray on his head with dishes and the model of a castle, presumably in token of submission, while another leads a fine pair of horses. The style is more detailed and lively than ninth-century examples.

Some Assyrianizing panels

In 1852 Henry Rawlinson visited Nimrud and reopened some of Layard's excavations. He found 'a set of ivory ornaments, some of them very beautifully carved, but all more or less injured'.[21] These were probably found in the North West Palace, but exactly where is uncertain, possibly in or near Layard's 'ivory store'. The fragmentary panels are very handsome, and depict tall, beardless youths with long hair, bound by diadems and falling in ringlets in front of their ears. They are clad in long garments made of a pleated material, with fringed hems, and wear fringed shawls wound round the waist and across the shoulders; double straps cross their chests. They are either standing below winged discs of an unusual form and plucking fruits (BM 118109, 118115, **47**),[22] or flanking a stylized tree, raising one of their hands in salutation and holding a mace in the other. Registered in 1856 with the panels of the youths, and probably forming part of the same set, is a fragment with a fine, feisty lion, his hind legs grasped by a pair of 'heroes', of whom all that survives is the foot of the one on the left, and part of the leading leg and garment of his companion on the right (BM 118117, **48**).[23]

Although superficially Assyrian in style, these panels are Assyrianizing rather than Assyrian. This is not surprising, as Assyria was the superpower of the time, and versions of Assyrian art were popular, especially from the eighth century, across a wide area from north Syria to Urartu in Anatolia to western Iran. There is no agreement as to their origin, though comparisons with ivories from Toprak Kale near Lake Van may suggest that they were Urartian.

Small inlays, statuettes and furniture pieces

Precious material was often in short supply in Mesopotamia, as it had to be imported. To economize on its use, an old technique, known from the third millennium BC, was to carve only the figure in shell, ivory or bone, and then to set it in a wooden backing. Three small silhouettes or inlay figures continue the old tradition and are, like the panels, either incised or modelled. An incised figure of a beardless courtier (ND 7667, **49**),[24] was found in the Throne Room in the Residency of the Fort, while the other two inlays, found in the *rab ekalli*'s suite, show winged genies (ND 7584 and 7642, **50–51**).[25]

The flood of tribute and booty entering Assyrian warehouses by the eighth century resulted in a much greater use of ivory; this may also have been linked to the employment of foreign craftsmen, familiar with problems

LEFT AND ABOVE **47–48** Fragments of two Assyrianizing panels, found by Henry Rawlinson in the 19th century: one shows a pair of handsome youths with long hair, plucking fruits from a tree (16.6 × 10 × 0.4 cm; 6½ × 3¹⁵⁄₁₆ × ¼ in.), and the other shows a lion fought by a pair of heroes, of whom only parts of the feet survive (7.9 × 4.1 × 0.4 cm; 3⅛ × 1⅝ × ¼ in.). London, British Museum, inv. nos 118109, 118115, 118117.

RIGHT **49–51** Ivory silhouettes or inlays for setting in wood – an old technique for economizing on the use of precious material: (left) incised figure of a courtier (3.9 × 1 × 0.5 cm; 1½ × ⅜ × ³⁄₁₆ in.); (centre) incised figure of a kneeling, winged genie, wearing a horned crown (4 × 2.6 cm; 1⁹⁄₁₆ × 1 in.); and (right) modelled fragment of a winged genie (4.9 × 1.9 × 0.8 cm; 1¹⁵⁄₁₆ × ¾ × ⁵⁄₁₆ in.). ND 7667, 7584, 7642. London, British Museum.

52 Winged, eagle-headed genie, carrying bucket and cone; 8th-century openwork panel in Assyrian style, found in Fort Shalmaneser (11.7 × 6 cm; 4⅝ × 2⅜ in.). ND 10328, Baghdad, National Museum of Iraq.

of carving hard wood and ivory. An openwork piece, carved in the round and depicting a winged, eagle-headed genie, was found in a workroom in the Fort (ND 10328, **52**).[26] He has an upright crest, hanging curls and a necklace, and is equipped with the usual bucket and cone. He can be dated to the eighth century BC because of the short, kilted skirt with a pendant fishtail fringe, first seen on Assyrian reliefs during the reign of Tiglath-pileser III (r. 745–727 BC).

But once again it is a find from Well AJ that illustrates the marked change in ivory usage that occurred during the eighth century, and shows just how magnificent Assyrian statuary may have been. This consists of parts of a composite statuette, made up of many pieces carved in ivory, fitted together with tenons and mounted on a wooden core; it was doubtless originally richly gilded and clothed. This statuette, representing an Assyrian courtier or eunuch, when restored, would have measured some 53 cm (21 in.) in height. The surviving parts of the ivory consist of a massive head, carved in one piece, the two shoulders and upper arms, the right side of the body and the two sandalled feet (IM 79520, **53**).[27] They were found close together at a depth of about 23 metres (75½ ft). The head is carved from a huge tusk, the distance between the upper ends of the ears measuring 18.2 cm (a little more than 7 in.). The hair is waved over the head and behind the ears, falling onto the shoulder in a heavy roll of spiral curls. The face is round and smooth with heavy eyebrows, large, almond-shaped eyes with pronounced rims, a curving fleshy nose, a small mouth, rounded cheeks and a firm chin. The hair, eyebrows, eyelashes and pupils of the eyes were originally coloured black. The neck is short and thick, and at the base is encircled by a torque with many herringbone pendants. The face is typically Assyrian and is similar to those on a panel with courtiers from Well AJ (IM 79537, **10**, p. 15).[28] The shoulders are covered in a short-sleeved garment, decorated with chevrons and rectangles. The feet, which are more than 11 cm (4¼ in.) long (**54**), are carved naturalistically with the toes and toenails carefully delineated; they are shod in heeled sandals secured by straps around the big toe and tied on the top of the foot.

53-54 One of the most remarkable discoveries in Well AJ consists of parts of a statuette of a beardless Assyrian courtier, carved in ivory and wood and then presumably gilded and clothed (it would have been c. 50 cm, 19½ in. tall). The massive head (18.2 × 12 cm; 7³⁄₁₆ × 4¾ in.) was carved in one piece; the hair is waved over the head, ending in a heavy roll, and the face is round and smooth, with strong brows, almond-shaped eyes, a large nose and a small mouth. The feet (11.6 × 4.4 × 3.4 cm; 4⁹⁄₁₆ × 1¾ × 1⅜ in.) are sensitively carved and shod in sandals; traces of black paint suggest that they were painted. IM 79520, Baghdad, National Museum of Iraq. Photograph Mick Sharp.

ABOVE 55 One of a pair of circular furniture fittings in the form of palm capitals, carved from a large tusk; these decorated the legs of a throne or bed, and examples were also worked in bronze or stone (H 5, dia. 13.4 cm; H 2, dia. 5¼ in.). IM 79546, Baghdad, National Museum of Iraq.

LEFT 56 By the 8th century, supplies of ivory were plentiful and it was even used for hidden fitments, such as this plain cylinder with a series of interlocking tenon slots, found in Well AJ (H 8.5, dia. 7.6 cm; H 3⅜, dia. 3 in.). IM 79595, Baghdad, National Museum of Iraq.

By the late eighth century BC ivory was being used even for large furniture elements, such as a pair of circular fittings in the form of palm capitals, found, again, in Well AJ. One of these (IM 79546, **55**)[29] has a diameter of some 13.4 cm (5¼ in.) and a depth of 5 cm (2 in.), and was fixed by a large rectangular tenon passing through a slot in the centre. Similar fittings have been found in bronze and stone and formed parts of the legs of Assyrian thrones, stools and footstools. By comparison with the economic use of ivory in the ninth century, this piece shows a fundamentally different approach and suggests the greater availability of large tusks, which were often listed in descriptions of tribute or booty. Pieces were even used for interior fittings (IM 79595, **56**). Layard found the 'remains of several entire elephants' tusks, the largest being about 2 feet 5 inches long' in his Treasure Chamber,[30] and Mallowan also found tusks.[31] This change in Assyrian ivory-working may also have resulted from the presence of imported craftsmen: skilled foreign craftsmen were highly valued, and there are many references to instances of a craftsman being lent. However, they would have been carefully controlled and would have worked to Assyrian orders and in the Assyrian style.

The importance of context

As significant as their style are the locations in which the ivories were found. It is notable that the distribution of Assyrian ivory panels showing narrative scenes is entirely different from that of Levantine ivories: they were found in areas with official or royal connections, in throne rooms, near throne daises or in royal or ceremonial suites. In the

North West Palace, for example, narrative panels were found in and adjacent to the Throne Room, and some had been thrown down Well AJ, close to the king's suite. Elsewhere on the citadel, a fine collection was found around the throne dais in the Nabu Temple, while panels found by Loftus were probably from the Central Palace.

The same pattern of distribution occurs in Fort Shalmaneser. The relatively few narrative Assyrian ivories were clustered in prime ceremonial and residential areas, such as the rooms of the principal suite in the Residency and the room next to the throne dais in the great South East Courtyard, locations where imported ivories were notably absent. An assemblage of incised, modelled and miniature burnt fragments was found in Room T10, a furniture store, conveniently sited between the main Throne Room (T1) and the reception suites in the T wing. This is one of the few locations where local and imported ivories occur together.

The situation in the *rab ekalli*'s suite is slightly different. His rooms are one of the few 'residential' units that contained ivories. Like T10, these rooms had been burnt, and objects had fallen down from the upper storey. The ivories found here include a few Assyrian fragments, as well as a range of Levantine pieces. Furthermore, a room probably forming part of the suite (Room NE2) contained one of the finest groups of ivories found at Nimrud. The statuettes are carved in the round and show men – Syrians or Africans – each leading an animal and carrying a second on his shoulders (**98–100**, pp. 86–87). They are superb works of art, items of booty clearly enjoyed by their new owner. This appreciation of 'foreign' art appears to have been rare, though from such a small sample it is not possible to be certain whether the *rab ekalli* was unusual in valuing it. Certainly, there is a marked absence of foreign pieces in the elite Assyrian areas, and further evidence of this likely indifference is provided by the fact that the majority of the Levantine ivories throughout the Fort were simply stored, stripped of their gold overlays, in a broken state.

The division between the two types of ivory is clear. In official or ceremonial areas, Assyrian art was standard. This distribution indicates that the furniture used in primary contexts was decorated with Assyrian art, complementing the art of wall reliefs, paintings and bronze bands on doors. Nevertheless, relatively few Assyrian ivories have survived – certainly not a sufficient number to have decorated all the items of furniture in the royal suites. It seems probable, therefore, that ivory was relatively little used on Assyrian furniture, which was more frequently decorated with bronze, or with a mixture of bronze and ivory. Layard found the remains of just such a throne in the North West Palace:

> with the exception of the legs, which appear to have been partly of ivory, it was of wood, cased or overlaid with bronze. . . . The metal was elaborately engraved and embossed with symbolical figures and ornaments, like those embroidered on the robes of the early Nimroud king, such as winged deities, struggling with griffins, mythic animals, men before the sacred tree, and the winged lion and bull.[32]

It is unclear why the Assyrians bothered to bring back so much ivory booty to Kalhu, and having done so why they did not actually use it. Resurgent Assyria was the superpower of the area. Its arms were unbeatable, and defeat by them was terrible – people were slaughtered, or carried away into captivity and resettled within the empire. The Assyrians had developed their own distinctive and characteristic art from the late second millennium BC. From the beginning it had a narrative element, steadily developed during the early first millennium. The stories of victory and the total defeat of enemies, told on their sculptures, bronze bands and ivory panels, proclaimed a propaganda message to all those who visited Kalhu.

However, another, even more important, aspect of Assyrian art was that of protection against evil. The Assyrian king was surrounded by his own art, from great gateway figures at the entrances to important rooms, to the relief sculptures and metalwork, to wall paintings, furniture, clothing and jewelry and magical foundation figurines. The art of defeated peoples, by contrast, had clearly failed to protect them. This may be one reason why the imported ivories were simply stored: they had no power.

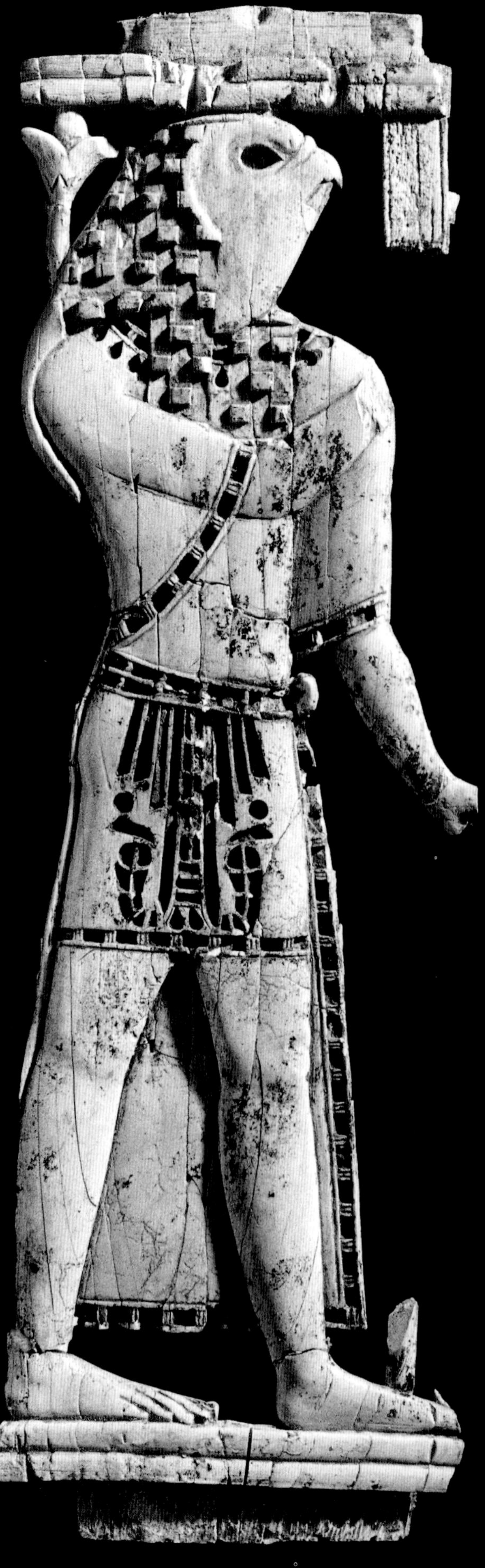

Chapter 3

The Phoenicians: Master Craftsmen

Now I [King Hiram of Tyre] have sent a skilled man, endued with understanding, Huram-abi.... He is trained to work in gold, silver, bronze, iron, stone, and wood, and in purple, blue, and crimson fabrics and fine linen, and to do all sorts of engraving and execute any design that may be assigned him[.]*

The Phoenicians are essentially a lost civilization. We learn about them only through accounts in the Bible, the Assyrian records and classical sources, each of which has its own agenda. The prophet Isaiah, who wrote a long account the main purpose of which was to exult over the possible fall of Tyre, described the Phoenicians as famous for their wealth, their seamanship and the quality of their craftsmanship: 'Tyre, the crowning city, whose merchants are princes, whose traffickers are the honourable of the earth' (Isaiah 23:8).

Remarkably little is known about the Phoenicians. Even their name, *phoenikes*, which is what the Greeks called the merchants of the Levant seaboard,[1] is misleading: first, it is not what they called themselves, and, second, it suggests that there was a Phoenician state, for which there is no evidence. Like so many Near Eastern peoples, the Phoenicians were city dwellers and their loyalty was to their city: the men of Sidon were Sidonians, the men of Tyre Tyrians. This focus on the city was reinforced by their geography. Phoenician territory consisted of a narrow, fertile coastal fringe, stretching from north of Arvad to Akko (or Acre) south of Tyre, an area with the sea to the west and the Lebanese mountains to the east. It was made up of compartmentalized regions, separated from one another by rivers and mountain spurs, conditions that favoured the development of independent political units.

Maritime merchants

The principal Phoenician cities were located either on promontories dominating a bay or on small natural inlets that provided shelter for their ships; two, Tyre and Arvad, were on islands. Their focus was on trade and the sea, rather than on the formation of a state. Their cities were rich in resources: forests of cedar, pine and cypress grew on the mountains, fish were plentiful in the sea, and they exploited the remarkable *murex*, a sea snail, from which they made the famous 'Tyrian purple' dye. Vines and olives flourished in the fertile hinterland, but they were always short of corn. The cities were ruled by kings, supported by councils of elders, or representatives of the most renowned and powerful families in the city, whose power probably lay in their mercantile interests.[2]

Phoenician wealth was based on maritime trade. As early as 2600 BC, Egyptian inscriptions mention 'ships of

---

57 A superbly preserved, falcon-headed male deity of the Phoenician Ornate Group, coloured with red and blue inlays; he has a tripartite wig, a shawl-sleeved garment and skirt with an elaborate apron, typical markers of the group. ND 10476, Baghdad, National Museum of Iraq (27.5 × 8.7 × 1 cm; 10¹³⁄₁₆ × 3⁷⁄₁₆ × ⅜ in.). Photograph Mick Sharp.

Byblos' transporting wood and oil. At this time Byblos was the principal Phoenician city. Later the prophet Ezekiel praised the Phoenicians' seamanship: 'The inhabitants of Zidon and Arvad were thy mariners: thy wise men, O Tyrus, that were in thee, were thy pilots' (Ezekiel 27:8). Long before the invention of the mariner's compass, Phoenician sailors mastered the sea, braving treacherous winds and reefs. The Mediterranean was their domain, and they founded commercial bases at Memphis in Egypt, in Cyprus, Crete, Sicily, Sardinia, France, Spain and north Africa. They ventured through the Straits of Gibraltar, the ancient 'Pillars of Hercules', and along the Atlantic coasts of Spain and Morocco. According to Herodotus, they even circumnavigated Africa, a task that took three years and was not to be repeated for another 2,000.

The foundation of the Phoenicians' success was their ships: there were three types, each illustrated on the Assyrian reliefs. The smallest ones, *hippoi*, used for local transport and fishing, were rowed by one or two men; they had rounded ends, and figureheads in the form of horses' heads. On a bronze frieze on the famous Balawat Gates of Shalmaneser III (r. 858–824 BC), the Tyrian king, Ithobaal (r. 887–856 BC), can be seen loading *hippoi* with tribute (**58**); the scene is identified in an epigraph: 'I received tribute from the cities of the people of Tyre and Sidon: silver, gold, tin, bronze, wool, lapis lazuli (and) carnelian.'[3] The principal merchant ship was the *gaulos*, a larger, round-bottomed sailing ship with symmetrical upright stem- and sternposts. It was well suited to deep-water, long-distance commerce and could carry large cargoes. Averaging between 20 and 30 metres (65–100 ft) in length, it had a sturdy mast that supported a broad rectangular sail. Towards the stern was a quarterdeck, which provided shelter for the crew and the ship's galley.[4] The third ship, the Phoenician war galley, was highly respected for its speed and agility. The triaconter and penteconter were single-banked vessels with thirty and fifty oarsmen respectively. During the eighth century BC the invention of the raised deck made possible the creation of a double-banked galley, with two staggered rows of oarsmen, one above the other, working their oars from inside the vessel, the upper row on the gunwale itself, the lower through ports in the hull.[5] This innovation was a great improvement, as it made the ship more compact and shock-resistant. As with all war galleys, at the waterline the prow of the vessel extended to a point, which was shod with bronze for ramming and disabling enemy craft. Both types of vessel – the merchant ship and the warship – can be seen on a relief from the Palace of Sennacherib at Nineveh, depicting a scene identified as the flight of King Luli of Tyre to Cyprus. On the right can be seen the city walls, with a building that is perhaps the temple of the principal Tyrian deity, Melqart, above (**59**).

BELOW **58** Ithobaal, king of Tyre, loading tribute onto small boats known as *hippoi*, on the Balawat Gates of Shalmaneser III, mid-9th century BC. London, British Museum, inv. no. 124657.

RIGHT **59** The flight of King Luli from Tyre, on a sculpture from the Southwest Palace of King Sennacherib at Nineveh, early 7th century BC; the scene clearly shows the Phoenicians' round-bottomed merchant ships and their double-banked warships with rams. Barnett et al. 1998, pl. 38, 30a.

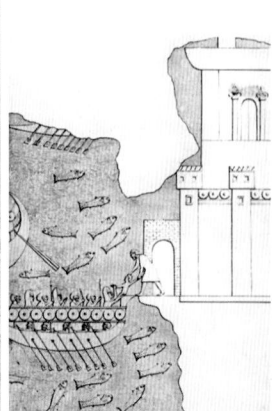

The Phoenicians used their maritime skills to procure and transport quantities of valued raw materials over long distances, both for their own use and for re-export. As recorded in the early eleventh-century account of the Egyptian envoy Wen-Amon to King Zakar-Baal of Byblos, in exchange for valuable cedars to build 'the great and august ship of Amon-Re, sovereign of the gods',[6] Egypt provided gold and silver, linen, papyrus rolls, cow hides, ropes, lentils and fish;[7] the quantities of goods traded in such transactions were based on a predetermined exchange rate, set against the price of cedar wood.[8] Long-distance trade involved the importation of copper from Cyprus and silver from Sardinia and Spain. Tyre also had extensive inland trading connections – with Israel and Judah, Damascus, Arabia and Mesopotamia. The primary commodities that Tyre acquired were precious metals and minerals, ivory and ebony, elephant hides, dyed and embroidered garments, linen and wool, spices, wines, corn and livestock.

Both Tyrians and Sidonians (the names were used interchangeably so do not necessarily give a reliable indication of place of origin) were known as skilled craftsmen, particularly in bronze. They are mentioned in both the biblical book of Kings and the *Iliad*. Perhaps the most famous story about the Tyrians is the series of exchanges between Hiram I of Tyre (r. 971–939 BC) and King Solomon: when Solomon was building the Temple in Jerusalem, he asked Hiram to provide him not only with cedars but also with craftsmen to help him (1 Kings 5:1–12; 2 Chronicles 2); Hiram sent a skilled man 'to work in gold, silver, bronze, iron, stone, and wood' (2 Chronicles 2:14). Another story concerns a trading partnership between Solomon and Hiram: 'Once every three years the fleet of ships of Tarshish used to come bringing gold, silver, ivory, apes, peacocks' (1 Kings 10:22).

Unfortunately – as is the case with so much about the Phoenicians – there is considerable dispute as to whether these attractive stories are myth or reflect reality. There is little archaeological proof of a flourishing united monarchy of Israel and Judah in the tenth century. As Jonathan Tubb, Keeper of the Middle East Department of the British Museum (among many others), points out, it was not until the early ninth century that Omri (r. 885–874 BC) formed the first Israelite kingdom and made Samaria his new capital. This is the earliest evidence of a well-constructed capital city, and there are uniform architectural plans of the defences and gateways at Samaria and at the biblical cities of Hazor, Megiddo and Gezer. Debate will undoubtedly continue on this divisive topic. Omri was succeeded by his son Ahab (r. c. 874–853 BC), who, according to the Bible, married the Phoenician princess Jezebel, daughter of Ithobaal of Tyre, and is castigated in the book of Kings for 'the ivory house which he built' (1 Kings 22:39).[9]

Phoenician literature and art

Although the Phoenicians bequeathed the alphabet to humanity, none of their literature has survived. Phoenician histories, economic records and mythologies, diligently recorded on papyrus rolls and stored in palace and temple archives, are referred to time and again in the Bible, and in the texts of other cultures, such as the Assyrians and the Greeks, but they have all disappeared: not one Phoenician manuscript has survived. This appalling loss is matched by a similar loss of their artistic heritage. Because their cities along the Levant coast were so brilliantly sited, they have continued in occupation to the present day, so that little excavation has been possible. No examples survive of two of the Phoenicians' most valued commodities, fine textiles and carved woodwork. Most of their worked precious metals have also disappeared, the victims of human and environmental intervention.[10] That their metalwork was highly esteemed, not only as an initial purchase but also as it acquired value through its history, is illustrated by a story in Homer. A large silver crater, offered by Achilles as a prize at the funeral games for his friend Patroclus, was 'a masterpiece of Sidonian craftsmanship', the 'loveliest thing in the world', which had been 'shipped by Phoenician traders across the misty seas' (*Iliad* XXIII:740–45).

Any attempt to discover Phoenician art has to be based on finds from the outlying regions that formed their markets, and above all on the tribute and booty seized by the Assyrian kings and deposited in their new capital city. Phoenician cities provided 'gifts' or tribute to most Assyrian kings. Although Tiglath-pileser I (r. 1114–1076 BC) received gifts from Sidon, it was not until the early ninth century that Assyrian kings actively campaigned in the west. Ashurnasirpal II (r. 883–859 BC) marched to the Mediterranean, where he received the tribute of 'the kings of the sea coast, from the lands of the people of Tyre, Sidon, Byblos...and the city Arvad'.[11] Among the 47,074 able-bodied men and women 'summoned from all the districts of my land' by Ashurnasirpal II to Kalhu and invited to the great feast to celebrate the completion of the North West Palace were men of Tyre and Sidon.[12] Until the mid-eighth century, Tyre continued to flourish, paying a reasonable tribute to Assyria. However, with the accession of Tiglath-pileser III (r. 745–727 BC) there was a change of Assyrian approach: the Levantine cities were conquered, Assyrian officials were installed to control them and a heavy tribute was imposed. This policy continued throughout the remaining years of Assyrian rule. Esarhaddon (r. 680–669 BC) besieged Tyre, which had rebelled, along with the pharaoh Taharqa of Egypt, and captured the two kings; his victory is recorded on a stela found at Zinjirli. He seized the wealth stored by the Tyrian king:

gold, silver, precious stones, elephant hides, ivory, maple, boxwood, garments of brightly colored wool and linen, of every description, the treasure of his palace, I carried off en masse. His people, from far and near, which were countless, (with their) cattle, flocks and asses, I deported to Assyria.[13]

The cities of the Levant coast had been in regular contact with Egypt since at least the third millennium BC, and at times were under direct Egyptian control. This debt is already evident in Late Bronze Age material from Ugarit (modern Ras Shamra):[14] Egyptian metalwork and ivories offer many parallels with Phoenician work of the early first millennium. Continuing contact with Egypt between 945 and 850 BC is shown by busts and statues sent to Byblos as diplomatic gifts by the Tanite pharaohs Sheshonk I and Osorkon I and II.[15] The first clue, therefore, to identifying Phoenician ivories is a debt to the art of Egypt.

Perhaps the most famous early Phoenician artefact is a great sarcophagus, found in the Royal Cemetery at Byblos (**60**). This massive stone coffin is decorated on both the top and the sides, and carries an inscription on the lid by Ithobaal, dedicating it to his father, King Ahiram (c. 1000 BC). Despite the inscription, the date of the sarcophagus is hotly

60 Massive limestone sarcophagus found in the Royal Necropolis at Byblos with an inscription dedicating it to King Ahiram (c. 1000 BC); it is one of the most important examples of early Phoenician art. National Museum of Beirut. (See also **257**, p. 165.)

58   ANCIENT IVORY

disputed, some scholars suggesting that it was re-used and was originally made in the early twelfth century, while others accept a date in the tenth or even eighth century. While the dispute will continue, a date in the eleventh century seems reasonable. The scenes on the sides of the sarcophagus show a dead king seated on a magnificent throne, the side of which is in the form of a sphinx. The table in front of him is loaded with funerary meats; an attendant holds a fly-whisk and a towel, and is followed by a line of mourners. The banquet scene was a popular motif, usually associated with funerary rites. Nevertheless, it is remarkable that this particular version was copied on a tenth-century ivory pyxis, carved in the North Syrian 'flame and frond' style, which was found in Well AJ of the North West Palace (**264**, p. 169). Such parallelism, apart from the obvious differences in style, scale and material, suggest the use of some form of pattern book.

The Phoenician ivories found at Nimrud

More than a thousand pieces from Nimrud have been identified as Phoenician. They can be divided into a number of style-groups, such as the Egyptianizing, the 'Ornate Group', the 'Finely Carved' and so on. Some of these groups share so many stylistic and technical features that it seems possible they were carved in the workshops of a single centre. In view of the quantity of ivory produced, such a centre must have had a number of workshops, with teams of craftsmen specializing in ivory, wood, gold and inlay work. However, not all Phoenician ivories would have been carved in a single centre. Others, particularly those lacking the colourful inlays that are such a hallmark of the finest ivories, would probably have originated in one of the many other Phoenician cities along the Levant coast.

Phoenician ivories are among the most beautiful and superbly worked pieces found at Nimrud. They are unified by a strong sense of elegance, balance and symmetry, and are often gilded and inlaid with coloured glass or occasionally stone. The range of subjects is limited: they consist of Egyptianizing scenes or slender figures harmoniously disposed in the available space. The figures are mostly deities, both male and female, young males, especially pharaoh figures, and mythical creatures, such as sphinxes and griffins. Another favourite motif was the stylized tree, and there are also animal scenes. There is a marked absence of any sort of narrative, despite there being a strong tradition in Egypt, from whom the Phoenicians borrowed so much, and the presence to the east of Assyria, with its own highly developed narrative tradition.

Egyptianizing ivories

About a hundred of the Phoenician ivories discovered at Nimrud show such strong Egyptian influence that they are called 'Egyptianizing'. The first examples were found in 1846 by Layard in the North West Palace. Being remarkably perceptive, he recognized that the Egyptian characteristics of these pieces were 'not quite right'.

The most interesting are the remains of two small tablets, one nearly entire [BM 118120, **61**],[16] the other much injured, representing two sitting figures, holding

61 A splendid Egyptianizing ivory, found by Layard in Room V of the North West Palace, still showing traces of the original inlay and gold leaf; deities are seated on either side of a central cartouche, the hieroglyphs of which can be read as the commonplace phrase 'Shu, son of Re' (7.4 × 15.9 × 0.4 cm; 2$^{15}/_{16}$ × 6$^{1}/_{4}$ × $^{1}/_{8}$ in.). London, British Museum, inv. no. 118120.

The Phoenicians: Master Craftsmen

62 An Egyptianizing ivory panel, showing a two male figures (partly preserved), kneeling on either side of a central feature (misunderstood by the sculptor) in the form of a hieroglyph for 'temple' (5.1 × 13.8 × 0.7 cm; 2 × 5 7/16 × 1/4 in.). ND 13026, Baghdad, National Museum of Iraq. Photograph Mick Sharp.

in one hand the Egyptian sceptre or symbol of power. . . . The forms and style of art have a purely Egyptian character, although there are certain peculiarities in the execution and mode of treatment that would seem to mark the work of a foreign, perhaps an Assyrian, artist. The same peculiarities – the same anomalies – characterized all the other objects discovered; . . . In all these specimens the spirit of the design and the delicacy of the workmanship are equally to be admired.[17]

Shortly after Layard's rapid publication of his discoveries, some French scholars suggested that the workmanship of these ivories was not Egyptian but Phoenician, a conclusion followed in 1912 by Frederik Poulsen and recently shared by Professor Ken Kitchen of the University of Liverpool:

Did any of this considerable collection of Egyptian-influenced ivories actually originate in Egypt, i.e. were any of them carved there? Frankly, this possibility seems very doubtful indeed. It is perfectly possible that Levantine craftsmen worked in Egypt, either in such East Delta centres as Tanis or even Bubastis, or most likely at the capital, Memphis, where even Herodotus alludes to Tyrians, and where there was certainly a cosmopolitan element from at least the New Kingdom onwards. That any Egyptian craftsman carved any of these pieces seems almost impossible. Almost throughout, non-Egyptian treatment of motifs (not to mention the signs) and styles of workmanship exclude a strictly Egyptian origin. Even so fine a piece as No. 1003 [ND 13026, **62**],[18] rivaling Egyptian style and carving, cannot be so attributed because of the treatment of subject-matter: the plinth with *shen* and [lotus] is not an object of worship in Egypt. . . . But what of foreigners working in Egypt? Here too I am sceptical. The one part of the ancient world where these Levantine ivories are not attested is Egypt herself. No tomb, no occupation site, no temple cache has yielded any such object yet, as far as I know.[19]

Egyptianizing ivories were found both in the North West Palace and in Fort Shalmaneser, and form a particularly coherent group. The designs are clearly derived from Egyptian originals and consist of complete compositions carved on single panels. They illustrate a larger range of subjects than other Phoenician ivories and focus on scenes set in boats that have prows in the form of papyrus flowers and are often navigating papyrus marshes, or on scenes centred on the *djed* pillar altar (a symbol of Osiris) or on a cartouche (an oval frame containing hieroglyphs). A number of Egyptian-derived features, such as the *wedjat* eye (or Eye of Horus) and the *aegis* (symbols of protection and healing), occur only on Phoenician ivories, not on other Levantine pieces. Many Egyptianizing examples are unique, though there are some paired panels; this, too, is in contrast to other Levantine ivories, which usually form sets of identical panels. Technically, 'Egyptianizing' ivories share many features, from the unusual forms of the panels to the extensive use of colouring and gilding. Like the designs, the technique of gilding and inlaying was borrowed from Egypt, where it was applied across the board, from furniture to jewelry. The majority of the ivories were decorated with glass inlays, set on a frit bedding within cloisons covered with gold foil, but some were simply modelled and gilded. Some of the glass inlays, such as wigs or flowers or the body parts of scarab beetles, were specifically shaped to fit the cloisons, a technique that occurs only on Egyptianizing and Ornate Group ivories.

BOAT SCENES

Designs set in boats usually include a central motif, such as the four-winged scarab beetle of ND 10701 (**129**, p. 99).[20] The beetle is holding a sun disc between its forelegs and a *shen* sign (symbolizing protection) between its hind legs, and represents the (re)birth of the sun god each dawn. The prow and stern of the boat are decorated with falcon heads, and it is floating on a zigzag line, the sign for water. Specially shaped pieces of glass were used for the inlays of the prows, the sun disc and the body of the beetle, while more regular pieces were employed elsewhere. Like many Egyptianizing panels, this one is slightly narrower at the top than at the bottom and was held by tenons at the sides.

Another boat scene (ND 10702, **124**, p. 98)[21] has *ba*-birds flanking a complex central motif. The birds are human-headed, bearded and wear Egyptian double crowns set upon *nemes* (headcloths). They have human arms, flexed and raised to the central crown, and are standing on platforms. The bird is a symbol of a person's soul; adding a crown to its head is not an Egyptian feature, but echoes kingly figures seen in late Egyptian parallels in Nubia. The birds salute the central motif, a *hmhm* or triple *atef* crown set on a sun disc rising over the horizon. The sun disc contains a *wedjat* eye and is flanked by a pair of crowned *uraei* (sacred cobras). This design, with its 'piling up' of religious motifs, is reminiscent of complex theological jewelry from Tutankhamun's tomb.

Perhaps the most complicated scene set in a boat is on a poorly preserved rectangular panel found in Room SW37 in Fort Shalmaneser (ND 10566, **63**).[22] The boat is being paddled in the marshes by a figure wearing an ibis headdress with a crown, consisting of a crescent moon encircling the full moon, a wig and a short skirt. He uses two paddles to propel

63 Poorly preserved Egyptianizing ivory panel from the Fort, showing a fascinating scene of two deities in a boat in the marshes; in Egyptian iconography, the figures would represent the enthroned sun god Re being paddled by Thoth, the god of wisdom (6.4 × 11.7 × 0.8 cm; 2½ × 4⅝ × 5/16 in.). ND 10566, Baghdad, National Museum of Iraq. Photograph Mick Sharp.

the boat along a waterway lined with flowering papyrus. Seated on a typical Egyptian chair, with a cushioned back, and sides decorated with scales, is a figure wearing a falcon headdress and crowned with a sun disc set on a crescent. He wears an ankle-length skirt, the upper part of which is pleated, the lower plain. In his left hand he holds a *was* sceptre, in the right an *ankh* (the sign of life) resting on his knee. In Egyptian art, this image would represent the enthroned sun god Re with Thoth, the god of wisdom and hieroglyphs and the scribe of the gods. The employment of Thoth as navigator occurs as early as the Twelfth Dynasty. The papyrus reeds are inlaid with alternating sections of raised ivory and glass cylinders, a technique known as 'alternate inlay', which is another feature unique to ivories of the Egyptianizing and Ornate groups.

Essentially the same pair of central figures is represented on a trapezoidal plaque, also found in Room SW37 (ND 10562, **64**).[23] There are three registers. At the top is a four-winged scarab beetle, falcon-headed with human arms, helping to support the Osiride crown; its hind feet hold a disc resting on a lotus blossom. The lotus is flanked by a pair of birds, with another bird to the left and a seated animal, perhaps a dog, to the right. The central register shows four different birds, walking towards the left. Two male figures walk towards the centre of the bottom register. The man on the left wears a falcon headdress, crowned with sun disc and *uraei*, and presumably represents the sun god Re, while that on the right is Thoth, wearing an ibis headdress, crowned with a lunar disc on a crescent, and carrying a pen in his raised right hand and a roll in his left. Between them is a monkey, or perhaps an ape (the baboon was the sacred animal of the god Thoth). Above the monkey is a rectangle with incised hieroglyphs, which are simply pseudo-signs or 'gibberish'.

64 A Plaque in Phoenician style, found in Room SW37 in Fort Shalmaneser, showing a crowned scarab beetle above a frieze of birds, and a lower scene with the sun god Re and Thoth, the god of wisdom; the central hieroglyphs are meaningless (13.3 × 8.4 × 1.6 cm; 5¼ × 3⁵⁄₁₆ × ⅝ in.). ND 10562, London, British Museum. Photograph Mick Sharp.

62   Ancient Ivory

THE SCARAB BEETLE

The scarab beetle was one of a number of Egyptian motifs (also including the *wedjat* eye, the *aegis* of the goddess Bastet – a broad collar-like necklace, symbolizing protection – and the dwarf god Bes) that formed part of the Phoenician artistic vocabulary. The scarab beetle can be seen on a pair of tall openwork panels (unfortunately fragmentary) from Room SW11/12, which are unusual as they are beautifully carved on both sides.[24] They originally consisted of at least three registers: one of the panels (ND 13864, **65**) shows a four-winged scarab beetle above a deity wearing a tripartite wig, over which is a ram headdress, crowned with a sun disc with a central *uraeus*. The god has both arms and wings extended, the surviving hand holding what appears to be the thick stalk of a plant. He is dressed in a short kilt and open overskirt with sloping hem.

The beetle was a popular motif on bridle harness, both on shield-shaped blinkers (an Egyptian form of blinker) and on matching triangular frontlets (ornaments attached to the brow-band of the bridle). The beetle of ND 10388 carries the sun disc and *shen* sign between (respectively) its forelegs and hind legs (**66**).[25] The aim of decorating a bridle harness with this image would have been to protect the horse's owner. An unusual version of the scarab beetle is shown on a fragment from Room SE9, a secondary entrance to the Residency. Here, a beautifully modelled and richly inlaid beetle (ND 7568, **67**)[26] is represented between two crowned lion heads of the dwarf god Bes, an Egyptian deity adopted by the Phoenicians and associated with healing, fertility and magical protection. On the right edge is a flexed human arm, resting on an *ankh*.

ABOVE **65** One of a pair of Phoenician panels, unusually carved on both sides; a four-winged scarab beetle is set above a four-winged deity who wears a ram headdress (16.5 × 6.1 × 1.3 cm; 6½ × 2⅜ × ½ in.). ND 13864, Baghdad, National Museum of Iraq.

BELOW **66** A Phoenician-style, shield-shaped blinker, one of a pair that would have been fixed to the leather bridle; it carries a winged scarab beetle, holding the sun-disc and *shen* sign between its legs (7.9 × 7.7 × 0.8 cm; 3⅛ × 3 × 5/16 in.). ND 10388, Baghdad, National Museum of Iraq.

RIGHT **67** An unusual inlaid fragment from the Residency at the Fort; a central scarab beetle is flanked by a pair of crowned leonine heads representing the dwarf god Bes (7.2 × 13.4 × 0.6 cm; 2 13/16 × 5¼ × ¼ in.). ND 7568, London, British Museum.

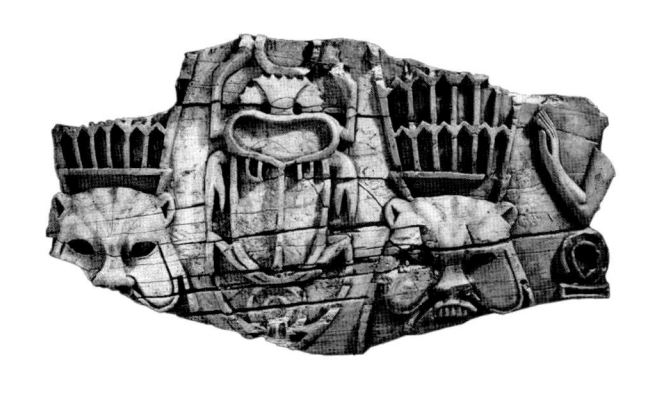

The Phoenicians: Master Craftsmen

THE DJED PILLAR AND THE CARTOUCHE

Figures flanking a central motif, such as the *djed* pillar altar, a crowned cartouche or the god Horus on a lotus, were popular designs. The *djed* pillar is set on a lotus and surmounted by sun discs and plumes, sometimes mounted on a ram's horns. The strongly carved, tenoned panel ND 9470 (**128**, p. 99)[27] shows falcons and *uraei* flanking the altar. The falcons are crowned with sun discs, hold flails and are standing on the tails of the *uraei*. This panel is one of the few Egyptianizing pieces with a fitter's mark – the letter *beth* of the West Semitic (or Aramaic) alphabet, carved on the back.

A cartouche often occupies the centre of a panel. The long tenoned panel ND 11023 (**122**, p. 98)[28] was found near the west wall of Room SW12 at a depth of some 2 metres (6½ ft). The human-headed sphinxes flanking the central cartouche have shaved heads except for the side-lock of childhood and two tufts of hair extending over the foreheads and backs of the heads. They wear jewelled collars and aprons decorated with chevrons. The text on the cartouche is read vertically and can be interpreted as triumphal epithets accorded to a king – one who 'seizes all lands, the head over. . .'.[29] The long borders at top and bottom, with their alternate sections of raised ivory and inlays, are unusual.

The rather corrupted hieroglyphs on the cartouche of the well-known Egyptianizing panel found by Layard (BM 118120; **61**, p. 59) have been misread since the nineteenth century as the name of an exceptionally obscure Egyptian pharaoh. However, Professor Ken Kitchen has corrected the reading and has established that Phoenician artists regularly employed garbled phrases borrowed from formal speeches of the gods. The hieroglyphs on a second panel with kneeling figures flanking a cartouche (ND 12034, **123**, p. 98)[30] should be read in the same way. Kitchen comments:

> The reading 'Shu, son of Re' is the most banal and commonplace phrase one could ever find relating to that deity. Thus, if the Phoenicians knew of Shu through their incessant Egyptian contacts (as his occurrence elsewhere on these ivories would indicate) then this phrase would be known.[31]

The kneeling youths of ND 12034 offer divine figures to the crowned cartouche, which is set on the sign for gold, *nwb*, and associated with crowned *uraei*. The divine figures are seated on baskets and hold stemmed circles on their knees.

Part of a similar panel was found at Samaria, where a number of ivories, many fragmentary, were recovered within the royal compound, though sadly not from a stratified context.[32] The Samarian ivories are, predictably, a mixed collection, consisting of Phoenician, Syro-Phoenician and North Syrian material: many are similar to, but not identical with, the Nimrud material. Samaria was made the capital of Israel by Omri (r. 885–874 BC) and there were close links between Israel and Tyre in the early first millennium. The kingdom survived, despite predictable problems with Assyria, but was conquered by Sargon II in 722 BC and turned into an Assyrian province.

THE SUN GOD HORUS AND SCENES OF SUCKLING

Horus squatting on a lotus was a popular subject on Egyptianizing ivories. He is identified by the side-lock of childhood and is often shown with his hand raised to his mouth. He may be shown being worshipped by a pair of goddesses or being suckled by his mother, Isis, in the papyrus marshes. In the Book of the Dead, a hymn of adoration to 'Re (sun-god) at his rising from the eastern horizon' contains the phrase 'Hail to (you), O Child, in the same way as yesterday(?), who has risen from the lotus. . .'.[33] In Egypt, therefore, this image represents the sun god rising daily from the primeval lotus. When Isis is suckling Horus, they are shown either standing or sitting, but always in a papyrus thicket. The setting represents the delta marshes at Chemmis, supposedly an island near Buto, where Isis, fleeing from Seth, the murderer of her husband, Osiris, brings up Horus. This scene reflects the Osiris–Isis–Horus myth, popular particularly in the New Kingdom (sixteenth to eleventh centuries BC): it was ubiquitous in Egypt from before 1000 BC.[34]

At Nimrud a number of panels found in Room SW37 show Horus worshipped or suckled by goddesses. On IM 74825

(**68**)³⁵ he wears a composite crown of sun disc and plumes set on ram's horns and has an *usekh* collar. The goddesses are lion-headed with tripartite wigs and *usekh* collars. Their wings are folded round their bodies to form skirts. Their nearer arms are raised in adoration; in their further hands they hold tall papyrus columns. They may be meant to represent Sekhmet or Bastet. The surviving hieroglyphs can be read as 'Words spoken by (goddess/Nut?)'.³⁶

On a fragmentary panel, Isis is shown suckling Horus in a semicircular field of papyrus (ND 9475, **126**, p. 99).³⁷ Only the upper body of the goddess survives. She is standing, and cups her left breast in her right hand to help the child suckle, holding him to her chest with her left arm. She wears a crown with sun disc and Hathor horns, set on a vulture headdress and tripartite wig, and has an *usekh* collar. Of the child, only his head and a trace of his arm survive. Winged and taloned *wedjat* eyes are set in the top corners. Another incomplete panel depicts a maned lioness suckling her maned cubs, again in a field of papyrus (ND 10535, **69**).³⁸ One cub is jumping up at her chest, while a second, of which only the top of the head survives, is suckling. In the top corner there is a duck rather than the *wedjat* eye of ND 9475. The

RIGHT **68** The sun god Horus squatting on a lotus; he is wearing the triple atef crown and is identified by the side-lock of childhood. A pair of lion-headed goddesses, one in front and one behind, their wings folded round their bodies and holding papyrus columns, adore him; they may represent Sekhmet or Bastet (7.7 × 11.2 × 0.7 cm; 3 × 4⅜ × ¼ in.). IM 74825, formerly Mosul Museum of History. Photograph Mick Sharp.

BELOW **69** A maned lioness suckles her cubs in a semicircular field of papyrus and lily flowers, with a duck flying overhead (upper left corner); the shape of the panel, with sloping sides and semicircular sections cut out of the bottom corners, is unusual (7.9 × 18 × 0.8 cm; 3⅛ × 7¹/₁₆ × ⁵/₁₆ in.). ND 10535, Oxford, Ashmolean Museum.

The Phoenicians: Master Craftsmen   65

shape of these two panels is unusual: they narrow slightly at the top and have curving sections cut out from the lower sides. This form of panel may have been reserved for scenes of suckling in the marshes. These two examples would have been gilded, and coloured with glass inlays set on a frit bedding, but there are also versions of both designs that are simply modelled and highlighted with gold overlays. It was formerly suggested that inlaid ivories were worked at a different time and in a different place from those that were only gilded,[39] but this hypothesis is incorrect. There are many Phoenician examples of coloured and plainer versions of the same designs.

HEH WITH NOTCHED PALM BRANCHES
A kneeling figure holding notched palm branches probably represents Heh, the god of 'millions of years' or eternity, and the curving palm branches end in an *ankh* (the sign of life); the dual reference to eternal life is clear. The fragment ND 7683 originally showed two or more repeats of the design, the kneeling male being crowned with the sun disc resting on a tripartite wig: he has an *usekh* collar and a belted, pleated skirt (**70**).[40] Traces remain of an oval tripartite object of uncertain significance, on which his outer elbow rests: 'this probably represented the *sa* sign, or "magical protection"'.[41] Two poorly preserved panels from the gate chamber, Room SE9, in the Fort, show pairs of figures wearing falcon headdresses.[42] A similar fragmentary panel was found at Samaria,[43] while a strip consisting of six panels with gilded Heh figures was found in the richly equipped Tomb 79 at Salamis in Cyprus.

In the 1960s some tombs were excavated at Salamis that are of considerable importance to the study of the ivories at Nimrud, because they contained pieces of actual furniture and Phoenician ivories, and because of the late eighth-century date of two burials. The city and kingdom of Salamis were already established in the eleventh century BC, having superseded the Late Bronze Age city of Enkomi, 5 km (3 miles) to the south. As the archaeologist Vassos Karageorghis wrote: 'The region round the bay of Salamis, on the east coast of Cyprus, is one of the most favoured in the whole island'.[44] During his excavations there, Karageorghis found some tombs that consisted of small rectangular chambers and long sloping *dromoi* (passageways), so that the chariots and hearses accompanying the dead could be driven to the door of the chamber. The richest was Tomb 79. Although the tomb chamber had been looted, the *dromos*, 16.8 metres (22 ft 4 in.) long, was found intact and contained two burials, from the end of the eighth century BC. The *dromos* contained the remains of two chariots, horses, a hearse, a bronze cauldron, a bed and three thrones decorated with silver and ivory, as well as a series of ivory panels, both gilded and inlaid. Thanks to Karageorghis's painstaking excavation, it proved possible to reconstruct the bed and two of the thrones or chairs (see chapter 6). There are many important parallels between the Salamis material and that from Nimrud. Most of the Salamis ivories belong to the Ornate Group (see below) and provide a date of the late eighth century for deposition (not manufacture). Karageorghis recognized that 'the Salamis ivories were not made in Cyprus but were imported from Phoenicia'.[45]

GODDESS PANELS AND THREE-SIDED FURNITURE PIECES
Egyptianizing ivories form an exceptionally coherent group, both because they are unusual in showing complete scenes, which are normally unique, and because they are stylistically

70 Kneeling figures, holding notched palm branches ending in *ankhs*; the better-preserved figure (left) is crowned with the sun disc set on a tripartite wig and wears an *usekh* collar (6.2 × 11 × 0.4 cm; 2⁷⁄₁₆ × 4⁵⁄₁₆ × ⅛ in.). ND 7683, London, British Museum.

66 Ancient Ivory

and technically so similar. By contrast, a small group of upright panels, decorated with a single figure of a goddess or a queen, pose an interesting problem. These elegant ladies either wear a long dress with a curving hem or are bare-breasted and have their wings wrapped round their bodies (ND 7580, **71**),[46] like the goddesses flanking the seated Horus (see fig. 16). Some are simply wigged, others wear the Hathor crown, and in some pieces there are rectangular frames containing hieroglyphs, which can be read as standard formulae – in this case, 'Re rises'.[47] The figures hold lotus flails over their shoulder and carry *ankh* signs in the other hand. They are superbly worked and beautifully inlaid. However, despite their stylistic and technical similarity to Egyptianizing panels, they are atypical of that group, for not only are the figures single, but there are a number of similar pieces.

The poorly preserved remains of similar goddesses on the side panels of some three-sided furniture posts suggests a possible explanation. The goddesses frame central figures of youths, from which it becomes obvious that the goddess panels and the three-sided posts belong together, probably forming parts of the same pieces of furniture (see chapter 6).[48] The youths wear 'pegged wigs', *usekh* collars, short skirts with elaborately decorated aprons and thigh-length skirts with sloping overskirts (ND 10571, **139**, p. 102).[49] Two of these features, the pegged wigs and the elaborate aprons, are diagnostics of the next group of panels, the Ornate Group. The wigs consist of raised pegs, overlaid with gold foil, which held cylinders of blue glass bedded on a blue frit (**57**, p. 56; the aprons have a central patterned section, flanked by *uraei*, with six short ties pendant from the belt, which itself ends in a volute.

This small group, therefore, links the distinctive Egyptianizing ritual scenes with the even larger Ornate Group. Both groups share the technique of highlighting by means of sophisticated inlays, originally derived from Egypt and found at Nimrud only in these Phoenician ivories. The strong technical similarities between the two groups suggest that they were all made at the same centre, though not necessarily in the same workshop.

71 A beautiful inlaid, Egyptianizing panel, showing a goddess wearing the crown of Hathor; her wings are wrapped round her body and she holds a flail in one hand and an *ankh* in the other. The hieroglyphs can be read as 'Re rises' (15.9 × 5.2 cm; 6¼ × 2¹/₁₆ in.). ND 7580, Baghdad, National Museum of Iraq.

THE ORNATE GROUP

Names are more helpful than letters and numbers when visualizing a group of ivories, but it is always difficult to decide what to call a new group while it is being assembled. So when, in 1992, the similar characteristics of a large number of attractive, colourful and easily recognizable panels were noticed among the ivories found in the Fort, they were named the 'Ornate Group'.[50] In the 1980s Professor Dan Barag suggested that there were significant differences between 'non-inlaid and inlaid Phoenician ivories [which] might have a bearing on their chronology, the former perhaps dating from the late ninth–early eighth century BC and the latter only from the eighth century BC'.[51] Following this suggestion, plain and inlaid ivories were catalogued separately in 1986.[52] However, it became increasingly evident that this was not a meaningful division, as there are many examples of panels that differ only in being inlaid or not inlaid. Equally, there is no proof that these ivories were produced at different times.[53]

Ornate Group panels are among the most numerous found at Nimrud. With their balance and symmetry, their tall, well-proportioned figures and their rich use of colour, they are easy to recognize. Compared with Egyptianizing ivories, their range of subjects is relatively limited. Instead of complete ritual scenes, many Ornate Group panels depict single figures, and multiple panels were subsequently made up into a balanced composition. Typical of the ivories of this group is their rich embellishment with gold overlays and colourful inlays. The falcon-headed deity of ND 10476 (**57**, p. 56)[54] is a magnificent example. He is wearing a tripartite pegged wig. His garment has shawled sleeves, and a long open overskirt worn over a short skirt with an elaborate apron decorated with crowned *ureaei*. Many traces survive of red and blue inlays. Attached to the double frame at the top right is a small rectangular plaque, probably designed to contain some hieroglyphs. The panel thus exhibits many of the characteristics of the group: the double frames, the pegged wig, the elaborate apron, the use of hieroglyphs and sophisticated inlays.

INLAYS

Unsurprisingly, since there are so many Ornate Group panels, there are various sub-groups. For instance, one sub-group consists of carvings worked on thin panels and coloured only with blue, another is worked on thicker panels with polychrome inlays, another is exceptionally finely worked, and yet another sets the figures against dense floral backgrounds. The inlaying on the fragment ND 9516, showing the head and upper body of a pharaoh figure (**134**, p. 101),[55] belongs to an exceptionally fine sub-group. Unusually, small circular cloisons cover the surface of the red crown, while the collar is decorated with crescent- and droplet-shaped cloisons. Remains of blue survive in the eye and eyebrow. Other examples were found in the gate chamber, Room SW2, which links the North West and South West courtyards. They included fragmentary stylized trees and a cow suckling her calf, both popular motifs across the region. Traces of some of the gold overlays on the cloison walls and of blue glass survive in the lower part of the beautifully carved stylized tree of ND 6453 (**142**, p. 102);[56] the fluted papyrus flowers are elegantly worked and are typically Ornate Group in form, as is the carving of the back. ND 6310 (**138**, p. 101)[57] is one of the most elegant interpretations of a cow suckling her calf. Despite its extreme fragility the panel is more or less complete. The cow is standing in a field of tall fluted papyrus flowers and buds, the flowers carefully excised for inlay. She turns her head to lick the tail of her calf, who is sucking vigorously, its tail raised, resting on the cow's body. As usual in Ornate Group panels, the frames are double. A double frame may seem to be a minor point, but it is characteristic: the use of such frames is essentially confined to vertical panels of the Ornate Group.

Specially shaped inlays, set in gilded cloisons, as in the flowers of ND 13524 (**132**, p. 100),[58] are also characteristic. The young deity is holding flowers and standing in a field of papyrus flowers and buds. Balanced on a papyrus between his wingtips is a winged *uraeus*, crowned with a sun disc. In front of him are the remains of the central feature, a floral standard and a cartouche, both topped by sun discs and *atef* plumes. The panel would have been completed by a second winged youth on the left. The figures on this group of ivories are set in floral fields, are inlaid only with blue and are carved on thin panels, some 5 mm (3/16 in.) thick. These features, which distinguish the panels from others of the Ornate Group, suggest the output either of a different workshop, or of a different teams of craftsmen working in the same centre.

PHAROAHS, HEROES AND GRIFFINS

The same motif was often applied across various types of ivory within a style-group. For instance, elegant kneeling pharaoh figures are carved on small trapezoidal plaques and on furniture panels alike, as in a set of seven plaques with roughened backs,[59] originally mounted on a wooden backing (ND 9422, **74**).[60] Minor differences can be observed among the seven, and the backs are roughened in different ways, again suggesting that they were probably carved by a team of craftsmen. Similar versions of the kneeling pharaoh can be identified on a set of three solid panels with double frames, which have unusual wide dowel holes to aid fixing (ND 6315, **73**),[61] and a superb openwork example of the Ornate Group, which has exceptionally fine inlays (ND 7589, **72**).[62]

ABOVE 72 An exquisite openwork pharaoh figure, belonging to the Phoenician Ornate Group; the youth wears a version of the Egyptian double crown highlighted with intricate blue inlays (10.4 × 6.4 × 1 cm; 4 1/8 × 2 1/2 × 3/8 in.). There is a fitter's mark on the short tenon at the bottom. ND 7589, Baghdad, National Museum of Iraq. Photograph Mick Sharp.

RIGHT 73 The same figure of the kneeling pharaoh with arms raised in supplication, carved in relief on a rectangular panel, one of a set of three (8.3 × 4.4 × 0.6 cm; 3 1/4 × 1 3/4 × 1/4 in.). ND 6315, Baghdad, National Museum of Iraq.

FAR RIGHT 74 Another version of the supplicating pharaoh, this time carved on a trapezoidal plaque, one of a set of seven, originally forming part of a faceted cupstand; minor differences in the carving suggest that the seven were the work of a team of craftsmen (6.4 × 4.4 × 0.8 cm; 2 1/2 × 1 3/4 × 5/16 in.). ND 9422, Birmingham, City Museum and Art Gallery.

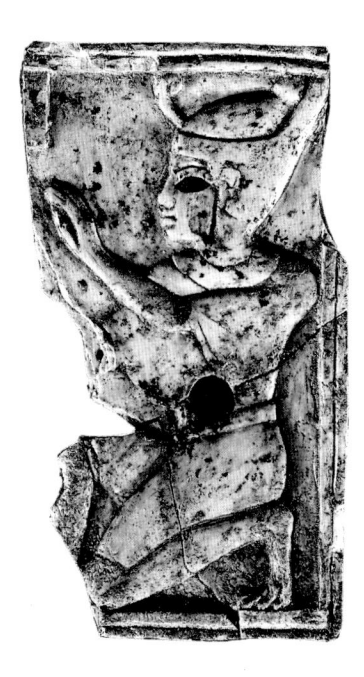

The Phoenicians: Master Craftsmen

75 An elaborately carved handle found in a Late Bronze Age grave at Enkomi in Cyprus, showing (left) a 'hero' fighting and killing a winged griffin and (right) a lion mauling a bull (20.2 x 8.7 x 2.2 cm; 7¹⁵⁄₁₆ x 3⁷⁄₁₆ x ⅞ in.); the design on the front of the handle, often known as the 'George and dragon' motif, probably originated in Cyprus and was later adopted by Phoenician and Syrian ivory carvers. London, British Museum, inv. no. 1897,0401.872.

The hallmark of Phoenician panels is elegance and balance, which are found even in scenes depicting a violent struggle, such as a hero fighting a griffin, or sphinxes striding over a fallen foe. The motif of a hero slaying a griffin, often known as a 'George and dragon', probably originated in Cyprus. An early representation is carved on a mirror handle found in 1896 at Late Bronze Age Enkomi in Cyprus (**75**). The struggle takes place in mountainous country. The warrior is face to face with a rampant griffin. His right arm is flexed, his legs tensed to take the thrust of his sword into the griffin's chest. The griffin's head is thrown up, its wings held down: it is supported on its hind legs with one forepaw resting on the warrior's hip.

The Phoenician version of this Cypriot design is completely different. The sense of dynamism is replaced by the calm dispatch of a griffin, which gracefully accepts its fate. This is beautifully illustrated on two Ornate Group panels, one inlaid with red and blue (ND 10500, **76**)[63] and the other modelled (ND 11036, **204**, p. 139).[64] In both pieces, the youthful pharaoh is striding forwards, framed by his wings,

70   Ancient Ivory

the curves of which are echoed by the wings of the griffin. He grasps its comb in one hand, turning its head, and thrusts the spear into its open beak. The panel of hieroglyphs at the top left of ND 11036 can be read as: 'enduring/abiding one: lord of radiance', an appropriate saying if the Phoenician originators realized it.[65]

The same motif can be seen on a plaque worked in another decorative technique, inaccurately known as 'champlevé'. In these examples the design is excised and then filled with colour, while the background is left higher and plain. This is a relatively small group; the technique was employed on plaques showing either a hero fighting a griffin (ND 10449, **149**, p. 103)[66] or a lion, winged youths or sphinxes with trees or floral friezes. Once again, this technique was borrowed from Egypt. Fragments of similar examples have been found at Samaria.

The most famous Phoenician contest scene is illustrated on a pair of plaques found by Mallowan in the sludge at the bottom of Well NN of the North West Palace (ND 2547 and 2548, **103–104**, pp. 90–91).[67] The excitement of their discovery is best described in his own words:

> The rich levels between course 320 and course 330 of the brickwork at the bottom of the well finally yielded two chryselephantine plaques, and the sight of them still leaves us amazed, for we can hardly believe the good fortune which has ensured their survival for posterity. . . . A dramatic episode unfolds itself before our eyes; a savage lioness mauling a dark 'Ethiopian' whom she holds in the embrace of death. This is the actual moment of the kill, when the victim, felled to the ground, knees still raised, leans upon his hands and proffers his neck in surrender as if in the ecstasy of sacrifice, for there is no sign of agony in his perfectly drawn features. The lioness, poised four-square and solid, gives, in its sinuous outline and the turn of its head, an impression of feline power well matched by the last tense resistance of its victim. This fearful scene takes place against a brilliant background, a meadow of Egyptian 'lilies' and

76 An inlaid openwork panel in the Phoenician Ornate Group style; in this beautiful and balanced version of the 'George and dragon' motif, which is set in a field of flowers, a winged hero grasps a griffin by its comb, turns its head and calmly dispatches it, without a struggle (14.8 × 9.1 × 1.1 cm; 5^{13}/$_{16}$ × 3^9/$_{16}$ × ^{7}/$_{16}$ in.). The piece was once inlaid with colourful red and blue glass; the hero's short, Egyptian-style wig has raised pegs of ivory that held blue glass cylinders set on blue frit. ND 10500, Baghdad, National Museum of Iraq.

> papyrus flowers with golden stems, blue and red in alternate rows, bending now one way, now the other, as if swaying before the wind. . . . The dazzling beauty of these two pieces gleams before one's eyes like a faceted polychrome jewel. The golden loin-cloth of the Ethiopian, closely moulded to his body; the golden spikelets of his hair and the vivid touches of lapis lazuli at the waist, on the arms, and on the head of the lioness are cleverly distributed to lighten the surface of the ivory.[68]

One of this pair of plaques belonged to the National Museum in Iraq and was stolen in the disastrous aftermath of the 2003 invasion: its present whereabouts are unknown. The other was presented to the British Museum, whose conservator, Dr H. J. Plenderleith, considered that 'the human figure was evidently intended to represent a negroid type and an effect of crisp, curly hair was obtained by fixing gilt-topped ivory pegs into the head, which was possibly stained black beforehand'.[69] Plenderleith's suggestion has been followed ever since: Mallowan called the youth a 'dark "Ethiopian"' and Barnett, a 'negro',[70] and other scholars have commented on his African features. However, there is no evidence to support this supposition. The pegged wig of the youth is a standard Ornate Group technique, his features are similar to those on many panels, and there is no trace of any black stain. In fact, what we have here is a Phoenician version of the familiar motif of pharaoh triumphant, the lion representing the pharaoh.

The purpose of these two jewel-like ivories, which are the only known examples with inlays of precious stones – lapis lazuli and carnelian – is uncertain. They were meant to be seen only from the front, the backs are curved and rough; they were fixed at the top and bottom, not the sides. Many suggestions have been made for their use, one of which is that they formed the central section of one of the Unusually Shaped Ivories, the dramatic scene having been set within the spreading branches of a tree, as on the exquisite ND 10409 (**77**).[71] Set in a field of flowers, this shows a pair of griffins, back to back, browsing on fronds growing from the tips of branches. The Unusually Shaped Ivories are the only group formed of curved panels, with rough backs and evidence of fixing at top and bottom.

While griffins are shown being slain in the hero and griffin panels, they are also seen browsing peacefully, as in ND 10409 or on a magnificent fragment from Well AJ (IM 79530, **78**).[72] This unique piece is carved on an exceptionally thin panel, only 4 mm (⅛ in.) thick, with a curved top edge; it survives to a height of some 20 cm (8 in.) but when complete must have measured more than 30 cm (12 in.). The griffin is browsing on a frond growing from a stylized tree, but this is not preserved. From a comparison with the inlaid griffin of ND 6311 (**131**, p. 100),[73] it is evident that it was depicted rampant, with one forepaw resting on the trunk of the tree. It has four crisp curls rising on its crest and four longer ones falling onto the shoulder and the chest, which is decorated with a collar of ribbed scales. The eye and beak are outlined, and there is a fine beaded collar round its neck. The wings curve upwards. This ivory is a true masterpiece.

LEFT 77 Concave panel, carved with winged griffins, set back to back within a frame of curving volutes, representing the branches of a tree, their beaks raised to nibble the fronds growing from the ends; the field around and between the griffins is filled with flowering papyrus (10.5 × 11.8 × 1.1 cm; 4⅛ × 4⅝ × 7/16 in.). The purpose of this jewel-like and colourful piece is uncertain. ND 10409, New York, Metropolitan Museum of Art.

OPPOSITE 78 Fragment of a large and very thin panel – a remarkable survival from Well AJ in the North West Palace – showing the front of a magnificent winged griffin browsing on a frond growing from a stylized tree (which was carved on an adjacent panel, now lost); the griffin's curls, eye and beak are subtly outlined, and it wears a necklace and a collar (20.1 × 11.2 × 0.4 cm; 7⅞ × 4⅜ × ⅛ in.). The piece is unique and superbly modelled, a true masterpiece. IM 79530, Baghdad, National Museum of Iraq.

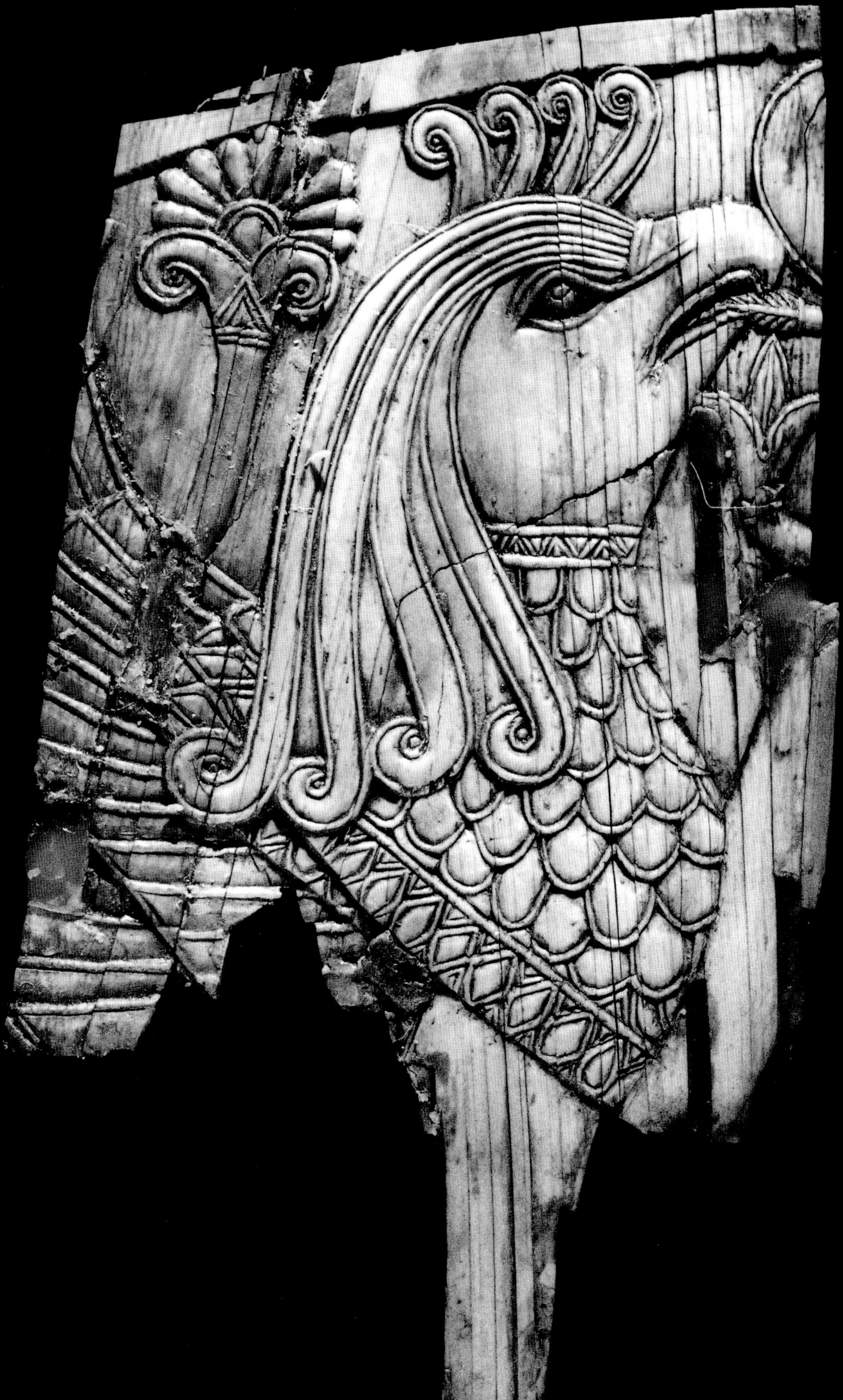

SPHINXES

Another popular Levantine subject, employed across the area, was the sphinx. It played a number of roles, and is shown in association with flora and stylized trees, or represents a pharaoh striding over his fallen enemies or even standing on the head of a squatting 'Egyptian'. A well-preserved and beautiful panel, one of a pair, shows a crowned falcon-headed sphinx marching through a scene of voluted palmette and lily flowers (ND 12033, **199**, p. 138).[74] The flower at the bottom left probably grew from a stylized tree (not preserved), which the sphinx is saluting.

Only the fronts survive of a pair of ram-headed sphinxes flanking a stylized tree on a handsome panel forming the centre of a three-panel design. The sphinxes are crowned with sun discs set on pairs of rams' horns and flanked by crowned *uraei*. They have Osiride beards, *usekh* collars and chevroned aprons (ND 9604, **79**).[75] Suspended from their chests are winged *uraei*, also equipped with the Egyptian double crown. The tree, with its mass of flowers, is typically Phoenician: in addition to the crown of flowers at the top, more grow from the branches up the tree; they include fine, fluted papyrus flowers, lilies and voluted palmette flowers. Not only is this type of tree a Phoenician marker, so also are the fluted papyrus flowers. A shorter version of a similar tree can be seen on a long rectangular panel, a richly inlaid ivory that is exceptionally finely worked (ND 10705, **80**).[76] Two winged, human-headed sphinxes flank a central stylized tree and are framed by two others.

Sets of matching panels would have been mounted to form long rails, like those on the famous couch of Ashurbanipal with its line of leaping lions on the relief of the Garden Scene from Nineveh, now in the British Museum (**240**, p. 152). A number of panels, especially those forming friezes, show sphinxes, usually falcon-headed, striding over fallen youths. This is another representation of pharaoh triumphant. In Egyptian iconography the foe should, of course, be an Asiatic – Egypt's traditional enemy. The fragment ND 13013 (**81**)[77] shows an authentic version of this originally Egyptian design: a pair of sphinxes proceed to the right, walking over the prostrate figures of Asiatics, recognizable by their headgear, beards and dress. Only one of the pair survives, though the tail of the leading sphinx is still preserved. They are separated by a *djed* pillar altar, crowned with a sun disc. The surviving sphinx has an unusual cheek marking, a *nemes* headcloth and an *usekh* collar. The Asiatic has a high and rounded hat, tied with a fillet. A lock of hair falls onto the shoulder, and traces survive of the beard. He is shown lying awkwardly on hip and arm and looking to the front and is wearing a long, pleated and fringed garment.

The tables are turned on the matching panel (ND 10362, **82**),[78] in which the fallen enemy is an Egyptian. The sphinx, his paw resting on the Egyptian's head, has the same cheek marking, *nemes* headcloth and *usekh* collar as in the

79 Panel, showing a stylized tree, with a crown of flowers and fine fluted papyrus flowers, flanked by ram-headed sphinxes, wearing elaborate crowns with sun discs and *uraei* set on rams' horns; the sphinxes have Osiride beards, and suspended from their chests are crowned and winged *uraei* (15 × 9 × 1.2 cm; 5⅞ × 3⁹⁄₁₆ × ½ in.). ND 9604, Cleveland Museum of Art. (See also **1**, p. 2).

ABOVE **80** Panel belonging to the Ornate Group, in which stylized trees frame winged, human-headed sphinxes, wearing headcloths, aprons, and unusual collars that outline their chests (3.7 × 22.4 × 0.9 cm; 1⁷⁄₁₆ × 8¹³⁄₁₆ × ³⁄₈ in.). ND 10705, Cambridge, Fitzwilliam Museum. Photograph Mick Sharp.

ABOVE AND RIGHT **81–82** Two fragmentary Ornate Group panels, showing falcon-headed sphinxes striding over defeated opponents lying on the ground, a scene derived from the common Egyptian motif of pharaoh triumphant over an Asiatic enemy. In the larger fragment (5.1 × 10.8 × 0.3 cm; 2 × 4¼ × ⅛ in.), two sphinxes (the leading one represented only by its tail) walk over an Asiatic, identifiable by his high hat, long garment, and the baldric passing over his shoulder. In the smaller piece (4.5 × 6.7 × 0.6 cm; 1¾ × 2⅝ × ¼ in.) the sphinx, which has unusual stylized wings running along its back and down its flank, rests its paw on the head of an Egyptian foe. ND 13013, 10362, Baghdad, National Museum of Iraq. Photographs Mick Sharp.

83-84 Cattle were a popular motif among ivory carvers of all the traditions. These two Phoenician panels show (LEFT) a cow suckling her calf in a field of papyrus flowers and buds, and (BELOW) a bull with a long curving horn, browsing in a field of lilies. ND 11094 (6.1 × 12.6 × 0.8 cm; 2⅜ × 4¹⁵⁄₁₆ × ⁵⁄₁₆ in.), Oxford, Ashmolean Museum. ND 10678 (4.8 × 10 × 0.5 cm; 1⅞ × 3¹⁵⁄₁₆ × ³⁄₁₆ in.), Baghdad, National Museum of Iraq.

preceding example. The inlays along his back and down his haunch are a residual representation of wings. The fallen Egyptian is wearing a tripartite wig and a long open overskirt and is lying awkwardly with his head turned to the front.

Two horizontal panels with backgrounds are Phoenician versions of the common Levantine motif of cattle. The first shows a cow suckling her calf and the second a browsing bull. The cow is standing in a field of papyrus with the flowers carefully worked and fluted (ND 11094, **83**):[79] it is similar to the fine openwork example ND 6310 (**138**, p. 101), though the body is a little heavier. The bull has a splendid head with horn curving forward, and a massive body (ND 10678, **84**);[80] he is ambling through a field of lilies.

Characteristics of Phoenician designs
SYMMETRY

A symmetrical design is typically Phoenician, as is the adaptation of Egyptian originals. A set of three small panels is based on a familiar Egyptian design, which shows Nile gods binding together the stems of the lily of Upper Egypt and the papyrus of the delta, thus symbolizing Egyptian unity. In the Phoenician version (ND 11015, **208**, p. 140),[81] two youths stand either side of a central column, formed of tied papyrus stalks, and grasp papyrus flowers growing on long stalks attached to the central column. Three small papyrus flowers rise from their short wigs, and they are wearing short skirts with open overskirts. A clear fitter's or maker's mark – the West Semitic letter *beth*, lying on its side, together with a single vertical stroke – can be seen on the bottom tenon. A second panel had the letter *aleph* and a single stroke. These could either be position markers or indicate different craftsman.

Winged deities again form part of a set of three panels, some 10–11 cm (*c.* 4–4½ in.) high (ND 11102, **209**, p. 140).[82] They are crowned with the Egyptian double crown set on a tripartite wig and are wearing a long open overskirt. Their further arms and wings are raised; the nearer ones are lowered and they hold voluted palmette flowers in their hands. The deities frame a central floral column, formed of a voluted palmette flower, and more palmette flowers fill the ground on either side. Resting on the column is the *aegis* of the goddess Bastet, the leonine head of which faces to the right. On a unique bridle frontlet, the *aegis* is set within an *usekh* collar, topped by crowned *uraei* and above a row of

76 Ancient Ivory

uraei (ND 12014, **85**).⁸³ The *aegis* became popular in early first millennium Egypt but is relatively rarely found on ivories. A number of originally Egyptian motifs are specific to ivories of the Phoenician tradition, including the *wedjat* eye, the scarab beetle and the use of hieroglyphs.

Another symmetrical and originally Egyptian design – a pharaoh figure holding a ram-headed sceptre and jug – was copied in increasingly misunderstood forms across the Levant; it was already at home in late second millennium Ugarit.⁸⁴ The finest examples are Phoenician and belong to a large Ornate Group set found in Room SW12 in the Fort.⁸⁵ The pharaoh figures of ND 11035 (**206**, p. 140)⁸⁶ have Egyptian double crowns, with spirals rising from the front and ribbons down the back, and Osiride beards. They wear beaded collars with pendant droplets, short skirts with elaborately decorated aprons, and open overskirts. Two lesser registers above show a row of *uraei*, crowned with sun discs at the top, and a Phoenician form of winged disc, flanked by *uraei*. This design is reminiscent of stone shrines or *naiskoi* found at Sidon: on these a row of *uraei* and a winged disc are carved above the central shrine, and flanking figures on the sides carry ram-headed sceptres and jugs. The Belgian scholar Eric Gubel dates the shrines to between 850 and 675 BC.⁸⁷

A different Phoenician version of this design,⁸⁸ also found in Room SW12 initially looks the same, but there are many differences between the two sets (ND 11098, **207**, p. 140).⁸⁹ First, they are carved on differently shaped panels: those of the Ornate Group set are of a standard shape and size, with double frames at top and bottom; the panels of the second set are of irregular size, narrower at the top than the bottom, and consist in some cases of more than one register. Furthermore, the backs of the Ornate Group examples have lightly incised fitters' marks and were fixed by means of keyhole slots, while the fitters' marks on the backs of the second set are deeply incised and there are no keyhole slots. There are also differences in the balance and proportions between the elements in the two designs. The tall, elegant pharaoh figures of the Ornate Group set are replaced on the other set by relatively squashed figures, lacking beards and differently dressed, and the *uraei* are taller.

85 Fragmentary frontlet from a bridle from the Ornate Group, decorated with the *aegis* of the goddess Bastet – the head of a lioness, crowned with the sun disc and horns – set within a collar and a pair of crowned *uraei*; this ensemble is set on three crowned *uraei*, above a stylized tree (11 × 5.6 × 1.7 cm; 4⁵⁄₁₆ × 2³⁄₈ × ¹¹⁄₁₆ in.). ND 12014, Baghdad, National Museum of Iraq.

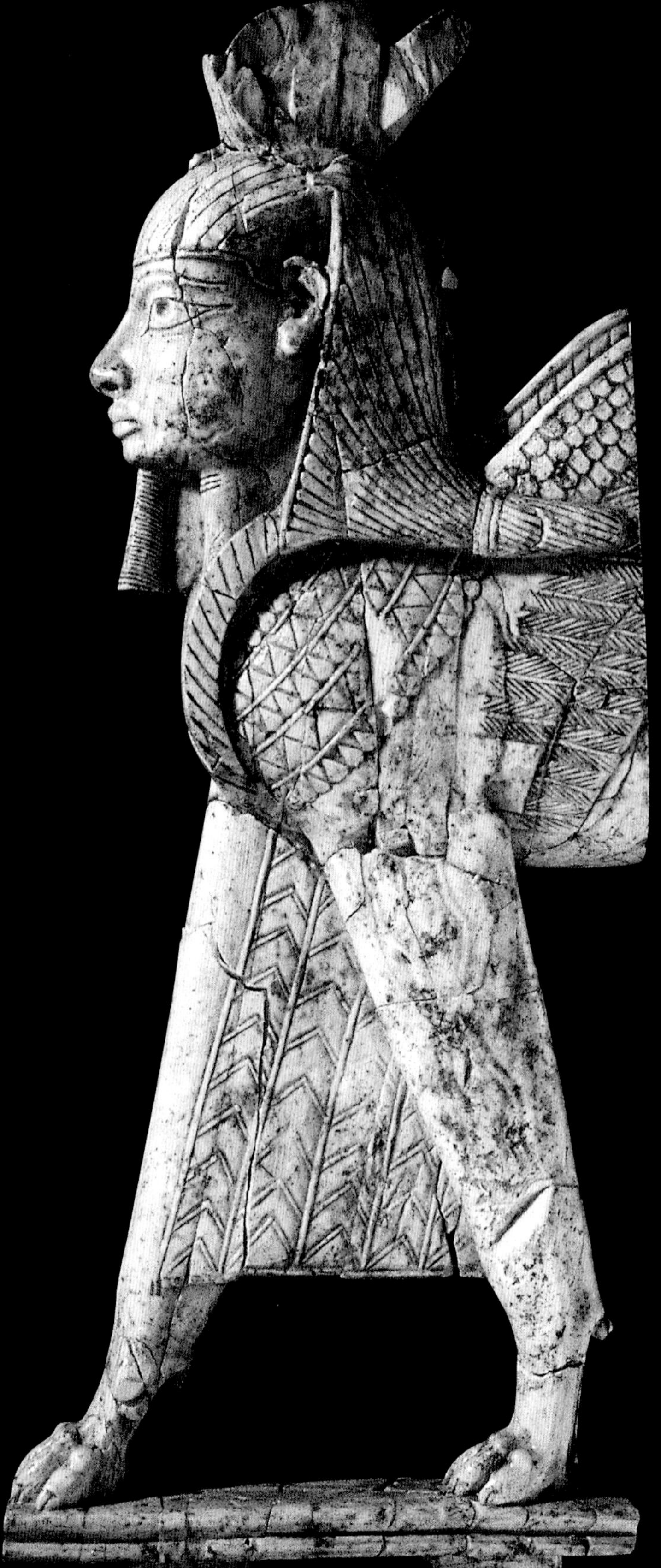

These differences, both in the carving of the design and in the technical features, such as the form of the panels and methods of fixing, suggest that not only was the second set carved in a different workshop from the first, but also that the workshop was probably sited in a different Phoenician centre. There were, of course, many Phoenician cities trading in the early first millennium and producing their own art works and manufactures.

ARTISTIC FREEDOM

It is interesting to attempt to establish the level of artistic freedom allowed to craftsmen within a workshop in respect of the inclusion or omission of specific details. The first fragments of some tall, elegant sphinxes were recorded in Room SW37.[90] They are winged, human- or ram-headed sphinxes, with the Egyptian double crown resting on the *nemes* headcloth, and wearing a collar and apron. Because some of them have a deep groove running down the cheek, representing the ties of an Osiride beard, they were named the 'grooved cheek' group. Many more examples were found in the adjacent Room SW12. ND 12115 is one of the finest (**86**).[91] The Egyptian double crown is fragmentary, but it is set on a beautifully carved *nemes* headcloth, with the unusual feature of an *uraeus* winding over the top. Although the sphinx has an Osiride beard, there are no grooves to represent the ties. It has a finely worked collar and apron and is set in the double frame typical of Ornate Group pieces. The equally finely carved but fragmentary ND 12324 (**87**)[92] also has the *nemes* headcloth with *uraeus*, collar and apron, but here the grooves for the ties are clearly marked. This pattern is repeated across the large and easily recognizable 'grooved cheek' group, in which some sphinxes have 'grooved cheeks' but others do not. The presence or absence of the grooves must have been a permitted variation. With ivories, after all, we are dealing not with 'factory' production but with the works of individual craftsmen. Variation can be documented again and again within sets of ivories, including the carving of individual features of faces.

A well-known Levantine design is the 'woman at the window', panels of which can be attributed to all three

86–87 Two Ornate Group human-headed sphinxes, offering an interesting illustration of the depiction of different details: in ND 12324 (ABOVE), a deep groove is excised along the curve of the cheek, representing the ties of the Osiride beard but this is not present in ND 12115 (OPPOSITE). ND 12115 (19.2 × 6.5 × 1.3 cm; 7 9/16 × 2 9/16 × 1/2 in.), London, British Museum. ND 12324 (13.9 × 6.8 × 1.1 cm; 5 1/2 × 2 11/16 × 7/16 in.), Mitaka, Tokyo, Middle Eastern Culture Center.

The Phoenicians: Master Craftsmen

88–90 Three examples from a set of Phoenician panels, found in Room S10 (the Queen's Treasury) in Fort Shalmaneser, showing the popular motif of the 'woman at the window'; the women look out over a balustrade, and each head is subtly different, as may be seen by comparing the details of carving of hair, eyes and mouth. ND 7754 (9.3 × 10.9 × 1.2 cm; 3⅝ × 4⁵⁄₁₆ × ½ in.), Baghdad, National Museum of Iraq. ND 8005 (7.2 × 7.2 × 1.3 cm; 2¹³⁄₁₆ × 2¹³⁄₁₆ × ½ in.), New York, Metropolitan Museum of Art. ND 7802 (3.6 × 3.3 cm; 1⁷⁄₁₆ × 1⁵⁄₁₆ in.), Baghdad, National Museum of Iraq.

Levantine traditions. Examples were found both in Layard's ivory store, in Rooms V and W of the North West Palace, and in various contexts in the Fort, especially in the Queen's Treasury (Room S10). The majority belong to the Syro-Phoenician tradition, but one set found in the treasury is outstanding and belongs to the Phoenician tradition. The lady of ND 7754 (**88**)[93] is the best-preserved of the seven examples and is exceptionally fine. She peers over the balustrade of her window, which is supported on four columns, framed by four reveals. Her hair is parted in the centre, held by a fillet with a central flower, and falls in ringlets, concealing her ears. Her face is gently rounded, eyebrows excised, and eyes outlined, with a drilled pupil. Her nose is damaged, but her mouth is carefully modelled and gently smiling. This piece was clearly carved by a master craftsmen, as was the burnt fragment ND 8005 (**89**).[94] In this example, the ringlets are more crisply carved, the eyes deeper set and the mouth fuller. The faces on the remaining fragments all vary subtly. What is perhaps the least competent fragment (ND 7802, **90**)[95] differs from the more refined pieces in the carving of the hair, the features and especially the rather clumsy mouth. It may have been carved by an apprentice.

These two sets demonstrate not only the freedom allowed to individual craftsmen in the selection of specific features, but also their varying competence, a pattern repeated across ivories from all traditions.

IS THERE AN ELEMENT OF PORTRAITURE?
Many faces and heads have been found at Nimrud. These would have formed parts of composite statuettes, either of pharaohs or of sphinxes, which were made up from a number of pieces. Despite considerable variation in size, they are technically similar and form part of the Ornate Group. One of the most charming is an exquisite face found in Room NE59 in the Fort (ND 10330, **91**).[96] The top and back of the head were carved separately. A raised ridge, divided into blocks round the forehead, forms the base of a crown, and part of the pegged wig can be seen behind and below the ears; a few of the cylinders and some of the blue

91 A refined and beautifully sculpted face, carved in the round, part of a pharaoh statuette or a sphinx; the crown and the back of the head (now lost) were carved separately (2.6 × 3 × 1.8 cm; 1 × 1 3/16 × 11/16 in.). ND 10330, New York, Metropolitan Museum of Art.

bedding of the wig survive, and traces of blue also remain in the deeply excised eyes and eyebrows. The face is well proportioned, with a fine nose, slim cheeks and a subtly modelled mouth and chin. This little masterpiece is only 2.6 cm high; it probably once formed part of either a sphinx looking forwards or a pharaoh statuette.

Only the curl linking the base of the crown to the ear survives of the pegged wig or headcloth of ND 11039 (**92**),[97] as the sides of the face are not preserved. Otherwise the piece is similar to ND 10330: the top and back of the head were carved separately, there is a ridged band round the forehead, and the eyes and eyebrows are excised. The eyes are outlined and elongated in a distinctive manner and traces of blue survive. This form of eye is typical of the group. However, the features differ from those of ND 10330, being plump and broad, and the mouth is wider above a dimpled chin. And this piece is more than twice the height of the other. A similar small face was found in the Idaean Cave in Crete, the most important cave sanctuary in Greece. Located high up on Mount Ida, and closed by snow for at least half the year, this was first excavated by Federico Halbherr in 1885, followed by the Greek archaeologist Yannis Sakellarakis in the 1980s. The little head formed part of a pharaoh statuette and has a band round the forehead, deeply excised eyebrows, elongated eyes and widely splayed ears (**93**; for another example see ND 11103).[98]

TOP LEFT 92 A plump, broad male face, with deeply excised eyes, small mouth and dimpled chin, part of a pharaoh statuette or a sphinx, carved in the round (6 × 5.2 cm; 2⅜ × 2¹⁄₁₆ in.). ND 11039, Baghdad, National Museum of Iraq.

ABOVE 93 Face plaque, probably part of a composite statuette, from the Idaean Cave in Crete, found by Yannis Sakellarakis (2.9 × 2.5 cm; 1⅛ × 1 in.). Heraklion, Archaeological Museum, inv. no. O-E 639.

LEFT 94 The face of a man, wearing a pegged wig, forming the front of a head carved in high relief; the eyes and eyebrows are deeply excised, the ears unusually large, the cheeks rounded and the full lips pursed (6.8 × 6.8 × 3 cm; 2¹¹⁄₁₆ × 2¹¹⁄₁₆ × 1¹³⁄₁₆ in.). IM 79523, Baghdad, National Museum of Iraq.

95 The head and shoulder of an openwork sphinx, carved in the round from a large tusk, the curve of which gives the figure a concave back; the eyes are almond shaped, the cheeks softly rounded, and the mouth smiling, and the sphinx wears a tripartite pegged wig and a large collar with inlaid borders (16.5 × 11.5 cm; 6½ × 4½ in.). IM 79522, Baghdad, National Museum of Iraq.

The same variety of features can be seen in more complete heads. Only the front of the head is carved on IM 79523 (**94**)[99] from Well AJ. It has the usual pegged wig, deeply excised, strongly arched eyebrows and downward-curving eyes. The ears are large with long lobes, the features rounded with a slightly pouting mouth and firm chin. The ivory has a flat back with a keyhole slot.

What remains of another masterpiece from Well AJ consists of the head and one shoulder of a large sphinx, facing forwards (IM 79522, **95**).[100] Surviving to a height of 16.5 cm (6½ in.), this must once have formed part of a large openwork panel or free-standing sculpture. It was carved from a massive tusk: the back is concave. The long wig is pegged, the face is rounded, the eyebrows arched, the deeply excised eyes slightly tilted and almond shaped, the ear is large, the nose has a narrow bridge and broad tip, and the lips are thin and curve upwards in an enigmatic smile. On the shoulder is a wide collar, plain except for inlaid borders. At the bottom can be seen some cloisons from the wing.

The largest and most remarkable surviving example is the relatively complete head and torso of a pharaoh statuette, which was found in two pieces in Room SW12 and restored in wax (ND 12000, **96**).[101] The top of the head is flat and contains a rectangular tenon slot for the attachment of the crown. The shoulder-length pegged wig is carved to stand free from the face, neck and shoulders. There is another tenon slot in the back of the wig, suggesting that

The Phoenicians: Master Craftsmen

96 A magnificent head and torso that formed part of a statuette of a pharaoh figure, carved in the round from a huge tusk (the lower body and lower arms were carved separately); it was found in pieces in Room SW12 in the Fort and restored by Nan Shaw Reade (17.7 × 10.3 × 8.9 cm; 7 × 4 1/16 × 3½ in.). The massive wig is pegged, the top flattened to receive a crown; the body, both back and front, is carefully worked, the navel is represented, and there are traces of the armlets at the ends of the upper arms. ND 12000, Baghdad, National Museum of Iraq.

the statuette was supported. Traces of blue survive in the wig and in the deeply excised, elongated eyes and eyebrows. The cheeks are subtly modelled and the full lips are slightly smiling. The features of the face are similar to those of some of the little heads discussed above, such as ND 10330, with the indented band around the forehead and the subtle form of the mouth. This remarkable piece is preserved to a height of 17.7 cm (7 in.), with a maximum width at the shoulder of 10.3 cm (c. 4 in.). When complete with crown and lower body, it must have stood to a height of nearly half a metre (20 in.), a massive piece.

At first glance, these heads and faces look rather different, though they are unified by technical features, such as the pegged wig, the excised eyebrows and elongated eyes, and can be assigned to the same style-group. However, in a recent study, the American scholar Marian Feldman pointed out that

> the mouths and ears exhibit quite different forms: IM 79522 has the so-called Archaic smile of thin lips and small, highly placed and delicately shaped ears; IM 79523 has full, fleshy lips pursed together in a straight line and large, heavily shaped ears that stick out from the side of the head.

She rightly comments on 'the exceptional range of variation that is found among first millennium Levantine ivories', and considers this 'a primary trait of the group as a whole'.[102] She draws, however, very different conclusions about workshop practices from those offered here – namely, that the finest Phoenician ivories were all worked in a single centre, by craftsmen who were allowed a degree of individuality, a trait well illustrated by these charming heads. Indeed, it seems possible that there is a real element of portraiture in these heads and faces, from the rather lugubrious IM 79523 to the smiling IM 79522. This pattern of variability of work can be demonstrated across the Levantine series.

Perhaps the most famous face found at Nimrud is the massive front of a head or mask found by Mallowan in Well NN (ND 2550, **102**, p. 89)[103] and immediately christened the 'Mona Lisa' of Nimrud (**20**, p. 29, as discovered). As Agatha Christie washed the mud from the head, she revealed the face of a beautiful young woman with doe eyes, smooth, rounded cheeks and chin. The eyes and eyebrows are coloured, the full lips are slightly parted and smiling. The thick black hair has a centre parting below the hairband and

84   ANCIENT IVORY

is tied to fall in separately bound and twisted locks below the carefully modelled ears. This large mask was cut from the longitudinal section of an abnormally large elephant's tusk, of which the curve can be seen in the side view. It is 16 cm high, 13.2 cm wide at the top, and 5.6 cm thick (6⅝ x 5³⁄₁₆ x 2³⁄₁₆ in.). The back is concave, slightly thicker in the centre, and left rough, with the tool marks visible. It was intended to be seen from the front. This is one of the largest and finest ivory heads to have survived from antiquity; it is a thing of rare beauty, a masterpiece of Phoenician carving. Tragically, it may no longer survive: photographs may be all we have to remember it by.

Carving in the round

As the great torso ND 12000 shows, some of these heads and faces formed parts of free-standing pharaoh statuettes. Unfortunately, none of these is complete, although together the remains provide sufficient evidence for it to be possible to reconstruct one. The figures are tall and stand to face the onlooker, with the left leg leading. Usually the left arm is flexed and the right held at the side, but this can be reversed. They are designed to be seen from the front or sides, the backs being left relatively rough. They wear the Egyptian double crown, an *usekh* collar and a short pleated skirt, belted at the waist, with the elaborate apron typical of the Ornate Group.

Like the faces, the statuettes are of varying sizes, and there are both inlaid and modelled examples. A reasonably well-preserved modelled statuette from SW37 is the tall and slender ND 7987 (**97**).[104] This figure lacks the head, arms and lower legs, but survives to a height of 17 cm (6¾ in.). He is wearing a short pleated skirt with the usual elaborate apron.

In surviving inlaid examples, the wigs, collars, belts and aprons were coloured. One of the most complete pieces, though unfortunately poorly preserved, is ND 9609 from Room SW37, which lacks only the head and crown and one leg.[105] He has an *usekh* collar and the usual pleated skirt and apron, belted at the waist. His right arm is at his side, his left arm flexed, the hand holding a staff on his chest. He still stands to a height of 20.4 cm (8 in.), so must originally have been more than 30 cm (12 in.) high, and is 6.3 cm (2½ in.) wide at the shoulder.

THE STATUETTES FROM ROOM NE2
While most ivories were deposited in store-rooms, a remarkable group of statuettes was found in Room NE2.

97 Statuette of a pharaoh figure, one of numerous examples of an Egyptian motif, most of which were highlighted with inlays (unlike this simply modelled version); they were usually made up of separate sections, according to the ivory available. This is a reasonably well-preserved specimen, though the head and crown, arms and lower legs are missing; it wears a short skirt with an elaborate apron (17 × 6.7 × 3.7 cm; 6¹¹⁄₁₆ × 2⅝ × 1⁷⁄₁₆ in.). ND 7987, Baghdad, National Museum of Iraq.

This room probably formed part of the *rab ekalli*'s suite, which occupied a number of rooms in the north-west corner of the South East Courtyard of the Fort. The *rab ekalli* was the palace manager, the official in charge of the Fort. Found in the debris of his rooms was a burnt alabaster jar, inscribed with the name of Esarhaddon (r. 680–669 BC), while his archive, found in and around his suite, covers a period of more than twenty years from *c.* 642 to 617 BC. These dates suggest that the rooms continued in use until the sack of the Fort in 614–612 BC.[106] An important collection of ivories, found in these rooms, is uniformly of a high standard and belongs principally to the Phoenician and Syro-Phoenician traditions, though there are also a few North Syrian and Assyrian pieces. This is one of the few contexts where there is evidence that an Assyrian official owned a range of Levantine ivories, as well as some Assyrian pieces.

Outstanding among the *rab ekalli*'s ivories are six statuettes, which are considered to be the finest Phoenician masterpieces. These were found in Room NE2; some were still set on a veneered ivory plinth in a niche, while others had fallen to the floor below. Both the subjects and the style of these figures are unique at Nimrud and they are among the few examples carved fully in the round. The statuettes represent a procession of men leading animals and carrying others on their shoulders. Four of them have short hair and are identified as Egyptian or African; they wear elaborately decorated short skirts with pendant ties, and jewelled collars and armbands. ND 9302 has a monkey perched on his left

98–100 Three of six superb free-standing Phoenician statuettes, found in and beneath a niche in Room NE2 in Fort Shalmaneser. The examples shown here represent an African (LEFT) and two Asiatics (CENTRE, RIGHT), differentiated by their features and their dress; each leads an animal (gazelles and an ostrich), and carries another on his shoulders (a monkey, a goat and a lion). ND 9302 (13.4 × 7.6 × 2 cm; 5¼ × 3 × ½ in.), New York, Metropolitan Museum of Art. ND 9306 (14.4 × 7.7 × 1.5 cm; 5¹¹⁄₁₆ × 3 × ⅝ in.), Baghdad, National Museum of Iraq. ND 9304 (12.8 × 6.3 × 1.3 cm; 5¹⁄₁₆ × 2½ × ½ in.), Baghdad, National Museum of Iraq.

shoulder, a leopard skin slung over his right and leads a gazelle (**98**);[107] the other three also have animals on their shoulders – a large monkey and gazelles – and they lead gazelles and a bovid. The two remaining figures are Asiatics. They have finer features and long, straight hair, arranged in ringlets, and they wear ankle-length overskirts, again richly decorated. One has a goat on his shoulders and leads an ostrich (ND 9306, **99**), the other has a lion, apparently crouching on his shoulders, with paws tied, and leads a gazelle (ND 9304, **100**).[108]

The *rab ekalli* must have been a considerable connoisseur, for in addition to these statuettes, arguably among the finest ivories found at Nimrud, another superb fragment was found in the niche. This beautiful hunter is grappling with a lion, of whom all that survives are its paws (ND 9398, **101**).[109] In the adjacent gate chamber, Room SE13, the burnt remains of the head and shoulders of a similar hunter and the heads of a pair of lions were found. These three fragments, together with ND 9398, presumably formed parts of a set of hunters and their prey, worked in the round and possibly set in the same niche in Room NE2. The youth's hair is coloured an orange-yellow, and is arranged in a curled fringe with long tresses falling on the shoulders. The eyes and eyebrows are excised for inlay, the eyes elongated as in the little masks discussed above; he has a fine straight nose and a carefully modelled mouth and chin. His upper body is naked, and his only covering is a short kilt decorated with zigzags and a cable pattern at the hem. He is holding a

101 Fragment of statuette found with the male figures with animals (**98–100**, pp. 86–87) and presumably part of the same fine Phoenician collection (7.5 × 4.6 × 1.3 cm; 2⅞ × 1¹³⁄₁₆ × ½ in.). The figure is a youthful hero or hunter, fighting a lion (of which only two paws remain); his head and hips are carved in profile, while the upper body is turned to the front. He wears a tight-fitting kilt and carries a weapon balanced on his shoulder, which would have pierced the lion's body. The fringe and long curled hair are coloured orange. ND 9398, Baghdad, National Museum of Iraq.

weapon and grappling with the lion, which he fends off with one arm. Fighting lions single-handed was an Arab tradition. Layard recorded how young Arabs captured lions by binding their right arms with strips of tamarisk, holding a strong piece of wood and advancing into the lion's lair. When the lion sprang the wood was forced into its jaws.[110]

In this chapter it has been possible to discuss only a few of the very large number of ivories attributed to the Phoenician tradition. These outnumber all the others found at Nimrud, which is not surprising, as the Phoenicians were famed as master craftsmen with a long history as wood-workers. There were copious supplies of cedars and other hard woods on the mountains inland from the coast, and ivory, of course, works like a hard wood. Furthermore, as active traders, they had access to plentiful supplies of ivory and gold. All the conditions were right for the production of luxury goods designed for court and temple. Since the status of ivory was extremely high at this time, much of the furniture decorated with ivory panels and the range of small objects, such as flasks, boxes and bridle harness, were probably designed for royal and ceremonial use.

The use of colour is relatively limited across the entire range of ivories. Phoenician ivories decorated with inlays include the beautiful and jewel-like ivories of the Egyptianizing and Ornate groups. Despite differences in the subjects depicted, their technical similarities suggest that the highly specialized work required to carve them would have been undertaken in a single, exceptionally wealthy centre, in workshops controlled by palace and temple. In addition to inlaid examples, there are also superb pieces belonging to both groups that were overlaid with gold but not inlaid.

Within the Phoenician oeuvre, there are numerous sub-groups, some superbly worked, others slightly less competent, as can be seen by comparing the two versions of pharaoh figures with sceptre and jug – the elegant Ornate Group version and the less sophisticated piece (**166–170**, pp. 114–15). It is probable that each of the independent Phoenician cities located along the Levant coast produced their own artefacts in their own workshops, but employing the same limited range of subjects and the same general style. The purpose of the motifs illustrated on the ivories – deities, pharaoh figures and mythical creatures – must have been to protect the owners, a protection that unfortunately failed. This may be why they were stripped of their gold overlays and thrown into storage by the victorious Assyrians.

OPPOSITE **102** The 'Lady of the Well' or 'Mona Lisa', one of the treasures found by Max Mallowan in Well NN of the North West Palace; the crown is pierced for decorative studs, and the back of the head, which is carved from a huge tusk, is concave (16 × 13.2 × 5.6 cm; 6⅜ × 5³⁄₁₆ × 2³⁄₁₆ in.). ND 2550, Baghdad, National Museum of Iraq. (See also **20**, p. 29.)

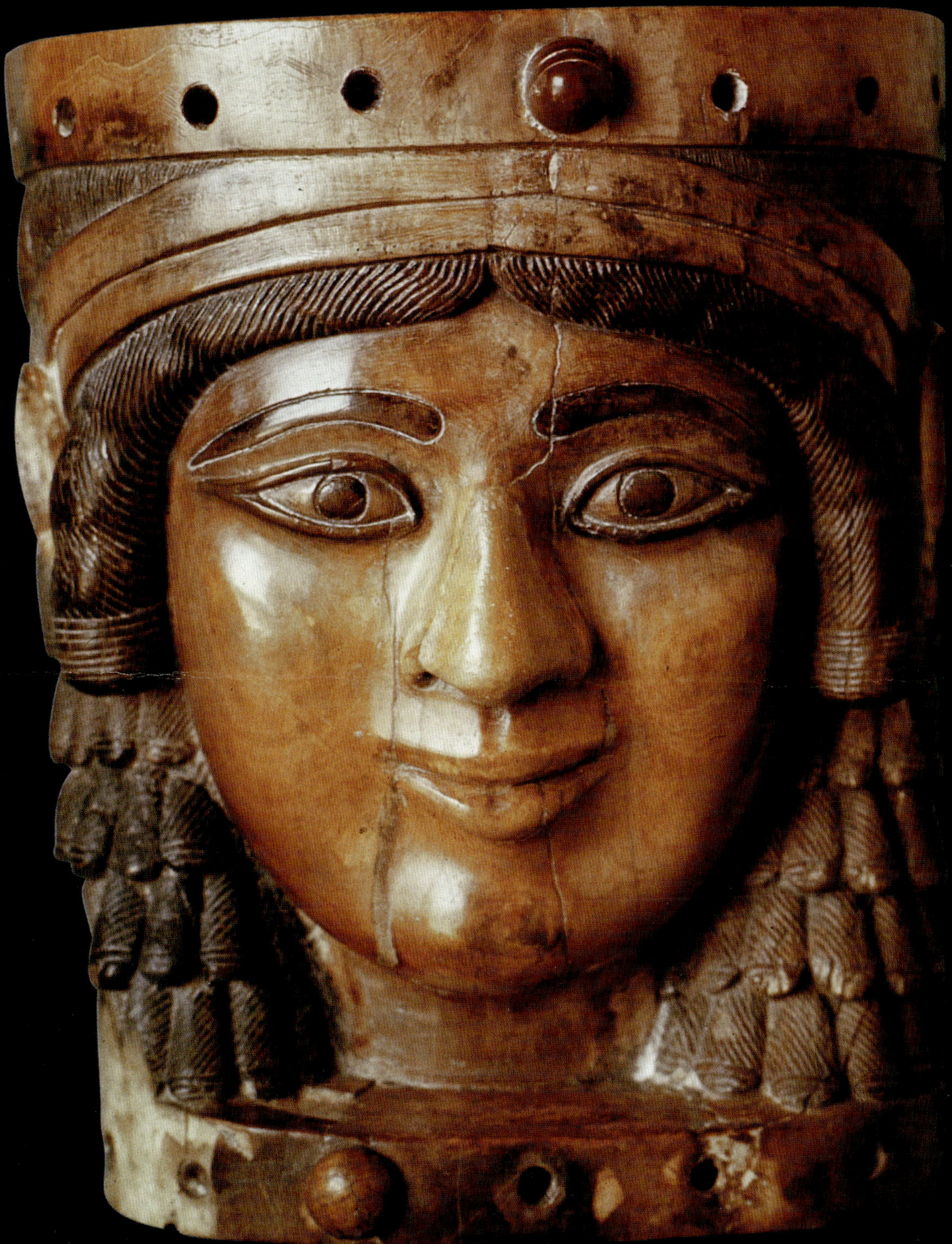

103 Violence in a meadow filled with lotus and papyrus flowers: a lioness mauls a youth, who offers himself to her, a design based on an Egyptian concept of the victorious pharaoh. This magnificent ivory, one of the finest carvings to survive from antiquity, is one of a pair found by Mallowan in Well NN in the North West Palace; carved by a Phoenician craftsman, it was highlighted with gold and inlaid with lapis lazuli and carnelian (10.5 × 9.8 × 2.8 cm; 4⅛ × 3⅞ × 1⅛ in.). ND 2547, formerly Baghdad, National Museum of Iraq.

104 The second of the pair of chryselephantine plaques found by Mallowan; the two, almost identical, pieces were carved by different craftsmen, both superb masters working in ivory, gold and precious stones. This panel is marginally less fine than the other, having only a single row of diamonds along the base; some of the inlays survive and traces of colour in the field of lotus and papyrus flowers (10.2 × 6.6–10.1 × 1.4 cm; 4 × 2⅝–4 × 9/16 in.). ND 2548, London, British Museum. Image © DEA/G. Dagli Orti/Getty Images.

ABOVE 105 Excavations on the citadel at Nimrud, directed by Max Mallowan in 1953 (his wife, Agatha Christie, is standing on the left), with the ziggurat and Tigris valley in the background. Photograph Joan Oates.

LEFT 106 The destruction with a sledgehammer of some of the carved panels of 'Mosul marble' decorating the great halls of the North West Palace, by a member of the group known as Islamic State, 2014. Still via Isis release/EPA.

ABOVE 107 The curved back of a Phoenician chair, with panels of openwork ivory scrolls, before conservation (33.3 × 54.5 × 0.3 cm; 13⅛ × 21⁷⁄₁₆ × ⅛ in.); the design is reminiscent of Homer's description of Penelope's throne (Odyssey XIX:55–57), which was 'inlaid with spirals of ivory and silver'. ND 7910, New York, Metropolitan Museum of Art. (See also **247**, p. 158.)

RIGHT 108 Agatha Christie Mallowan supervising the photography of one of the chair backs from Room SW7 in Fort Shalmaneser before conservation, 1958. Photograph, Dr Jorgen Laessoe.

LEFT 109 The antechamber of Tomb III, showing the double stone doors and the vaulted brick roof; the bronze coffin was found below a second one.

CENTRE LEFT 110 An exquisitely worked gold crown, found associated with a seal of Queen Hama in Tomb III, Coffin 2; magical winged figures, set on a roundel of daisies with pendant droplets of lapis lazuli, support a cap of vine leaves and bunches of grapes (H 16, dia. 245 cm; H 6⁵⁄₁₆, dia. 96⁷⁄₁₆ in.). ND 1989.309, Baghdad, National Museum of Iraq.

CENTRE RIGHT 111 Two sections from a remarkable hinged necklace, with designs of a date palm and a stylized tree; brilliant glass inlays are set in gold frames with hanging gold chains ending in pendants of pomegranates (H, inlay, 3 cm; 1³⁄₁₆ in.). ND 1989.32a–b, Baghdad, National Museum of Iraq.

BELOW LEFT 112 Four gold bowls from Tombs II and III (clockwise from top left): ND 1989.4, belonging to Ataliya, queen of Sargon II (dia. 20.4 cm; 8 in.); ND 1989.3, belonging to Yaba, queen of Tiglath-pileser III (dia. 20 cm; 7 ⁷⁄₈ in.); ND 1989.255, from Tomb III, Coffin 1, inscribed for Shamshi-ilu, an early 8th-century general (dia. 14.5 cm; 5¹¹⁄₁₆ in.); ND 1989.7, belonging to Baniti, queen of Shalmaneser V (dia. 12 cm; 4¼ in.). Baghdad, National Museum of Iraq.

BELOW RIGHT 113 A shallow Phoenician gold bowl, found in Tomb II, showing scenes of papyrus boats navigating the marshes, with princesses, horses and a crocodile in the centre; it is inscribed with the name of Queen Yaba (dia. 17.7 cm, 7 in.). ND 1989.6, Baghdad, National Museum of Iraq.

ABOVE 114 Five graduated agate eye pendants in gold mounts, set on a necklace with granulated spacer beads, found in Tomb II. ND 1989.120, Baghdad, National Museum of Iraq.

RIGHT 115 A superb gold necklace with subtle hinged shanks ending in animals' heads and twenty-nine pendant gold leaves; it was found on the upper skeleton in Tomb II. ND 1989.16, Baghdad, National Museum of Iraq.

TOP 116 Fragment of an incised Assyrian panel from the Nabu Temple, showing a procession of tributaries presenting gifts, including a bird, a bull with a bull-calf, and a horse, between crenellated borders (H 10.7 cm, 4¼ in. W, of whole panel as restored, 24 cm, 9⁷⁄₁₆ in.). ND 4193, New York, Metropolitan Museum of Art (fragment).

LEFT 117 Part of the handle from a fly-whisk or fan, carved on both sides, showing a pair of beardless human figures kneeling on either side of a stylized tree and plucking fruits from the palmette at the top (10.2 × 3.5 × 1 cm; 4 × 1⅜ × ⅜ in.). ND 2218, New York, Metropolitan Museum of Art.

CENTRE RIGHT 118 Two of a set of eight incised curved plaques, showing ostriches running with outstretched wings (each panel 3.5 × 5 × 0.2 cm; 1⅜ × 2 × ¹⁄₁₆ in.). ND 8006 London, British Museum.

BELOW RIGHT 119 Fragment of a curved trapezoidal plaque with an incised design, showing a spotted deer (probably a fallow deer) advancing to the left, followed by a second, of which only part of the antler and head survive (3.7 × 9 × 0.2 cm; 1⁷⁄₁₆ × 3⁹⁄₁₆ × ¹⁄₁₆ in.). ND 7742, London, British Museum.

ABOVE 120 The massive head and forequarters of a human-headed sphinx carved from a large tusk, found in Room T10 in the Fort; the piece is unique, more Syrian in style than either Assyrian or Phoenician, but with echoes of all three (21 × 8.1 cm; 8¼ × 3³⁄₁₆ in.). ND 11125, Baghdad, National Museum of Iraq.

RIGHT 121 Two Assyrianizing fragments of a carved panel, found by Henry Rawlinson, probably in the North West Palace: (above) part of an elaborate winged disc; (below) an almost complete figure of a beardless youth (originally one of a pair), plucking a fruit growing from the winged disc (his right hand is preserved in the upper piece) (as restored: 18.4 × 6.8 × 0.5 cm; 7¼ × 2¹³⁄₁₆ × ³⁄₁₆ in.). London, British Museum, inv. no. 118115.

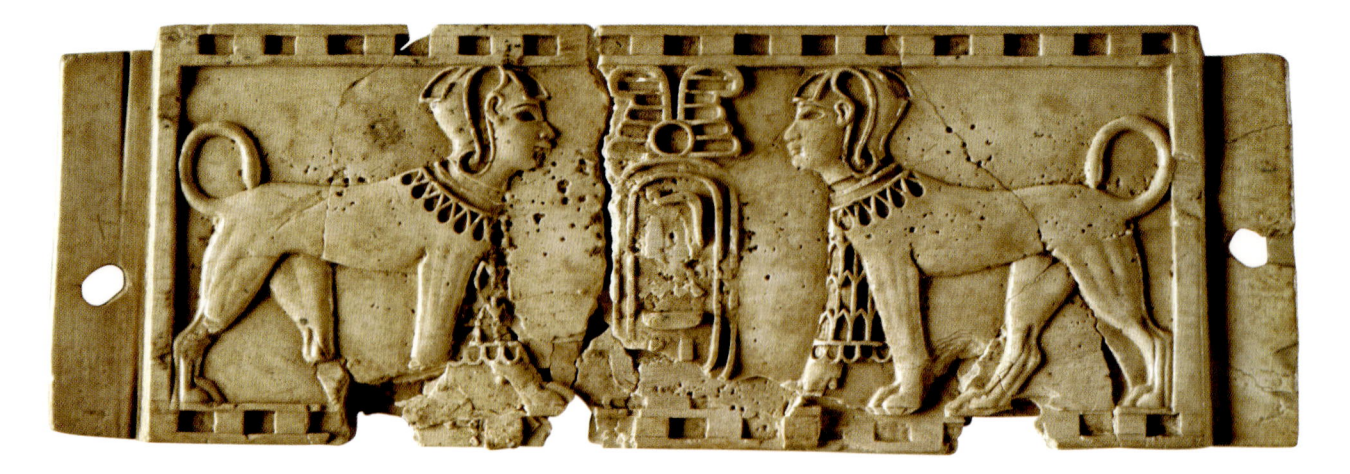

ABOVE 122 A long Egyptianizing panel, showing a pair of opposed, human-headed sphinxes with the side-locks of childhood, striding towards a central cartouche, which is crowned with a sun disc and *atef* feathers; some areas of the panel – the frame, hair, collars and cartouche – were inlaid (5.2 × 15.7 × 0.6 cm; 2¹/₁₆ × 6³/₁₆ × ¼ in.). The hieroglyphs in the cartouche can be read as a triumphal epithet. ND 11023, New York, Metropolitan Museum of Art.

CENTRE 123 Egyptianizing panel, showing a pair of kneeling youths, wearing wigs and kilts, who offer divine figures seated in baskets to a cartouche; set on the sign for gold, between *uraei*, the cartouche carries the triple *atef* crown (5.7 × 14 cm; 2¼ × 5½ in.). The hieroglyphs can be read as a corrupted version of 'Shu, son of Re'. ND 12034, Baghdad, National Museum of Iraq.

BELOW 124 Egyptianizing panel, showing a complicated theological scene, set in a richly inlaid boat with papyrus prows: in the centre is a sun disc rising over the horizon and containing the *wedjat* eye, flanked by crowned *uraei*, and carrying the triple *atef* crown set on a pair of ram's horns; to either side stand human-headed *ba*-birds with their flails (7 × 13.3 × 0.7 cm; 2¾ × 5¼ × ¼ in.). ND 10702, Baghdad, National Museum of Iraq. Photograph Mick Sharp.

FAR RIGHT 125 Part of a tapering cylinder, carved from the lower section of a large tusk in Egyptianizing style with inlays. The principal scene shows the pharaoh in his blue war crown, with a subservient figure kneeling in front of him; he is followed by an Asiatic, who carries a child-sized figure slung over his arm, and has a dog at his heels (14.3 × 11.6 × 1 cm; 5⅝ × 4⁹⁄₁₆ × ⅜ in.). Framing the scene but not shown are a pair of winged goddesses. TM 79516, Baghdad, National Museum of Iraq.

CENTRE LEFT 126 The upper section of an Egyptianizing panel with a scene set in a papyrus field, with winged *wedjat* eyes in the upper corners; the goddess, wearing a crown of horns and a central sun disc set on a vulture headdress, is suckling a child, of whom only the head, with the side-lock of childhood, and one arm are preserved (6.8 × 15.5 × 0.9 cm; 2¹¹⁄₁₆ × 6⅛ × ⅜ in.). The scene is based on the Egyptian motif of Isis suckling Horus. ND 9475, Baghdad, National Museum of Iraq. Photograph Mick Sharp.

CENTRE RIGHT 127 Inlaid Egyptianizing panel, showing a goddess standing in a field of papyrus and suckling her child, who has the side-lock and collar and holds an *ankh*; the goddess wears a close-fitting gown and an *usekh* collar. Part of her crown survives, set on a tripartite wig (8.1 × 6.8 × 0.7 cm; 3³⁄₁₆ × 2¹¹⁄₁₆ × ¼ in.). The scene is based on the Egyptian motif of Isis suckling Horus. ND 10509, Baghdad, National Museum of Iraq. Photograph Mick Sharp.

BELOW LEFT 128 A superbly carved and inlaid Egyptianizing panel, showing a pair of falcons, crowned with sun discs and carrying flails and each standing on the tail of a *uraeus*; they stand on either side of a central *djed* column, crowned with a pair of ram's horns and triple plumes (6.7 × 13.3 × 1.1 cm; 2⅝ × 5¼ × ⁷⁄₁₆ in.). ND 9470, Baghdad, National Museum of Iraq. Photograph Mick Sharp.

BELOW RIGHT 129 Inlaid Egyptianizing panel, showing a four-winged scarab beetle in a boat with papyrus prows decorated with falcon heads; it holds the sun disc between its forelegs and the *shen* sign between its back legs (5.6 × 12.5 × 1 cm; 2³⁄₁₆ × 4¹⁵⁄₁₆ × ⅜ in.). ND 10701, Baghdad, National Museum of Iraq. Photograph Mick Sharp.

ABOVE LEFT 130 A superbly carved fragment of an openwork panel, showing a winged god wearing a short Egyptian pegged wig, a collar, and a short skirt with open overskirt; between his wings is a hawk perched on a bud and holding a flail (25 × 10 × 1.1 cm; 9⅞ × 3¹⁵⁄₁₆ × ⁷⁄₁₆ in.). Numerous traces of red and blue inlays survive. ND 8068, Baghdad, National Museum of Iraq. Photograph Mick Sharp.

ABOVE RIGHT 131 A magnificent openwork panel, found in Room SW15 in the Fort; it is inlaid with red and blue beddings, and shows a winged griffin rampant in a field of flowers, reaching up to browse (13.5 × 8.2 × 1.2 cm; 5⁵⁄₁₆ × 3¼ × ½ in.). Some pieces of inlay and gold overlay survive. ND 6311, Baghdad, National Museum of Iraq. Photograph Mick Sharp.

LEFT 132 Fragment of an openwork, tenoned panel, with blue frit inlays, showing a winged deity standing in a field of papyrus flowers and buds and holding flowers in his outstretched hands; a winged *uraeus*, crowned with a sun disc, is delicately perched on a flower between his wings, and in front of him is a floral standard and a cartouche, both topped with sun discs and *atef* plumes (5 × 7 × 0.5 cm; 2 × 2¾ × ¹⁄₁₆ in.). ND 13524, Baghdad, National Museum of Iraq. Photograph Mick Sharp.

RIGHT 133 Fragments of an Ornate Group openwork panel, with intricate inlays, showing a human-headed, winged sphinx subduing a prostrate youth, who wears a short Egyptian pegged wig (8.5 × 5.1 × 1.0 cm; 3⅜ × 2 × ⅜ in.). This is a version of the familiar motif of pharaoh triumphant, but here the enemy is Egyptian. ND 13867a, Baghdad, National Museum of Iraq. Photograph Mick Sharp.

ABOVE LEFT 134 A beautiful fragment of the head and upper body of a pharaoh figure; he wears the Egyptian double crown and *usekh* collar, the cloisonné work of which is exceptionally fine (6.1 × 4.7 × 0.8 cm; 2⅜ × 1⅞ × 5/16 in.). ND 9516, Baghdad, National Museum of Iraq. Photograph Mick Sharp.

ABOVE RIGHT 135 The head of a pharaoh figure, wearing an Egyptian double crown on a short pegged wig; this elegantly carved and inlaid piece was found in the great storage room, SW37, in Fort Shalmaneser, during excavations in 1958 (10 × 4.1 × 1.4 cm; 3 15/16 × 1⅝ × 9/16 in.). ND 10364, Baghdad, National Museum of Iraq. Photograph Mick Sharp.

LEFT 136 A richly inlaid Ornate Group panel, showing a winged god wearing a sun disc and *uraeus* crown on a falcon headdress and tripartite wig; he holds a flower over his shoulder and would have been set in a floral field (11.6 × 5.5 × 1.2 cm; 4 9/16 × 2 3/16 × ½ in.). Unusually, the gold overlays covering the walls of the cloisons are well preserved, as is much of the blue frit bedding. ND 6328, Baghdad, National Museum of Iraq.

RIGHT 137 A section of an inlaid cylinder in Phoenician style, which shows a cow suckling her calf in a field of papyrus; the cow faces forwards, and both horns are shown, in the Egyptian manner (5.6 × 6.9 × 0.4, dia. c. 9 cm; 2 3/16 × 2¼ × ⅛, dia. c. 9/16 in.). ND 9412, Baghdad, National Museum of Iraq. Photograph Mick Sharp.

BELOW RIGHT 138 Openwork panel showing an exceptionally elegant and refined version of the popular motif of a cow suckling her calf in a field of papyrus flowers and buds (8.8 × 8.4 cm; 3½ × 3 5/16 in.). It is one of four Ornate Group panels found in Room SW2 at the Fort, which probably formed parts of the same set, a did the stylized tree ND 6453 (142); the fine polychrome panel of a rampant griffin (ND 6311, 131), found nearby in Room NW15, may also have belonged to the set. Some traces of gold overlay and glass inlays survive on these pieces. ND 6310, Baghdad, National Museum of Iraq. Photograph Mick Sharp.

LEFT 139 A furniture fitting decorated on three sides. The richly inlaid central panel shows a youth in a short pegged wig, *usekh* collar, short skirt with an elaborate apron, and open overskirt; he holds a lotus blossom in his raised left hand and an *ankh* in his right, and a bunch of lotus flowers is tied in front of him (13.2 × 6 × 2.6 cm; 5³⁄₁₆ × 2³⁄₈ × 1 in.). The side panels (now lost) showed goddesses. ND 10571, Oxford, Ashmolean Museum.

BELOW LEFT 140 Fragment of a unique piece, probably carved in a Phoenician workshop, found in a room in the domestic wing of the North West Palace. It shows part of the head of a male(?) figure; the hair is represented by fine lines, originally overlaid with hammered gold, the locks fall in deep curls on the forehead and were rendered by twists of ivory, and around the head was a triple diadem, decorated with rosettes (8 × 3.5 cm; 3¹⁄₈ × 1³⁄₈ in.). ND 765, Baghdad, National Museum of Iraq.

BELOW CENTRE 141 The right side of a modelled panel, from the group known as Unusually Shaped Ivories. In a field of lotus flowers and pads, the child Horus can be seen on the left, squatting on a lotus flower (9.1 × 5 × 1.3 cm; 3⁹⁄₁₆ × 2 × ¹⁄₂ in.). ND 13006, Baghdad, National Museum of Iraq.

BELOW RIGHT 142 Openwork panel with inlays, showing a stylized tree (5.7 × 3.4 × 1.1 cm; 2¼ × 1³⁄₈ × ⁷⁄₁₆ in.). It is part of the Ornate Group of panels from Room SW2, which also included a pharaoh figure. ND 6453, Baghdad, National Museum of Iraq.

A collection of fragments in which the design is excised and the background is left high; the hollowed areas were filled with a frit, which was moulded to form the figure. The moulding is mostly lost, leaving only the colour of the bedding, but a few traces survive on the fragment at top left – the raised arm of the male figure and the body of the sphinx or griffin. The pieces, all found in Room SW37 at Fort Shalmaneser, must have formed part of a consignment of booty; fragments worked in the same technique have been found at Samaria.

TOP LEFT 143 A male figure kneels above the wing and body of a sphinx or griffin; behind them stands a floral column and at the bottom left is part of a lotus flower (7.2 × 4.2 × 0.8 cm; 2 13/16 × 1 5/8 × 5/16 in.). ND 13067, Baghdad, National Museum of Iraq. Photograph Mick Sharp.

TOP RIGHT 144 A rampant, winged griffin advances towards a stylized tree, raising its paw to touch a branch; a frieze of lotus flowers and buds runs beneath (6 × 5.1 × 0.6 cm; 2 3/8 × 2 × 1/4 in.). ND 10654, London, British Museum. Photograph Mick Sharp.

LEFT 145 The left side of a stylized tree, which shows many traces of blue frit (9.7 × 3.3 × 0.3 cm; 3 13/16 × 1 5/16 × 1/8 in.). ND 13136, Baghdad, National Museum of Iraq. Photograph Mick Sharp.

CENTRE RIGHT, ABOVE 146 A stylized tree, showing traces of blue frit; on the left edge there are traces of red and perhaps part of a human leg. (4.3 × 3.3 × 0.6 cm; 1 11/16 × 1 5/16 × 1/4 in.). ND 10371, Baghdad, National Museum of Iraq. Photograph Mick Sharp.

CENTRE RIGHT, BELOW 147–148 An *uraeus* (LEFT) and part of a frieze with a lotus and bud design (RIGHT). (3.1 × 2.3 × 0.4 cm; 1 1/4 × 7/8 × 1/8 in.), ND 13525; (2.3 × 3.1 × 0.4 cm; 7/8 × 1 1/4 × 1/8 in.), ND 13526, Baghdad, National Museum of Iraq. Photograph Mick Sharp.

BELOW LEFT 149 Curved rectangular panel, stained red and blue, showing a hero grasping the comb of a winged griffin in his left hand, and a sword or dagger in his right; he wears a short skirt and long open overskirt (5.1 × 4 × 0.9 cm; 2 × 1 9/16 × 3/8 in.). ND 10449, Baghdad, National Museum of Iraq.

BELOW CENTRE 150 Curved plaque in two registers: a hunter stabbing a rampant lion, with a frieze of lily flowers and buds above (5.7 × 2.8 × 0.6 cm; 2 1/4 × 1 1/8 × 1/4 in.) ND 10450. London, British Museum, inv. no. 132940.

BELOW RIGHT 151 Curved plaque with a winged male figure, holding papyrus flowers (5.8 × 3.6 × 0.6 cm; 2 1/4 × 1 7/16 × 1/4 in.). ND 10398, New York, Metropolitan Museum of Art.

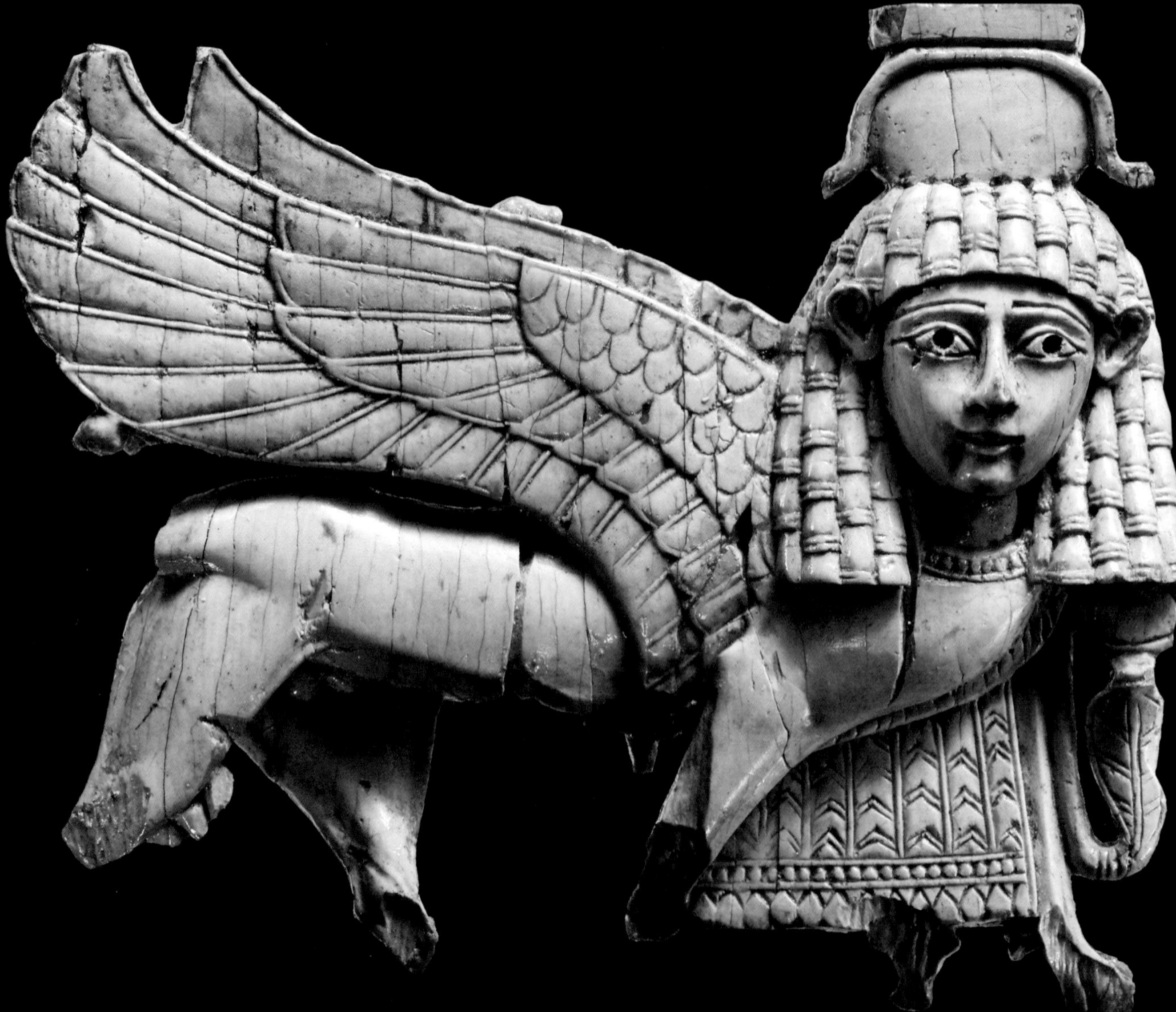

Chapter 4

Syro-Phoenician Ivories

[T]he riches of Damascus and the spoil of Samaria shall be taken away before the king of Assyria.*

In 1981 the American scholar Irene Winter began to question Frederik Poulsen's division of Levantine ivories into two groups, the Phoenician and the North Syrian, which had stood for seventy years. She pointed out that

> if one defines Phoenicia as corresponding more or less to the coastal strip west of the Lebanese mountains from the Carmel to Byblos, with the chief cities in antiquity as Tyre, Sidon, Arka, Arwad, Sarafand and Gebeil [Byblos], . . .and if one defines North Syria as comprising the city states north of the Orontes Valley and south of the Taurus, from the Habur to the Amanus, . . .then it will be noted that the territory occupied by these two regions in no way encompasses the entire Syro-Palestinian Levant.[1]

These two definitions omit southern Syrian centres such as Damascus, capital of the powerful kingdom of Aram, and Samaria, capital of Israel. Winter therefore began to build a group of ivories combining traditional Phoenician iconography in squat 'un-Phoenician' proportions, which she called 'South Syrian' and suggested might have been made at Damascus.

In the intervening thirty-five years this group has been variously refined, renamed and expanded. Here the term 'Syro-Phoenician' is used, as these ivories have proved to be Syrian versions of Phoenician originals, such as sphinxes, deities, pharaoh figures, the hero fighting a griffin, the 'woman at the window', bovids and stags. This borrowing and adaptation of Phoenician motifs can perhaps best be explained by the arrival of the Aramaeans, who in the early first millennium BC formed powerful new states in Syria that aspired to establish their independent identities. They wanted to create their own state arts, which was best achieved by borrowing and adjusting the arts of their wealthy and well-established neighbours. There were a number of these independent powers, not only the powerful kingdom of Aram centred on Damascus, and the kingdom of the Israelites with its capital at Samaria, but also other states such as Hamath and Lu'ash. And the style-groups within the Syro-Phoenician tradition reflect this diversity. Three of the easiest to identify are the 'wig and wing', the 'crown and scale' and the 'tall crown' groups, though there are a number of others.

152 A magnificent human-headed, winged sphinx, one of the finest examples of the Syro-Phoenician 'wig and wing' group. All the 'wig and wing' sphinxes look forwards and have gently curving, tripartite wings and a moulded muscle on the hindquarters; this one has a simple collar and a crowned and winged *uraeus* pendant (8.9 × 10 × 2 cm; 3½ × 4 × ¾ in.). ND 10594, New York, Metropolitan Museum of Art.

'Wig and wing' ivories

The name 'wig and wing' was given to this group because the figures wear distinctive wigs with tied locks and have wings that curve gently upwards. These features are well illustrated on a splendid sphinx from Room NW21 in Fort Shalmaneser (ND 10594, **152**).[2] 'Wig and wing' ivories form the most sophisticated and attractive group of Syro-Phoenician ivories. They have a distinctive style, are technically competent and are easy to recognize. They depict a surprisingly limited range of subjects, at present principally confined to sphinxes, the 'woman at the window' and deities, though more may be assigned to the group as time goes on. These ivories are not inlaid but were probably highlighted with gold overlays.

'Wig and wing' sphinxes have their heads turned to the front and are shown wearing a version of the sun disc and *uraei* crown, in which the sun disc is oval and the *uraei* form a horseshoe over the top. The locks of the wigs are either plain or hatched and may be tied with single or double ties. Most sphinxes wear the *usekh* collar and apron (though ND 10594 has just a simple collar). The gently curving tripartite wings start behind the chest and continue to the belly. The modelling is plastic: there are no muscle markings, but a raised muscle on the haunches is characteristic.

The Italian scholar Elena Scigliuzzo made a detailed study of the 'wig and wing' group, focusing on the motifs of the head of the sphinx and the 'woman at the window', all of which look to the front.[3] In addition to examples from Fort Shalmaneser, she was able to study a collection of similar sphinxes and 'woman at the window' designs discovered in the Nabu Temple, built by Sargon II (r. 722–705 BC) in the city he founded at Dur Sharrukin (modern Khorsabad). The ivories had presumably been given to that temple by the king as a dedication when he founded his new capital, and are typical of the ivories circulating in Assyria in the late eighth century BC. Using precise resemblances in the carving of eyes, eyebrows, cheeks and mouths, Scigliuzzo was able to identify the work of a number of different craftsmen. The fine sphinx discussed above, for instance, she assigns to Hand 2, as she also does ND 7872 (**153**).[4] She defines the faces as

> rather broad at eye level, jaw tending towards square, eyeballs more protuberant than those by other hands, eye groove almond shaped, elongated and raised towards the temple, lower lip full shaped like an orange segment, ear distinctive, butterfly-wing shaped.[5]

153 A less well-preserved version of a 'wig and wing' sphinx, possibly carved by the same hand as **152**, though this version is wearing the full *usekh* collar (7.6 × 8.4 × 1.5 cm; 3 × 3⁵⁄₁₆ × ⅝ in.). ND 7872, Baghdad, National Museum of Iraq.

154 Panel of a 'woman at the window', belonging to the 'wig and wing' group, found in the Queen's Treasury in Fort Shalmaneser (10.1 × 9.7 × 1 cm; 4 × 3¹³⁄₁₆ × ⅜ in.). ND 7739, Baghdad, National Museum of Iraq. It exactly matches a panel found in the Nabu Temple at Dur Sharrukin (now Khorsabad), the city of Sargon II; despite their very different locations, these two panels must originally have belonged to the same set and so must have been dispersed as booty.

An exact match can be made between two panels showing the 'woman at the window' motif, one found at Khorsabad (panel no. 29) and the other from the Queen's Treasury (, Room S10) in the Fort (ND 7739, **154**).⁶ They share a lengthened face, full lower lip with a dimple, puffy cheeks and similar ears. The form of the pilasters supporting the 'window' is also identical. So close are these two panels that they must have formed parts of the same set or matching sets.

Panels with faces in profile lack the full range of micro-variants established by Scigliuzzo, but she has attributed some of these to the 'wig and wing' workshop. They include a winged deity with the sun disc and *uraei* crown of typical 'wig and wing' form, set on a tripartite wig, with a small figure squatting between the gently curving wings (ND 8150, **212**, p. 142).⁷

Scigliuzzo's detailed study marks a real advance in our understanding of the production processes of ivory. She has proved that the same craftsmen carved different subjects – the 'woman at the window' and the sphinx – found at both Khorsabad and Nimrud. The same pattern can be observed in the ivories from Room V/W in the North West Palace, discovered by Layard and also assigned to the 'wig and wing' group. The Layard ivories, with youths saluting lotus plants and the 'woman at the window' motif, are discussed in chapter 1 (see **30–33**, p. 39); some of these can be attributed to specific craftsmen, who carved both types of panel.

The fragmentary four-winged deity of ND 7656 is unique in its design (**156**)⁸ but can also be assigned to the 'wig and wing' group. On his head is a version of the triple *atef* crown, and he holds out crowned *uraei* on either side, between his gently curving wings. Of particular interest about this panel

Syro-Phoenician Ivories 107

ABOVE 155 Fragment of a moulded plaque, one of a series attached to a large pottery jar found by Hormuzd Rassam (7.6 × 5.6 × 0.8 cm; 3 × 2³⁄₁₆ × ⁵⁄₁₆ in.). London, British Museum, inv. no. 92251. The jar was Assyrian, locally made, but the design on the plaque is typically Levantine, and was copied from a 'wig and wing' panel (156, right).

RIGHT 156 A fragmentary tenoned panel, carved in 'wig and wing' style, showing a four-winged deity wearing a composite crown on an Egyptian wig, and holding crowned *uraei* in his outstretched hands (7.6 × 5.6 cm; 3 × 2³⁄₁₆ in.). ND 7656, London, British Museum. The unique design served as a model for a group of pottery stamps applied to a jar (155 above).

is that its design was copied on a group of ceramic panels, which were attached to a large pottery jar (155), found by Layard's assistant, Hormuzd Rassam, at Nimrud. While the design of the ivory is typically Levantine, the jar is Assyrian and locally made, as has been proved by analysing the clay. This illustrates a new way in which designs might be copied in places far from their probable areas of origin. The potter must, presumably, have seen the ivory, liked the design, and made a mould, from which he prepared a series of plaques to attach to the jar. A fragment of another pottery mould was found at Zinjirli (ancient Sam'al); again, this is far from its probable source of production, as it shows part of a crouching lion, worked in the North Syrian 'flame and frond' style (see also chapter 5).

The majority of this attractive group of ivories have been found at Nimrud and Khorsabad, though there are a few examples from Arslan Tash (ancient Hadatu), about 30 km east of the Euphrates, and Tell Ahmar (Til Barsib), located near the Euphrates below Carchemish. Both these sites were absorbed into the Assyrian empire and became Assyrian centres. It is possible that the ivories found in them may have been booty redistributed by the Assyrians to their local governors.

'Crown and scale' ivories

Another distinctive group of Syro-Phoenician ivories, the 'crown and scale' group, employs a slightly greater range of subjects, as well as occasionally being highlighted with inlays. These ivories were so called because of two characteristic features: the figures wear misunderstood representations of Egyptian crowns, and the scales at the base of their tripartite wings are outlined or ribbed. The most common type of 'crown and scale' panel is an openwork sphinx, large numbers of which were found in Room SW37 and, especially, Room SW11. ND 12141 (**157**)[9] is a typical example of a human-headed sphinx, crowned with a squashed version of the Egyptian double crown, set over a headcloth. It has a fine face with a distinctive eye and a pronounced nose, an *usekh* collar, apron and tripartite wings, the lowest section of which consists of ribbed scales. The ground is filled with voluted palmette flowers, and the distinctive 'capped papyrus', typical of Syro-Phoenician ivories, can be seen above the wing: this is a much coarser version of the elegant, Phoenician fluted papyrus. The body is modelled with lightly incised markings on the haunches.

'Crown and scale' sphinxes were also carved with their heads facing forwards (ND 14534, **217**, p. 143).[10] Sometimes the head was carved separately and fixed to the panel by means of a keyhole slot or dowel (ND 9186, **158**).[11] Some sphinxes found in Room T10 in the Fort still had these separately carved heads attached (ND 14533).

In 1986 it was still thought that inlaid ivories might have been carved in different centres from modelled ones, and at a different date. However, the inlaid sphinx ND 10522, with its flattened sun disc surrounded by a pair of *uraei* in a horseshoe shape, is similar to many modelled examples (**221**, p. 143).[12] Once again, it is evident that both plain and inlaid ivories should be considered together as products

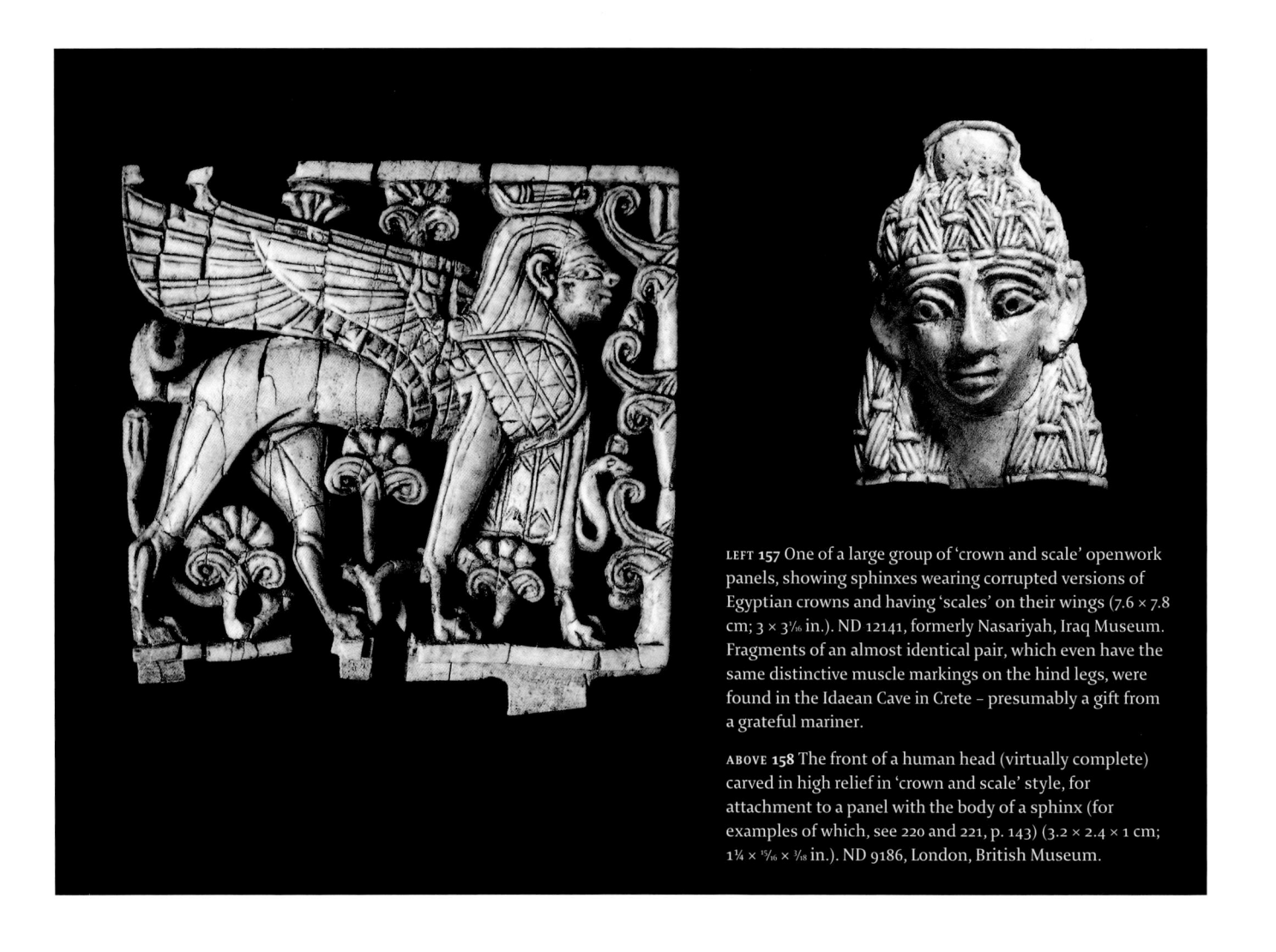

LEFT **157** One of a large group of 'crown and scale' openwork panels, showing sphinxes wearing corrupted versions of Egyptian crowns and having 'scales' on their wings (7.6 × 7.8 cm; 3 × 3¹/₁₆ in.). ND 12141, formerly Nasariyah, Iraq Museum. Fragments of an almost identical pair, which even have the same distinctive muscle markings on the hind legs, were found in the Idaean Cave in Crete – presumably a gift from a grateful mariner.

ABOVE **158** The front of a human head (virtually complete) carved in high relief in 'crown and scale' style, for attachment to a panel with the body of a sphinx (for examples of which, see 220 and 221, p. 143) (3.2 × 2.4 × 1 cm; 1¼ × ¹⁵/₁₆ × ⅜ in.). ND 9186, London, British Museum.

Syro-Phoenician Ivories 109

LEFT 159 Fragment of a panel, showing a kneeling deity holding a palmette flower (8.7 × 5.1 × 1.7 cm; 3⁷⁄₁₆ × 2 × ¹¹⁄₁₆ in.). ND 14531, Baghdad, National Museum of Iraq. Similarities between panels showing kneeling males, heroes killing griffins, and winged sphinxes, as well as the fact that the pieces were found in similar locations, led to the nomination of a single group, the 'crown and scale' group.

RIGHT 160 A well-preserved panel, showing a hero dispatching a griffin, forcing it to the ground with hand, spear and foot (9.9 × 5.6 × 0.8 cm; 3⁷⁄₈ × 2³⁄₁₆ × ⁵⁄₁₆ in.). ND 10471, New York, Metropolitan Museum of Art. This Syro-Phoenician version is dramatically different from the calm Phoenician depiction seen in **204** (p. 139).

of the same workshop or workshops. However, inlaying on Syro-Phoenician ivories is not only relatively rare but also considerably coarser than the fine Phoenician work.

Linking panels with different subjects is always complicated and subjective. The discovery of three fragmentary panels in T10 and SE10, showing kneeling youths, made it possible to enlarge the 'crown and scale' group to include both the youths and some hero and griffin panels. The youth of ND 14531 is wearing a sun disc and *uraeus* crown on a wig of twisted ringlets, and has the typical 'crown and scale' fine face with large eyes, slender nose and small mouth (**159**).[13] He wears a finely pleated tunic with a short skirt, held by a belt that ends in a volute, and holds the stalk of a flower over his shoulder. The hero of ND 10471 has a flattened version of the Egyptian double crown, with the frontal *uraeus* extended into a volute (**160**).[14] The crown is set on a wig of twisted ringlets. The face is fine, with a large eye and pointed nose. The hero is framed by the hatched wings of the griffin, which, still flying, is thrust to the ground and held down by hand and foot, its beak pierced by the spear. The designs using sphinxes, kneeling youths and heroes fighting griffins share many characteristics, such as the crowded compositions, the misrepresented crowns, the form of the wigs, the peaky faces and the pleated clothing with voluted belts, as well as technical features – the types of panel, framing and tenoning, and the occasional presence of fitters' marks.

A common location often reinforces the linkage of panels, and 'crown and scale' panels were found together in a number of rooms at Nimrud. Altogether, seven 'hero and griffin' panels were found in the Fort – four in Room SW37, two in Room SE10 and one in Room NE59. Found with the one in NE59 was the front of an inlaid sphinx, and an openwork, ram-headed sphinx. In SE10, in addition to the pair of hero and griffin panels, there was the front of another inlaid sphinx and one of the kneeling youths. Finally, there were both 'crown and scale' sphinxes and the four hero and griffin panels in Room SW37.

110 Ancient Ivory

161 A ram-headed sphinx of the Crown and Scale group, ND 12134, part of a numerous set found in Room SW11 of Fort Shalmaneser. He carries an unusual, truncated trapezoidal crown set on a head cloth: the muscle markings on his haunches parallel those on a sphinx found in the Idaean Cave, and he advances towards a stylized tree. 7.3 x 6.7 x 1.0 cm. Iraq Museum, Erbil, IM 65908. Photograph Mick Sharp.

'Crown and scale' ivories are known only at Nimrud, apart from fragments of two sphinx panels found in the Idaean Cave in Crete. These are so close stylistically to those at Nimrud, having exactly the same muscle markings on the haunches, that they must have been carved in the same workshop.[15] The gift of a pair of such luxurious panels must have been an impressive donation to Zeus, perhaps a gift from a grateful sailor.

An unusual sphinx

A bizarre interpretation of a sphinx, which may have been carved in a Syro-Phoenician workshop, was found in Room T10. ND 11125 represents the front part of a massive, human-headed sphinx, carved from a large tusk and measuring some 21 cm (8¼ in.) in height (**120**, p. 97).[16] The sphinx stares out to the front and exhibits traits from a number of different groups. A form of headdress or crown rises above the dense curly wig over the forehead. The ringlets, falling to the shoulders behind the ears, are reminiscent of 'wig and wing' tied ringlets. The eyes and eyebrows are deeply excised for inlay, as in Phoenician pieces. The mouth is sensitively carved, above a rich, curly, spade-shaped beard, possibly influenced by Assyrian models. A collar, decorated with ribbed droplets, curves round the beard, while another collar covers the chest, the collars being similar to 'crown and scale' examples. The usual chevroned apron with ribbed droplets can be seen in front of the foreleg. This is a unique piece and exemplifies the challenges of trying to understand this remarkable archive.

Borrowing

Recent studies have begun to demonstrate that the designs carved on Syro-Phoenician ivories are usually borrowed from Phoenician originals. However, this type of borrowing is evident not only in the choice of a design, such as the ever popular sphinx, but also in the use of specific motifs. For instance, a distinctive and unusual 'triple flower' is seen blooming above the wings of some sphinxes. It consists of a central voluted palmette flower, flanked by lilies. When first observed, this seemed to be a useful diagnostic to help define a style-group. It can be seen on the sphinx of ND 7616, which, with its double frame and tall proportions, Egyptian double crown and Osiride beard, is a typical Ornate Group panel (**162**).[17] It also occurs on the sphinx of ND 9737, which is very different (**163**).[18] The latter sphinx is considerably squatter and is carved in much higher relief, nearly in the round. It has a version of the Egyptian double crown, an unusually tall 'white crown' set on a striped headcloth; this form of crown accounts for the name of the 'tall crown' style-group. The face of ND 9737 is larger and heavier than that of ND 7616 and lacks the Osiride beard. It is a typical Syro-Phoenician version of a Phoenician design, and exemplifies borrowing not only of a design but also of

162–163 Two panels showing sphinxes, each with an unusual motif – a 'triple flower', consisting of a central palmette flower flanked by a pair of lilies – carved above the wings. The first, with its elegant proportions and sense of space, is clearly Phoenician, while the second is a cramped and crowded Syro-Phoenician version of the same design. ND 7616 (10.5 × 10.8 × 0.8 cm; 4⅛ × 4¼ × ⁵⁄₁₆ in.), Baghdad, National Museum of Iraq. ND 9737 (11.1 × 8.4 × 1.4 cm; 4⅜ × 3⁵⁄₁₆ × ⁹⁄₁₆ in.), London, British Museum.

a specific motif. A poorly preserved version of a similar panel was found at Samaria.[19]

A similar pattern of borrowing from Phoenician art can be seen on panels that show sphinxes standing on squatting figures. A tall Phoenician sphinx is supported on the heads and hands of a pair of squatting youths (ND 11024, **164**).[20] It wears an Egyptian double crown, set on a *nemes* headcloth that encloses an *usekh* collar, and an apron decorated with chevrons. Voluted palmette flowers grow up between the sphinx's legs and from the stylized tree forming one edge of the panel. In the Syro-Phoenician sphinx of ND 12146, not only are the proportions of the sphinx different, but so also is the dense packing of the ground between the kneeling youths and above the wings of the sphinx with voluted palmette plants and the triple flower (**165**).[21] It is a very 'busy' scene. This sphinx, like ND 9737 (**163**), belongs to the 'tall crown' group.

164–165 Another instance of borrowing, this time on two panels showing a design of a sphinx supported on a pair of kneeling male figures. LEFT ND 11024 (10 × 6.2 × 1.1 cm; 3 15/16 × 2 7/16 × 7/16 in.), New York, Metropolitan Museum of Art. RIGHT ND 12146 (14.9 × 6.2 × 1.2 cm; 5 7/8 × 2 7/16 × 1/2 in.), Baghdad, National Museum of Iraq. Photograph Mick Sharp.

Syro-Phoenician Ivories

Pharaoh figures with sceptres and jugs

Another design that was originally Egyptian is that of a pharaoh figure or worshipper with a ram-headed sceptre and jug. The earliest known representation in the Levant is at thirteenth-century Ugarit, while the latest is on a Roman altar from Baalbek: it occurs in various versions on ivories, seals, coins and bronze razors.[22] A typical Phoenician version shows pairs of pharaoh figures, holding ram-headed sceptres and jugs, standing on either side of stylized trees and below registers of *uraei* and winged discs, the whole representing a scene set in a shrine (ND 11032, **166**;[23] see also **206–207**, p. 140).

The design was widely copied on ivories, with single rather than paired figures, and became steadily more misunderstood as it travelled across the area. All elements of the shrine have disappeared in the three panels ND 10322, ND 10494 and ND 7579 (**166–168**).[24] The pharaoh figures are crowned with versions of Egyptian crowns and wear sleeved garments with short skirts and open overskirts. What unites these very differently carved versions is the presence of the ram-headed sceptre and jug, though the jug of ND 7579 contains a voluted palmette flower, apparently growing from it. These are all Syrian versions of the motif, which is even more unrecognizable in the provincial fragment ND 13438 (**160**). Here the crudely carved figure is crowned with a sun disc surrounded by a rudimentary *uraeus*. He is bearded and his hair is arranged in twisted ringlets. His nose is large and his cheeks fleshy. He wears a sleeved, thigh-length tunic and overskirt, and holds up an extraordinary form of animal-headed sceptre in one hand, with a jug in the other. The upper frame is decorated with circles.

LEFT **166** Panel showing a classic Phoenician version of an Egyptian motif of a worshipper with ram-headed sceptre and jug. In this symmetrical example, one of a set of five, the pharaoh figures flank a stylized tree, touching the upper branches with their sceptres; above is a winged disc and a row of crowned *uraei*, representing a shrine (12.2 × 7.7 × 1.1 cm; 4 13/16 × 3 × 7/16 in.). ND 11032, New York, Metropolitan Museum of Art.

OPPOSITE **167–170** Four panels, showing provincial (and increasingly misunderstood) versions of the motif of pharaoh with sceptre and jug, the last of which is identifiable only thanks to the attributes, though they are strangely rendered. CLOCKWISE FROM TOP LEFT ND 10322 (12.8 × 4 × 0.5 cm; 5 1/16 × 1 9/16 × 3/16 in.), Baghdad, National Museum of Iraq. Photograph Mick Sharp. ND 10494 (8.3 × 3.7 × 0.5 cm; 3 1/4 × 1 7/16 × 3/16 in.), Boston, Museum of Fine Arts. ND 7579 (11 × 6.4 cm; 4 5/16 × 2 1/2 in.), New York, Metropolitan Museum of Art. Photograph Mick Sharp. ND 13438 (5.7 × 3.6 × 0.7 cm; 2 1/4 × 1 7/16 × 1/4 in.), Baghdad, National Museum of Iraq.

114 Ancient Ivory

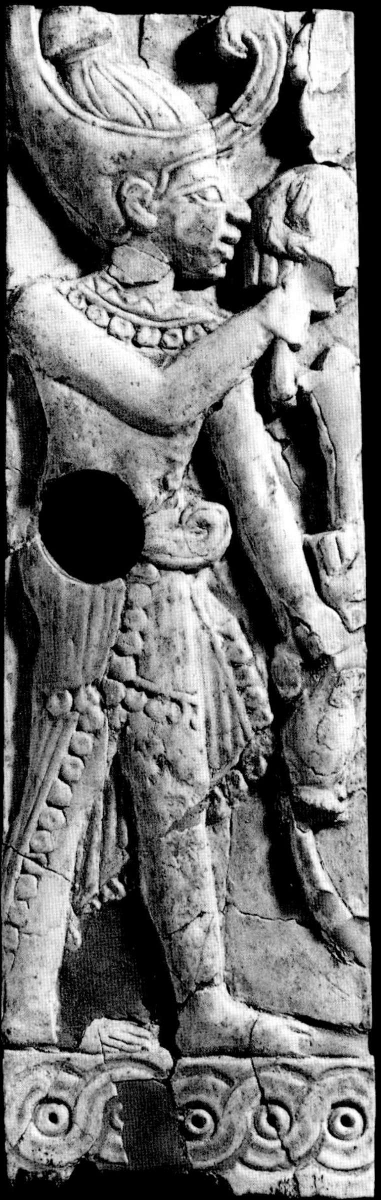
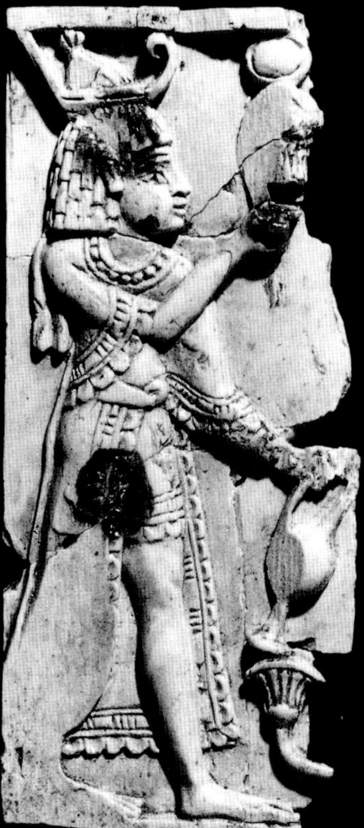
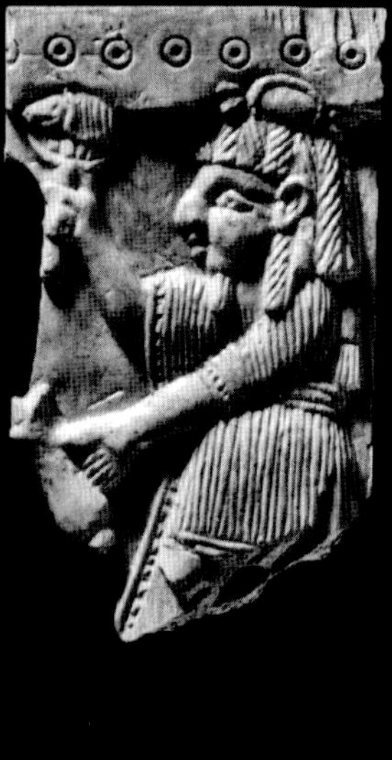
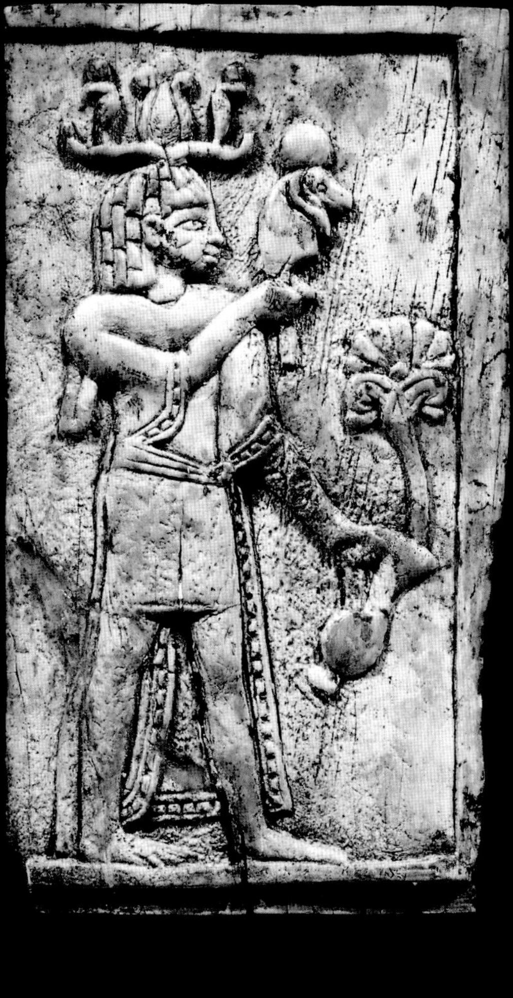

171 Sections of a long rectangular panel (originally a single piece with a semi-circular central element, now cut out), showing processions of worshippers advancing towards the centre; the leading figure on the panel on the right is, again, a pharaoh with sceptre and jug (panel reassembled: 6.8 × 23.6× 2.4 cm; 2¹¹⁄₁₆ × 9⁵⁄₁₆ × ¹⁵⁄₁₆ in.). ND, 10376, Baghdad, National Museum of Iraq.

The same pharaoh figure can be seen on one side of a long panel (now in two pieces) decorated with a complicated processional scene (ND 10376, **171**).[26] Five worshippers, four men and a woman, advance towards a (missing) central semicircular element. They wear eccentric versions of Egyptian crowns and carry a variety of attributes. The leading man raises a ram-headed sceptre in one hand and has a pitcher in the other. The second also raises a sceptre but holds an *ankh* in the other, while the woman at the end carries a duck. They are separated by lilies and are carved in high relief.

These five panels show the varied ways in which the same motif was used and the different styles in which it was worked.

Long panels

Long panels were used as furniture fittings, set along the base of couches, as can be seen on the frieze of fighting lions on the couch of Ashurbanipal on the famous relief from Nineveh (**240**, p. 152), or connecting chairs with their footstools. Popular motifs for such panels, which could be simply modelled or carved in openwork, included sets of browsing bulls, cows suckling their calves, and stags. They were often found in sets, such as those discovered in Room V of the North West Palace and in Room NW21 of the Fort. Room NW21 is one of three larger rooms along the north-western wall, and was probably used as a store-room, at least towards the end of the Fort's life. Most of the fine and varied collection of some sixty ivories found there were Syro-Phoenician, including at least a dozen stags and about ten cows suckling their young. The panels are all openwork, of a similar size, and were held in position by frames at top and bottom, reinforced by keyhole slots and having lightly striated backs, suggesting the use of a glue.

The browsing stags feed on fronds that grow from plants in front of them and twine under their bodies (ND 10582, **172**).[27] Although generally similar to Phoenician versions, the bodies of the cows are heavier. ND 10577 is a typical example: the head is turned back towards the calf, which is suckling vigorously, its tail curled up against the mother's belly (**173**).[28] Both stags and cattle have their eyes excised for inlays; there are markings on their necks and the cows' ribs are indicated, but little other musculature is delineated.

The Levantine ivory repertoire is relatively limited, consisting in the main of deities, pharaoh figures, youths, a few women, sphinxes and griffins, and cattle and cervids. Some of these designs were confined to the Phoenician and Syro-Phoenician worlds, while others were copied across the Levant. As with all ivories, there are stylistic and technical variations between the different groups.

Compared to the hundreds of ivories attributed to the Phoenician tradition, there are relatively few Syro-Phoenician examples, though a number of groups (more than the three discussed above) can be assembled. As far as can be determined to date – and ivory studies are ongoing – all the designs seem to be versions of Phoenician originals, carved in a different and perhaps more dynamic, but certainly less elegant and compressed, style. While many will have been highlighted with gold overlays, and possibly painted, the use of inlays is rare, having been identified so far only in the 'crown and scale' group, and relatively coarse.

While it is possible to form groups, it is not yet possible to decide where or when the Syro-Phoenician ivories were produced. Some were almost certainly made in Damascus, as Winter perceptively suggested back in 1981. Others, however, were probably carved in other Aramaean centres, production ceasing as the states were conquered by Assyria.

172–173 Two examples of a series of openwork pieces found in Room NW21 in the Fort, showing browsing stags and cows suckling their calves; these would have been made up into long panels.
ABOVE ND 10582 (5.7 × 19 cm; 2¼ × 7½ in.), Baghdad, National Museum of Iraq.
BELOW ND 10577 (5 × 9.4 cm; 2 × 3¹¹⁄₁₆ in.), Baghdad, National Museum of Iraq.

Syro-Phoenician Ivories 117

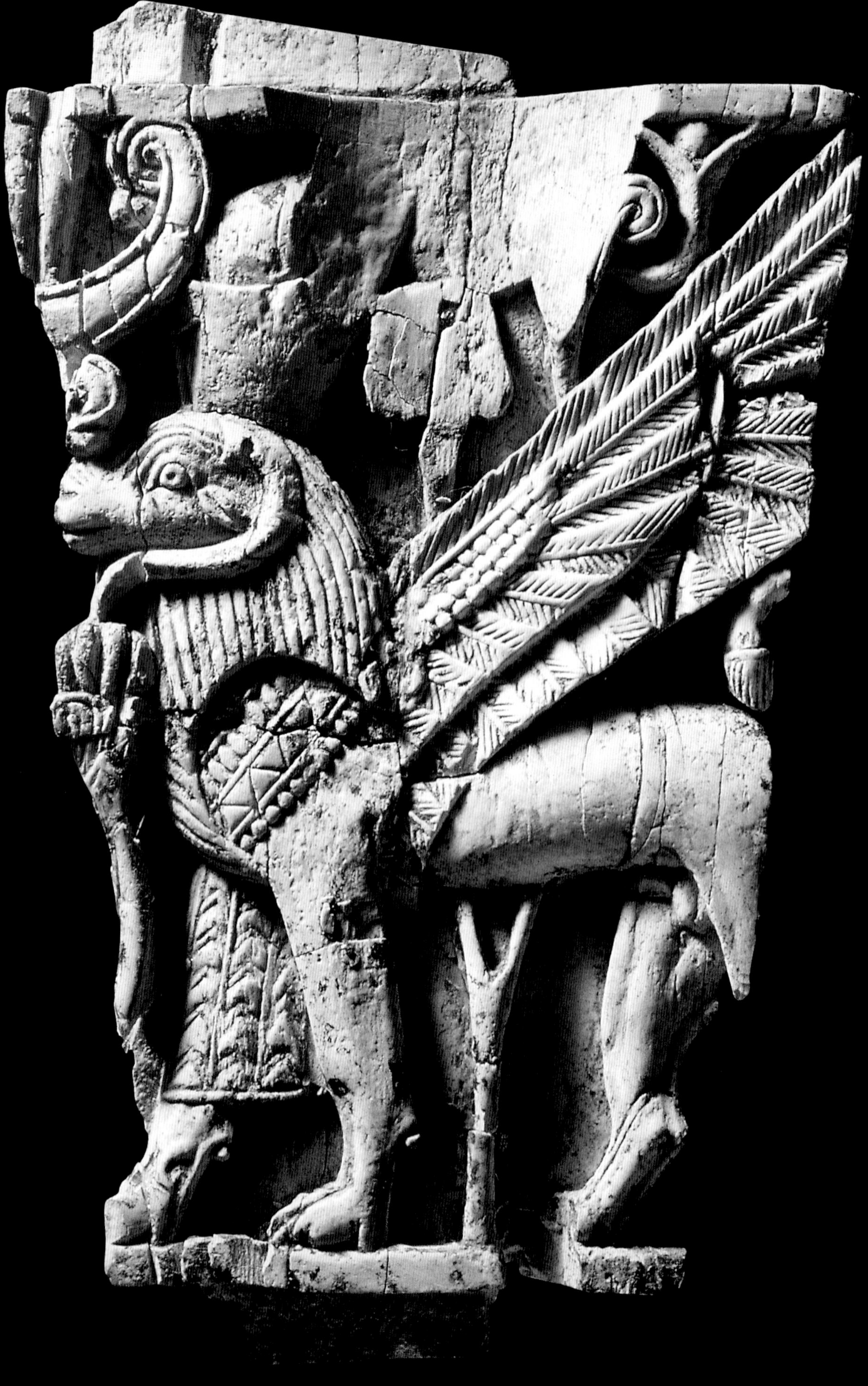

Chapter 5

The Ivories of North Syria

Surprises quite undreamt of fell to my lot; it was a turning point in my life. The spade was first of all applied at the spot where the Chechens had come upon those remarkable statues when they had tried to bury their dead....even in this short time [three days] I was able to lay bare part of the great principal face of the temple-palace.*

The last centuries of the second millennium BC saw considerable changes in the political world of the Near East. The relative stability that had resulted from alliances between the great powers of Hatti (the Hittites), the pharaohs of Eighteenth Dynasty Egypt, the kingdom of Mitanni (later replaced by emerging Assyria) and the Kassites of Babylonia collapsed. In about 1200 BC the Hittite cities of Anatolia were sacked and the Hittite empire ended, although a few Hittite cities, such as Malatya and Carchemish, in particular, continued as independent states with unbroken lines of kings of Hittite descent. At the same time there were movements of Semitic peoples from the desert. These included the Aramaeans, who over the next few centuries were to occupy much of the Levant and Mesopotamia, and the Israelites in Palestine.

We first hear of the Aramaeans in the reign of the Assyrian king Tiglath-pileser I (r. 1114–1076 BC), who 'crossed the Euphrates 28 times, twice in one year, in pursuit of the *ahlamu* [Aramaeans]'.[1] During the eleventh century BC they were consolidating their power and settling in large numbers across the Fertile Crescent, forming a series of states, the most important of which was the kingdom of Aram, with its capital at Damascus. The major centre of Carchemish continued under Hittite control, while others, originally Hittite, were Aramaized, such as Sam'al (modern Zinjirli), Bit Agusi (Tell Rifaat) and Hamath (Hama) in west and central Syria. Aramaean states included Bit Bahiani, the principal city of which was Guzana (Tell Halaf) on the River Khabur in east Syria.

Typically, these Aramaean states consisted of a capital city with dependent 'strong cities' and villages within a geographically distinct tract of land. Although the early first millennium was a time of constant manoeuvring for power, there are no records of conflict on ethnic grounds. The Aramaeans formed alliances both with and against other Syrian states, and then against the ever increasing threat of Assyria. Some of these states, including Guzana, were incorporated into the Assyrian empire by the end of the ninth century, and most had been absorbed by the end of the eighth century.

174 A Syro-Phoenician ivory from Room SW37 in Fort Shalmaneser, showing a winged, ram-headed sphinx of the 'tall crown' group (13.4 × 8.5 × 1.2 cm; 5¼ × 3⅜ × ½ in.). ND 7986, Birmingham, City Museum and Art Gallery.

Major and minor art in North Syria

Sculptures have been found at many of the sites along the Syro-Turkish border. It is generally agreed that minor arts reflect major, which helps to suggest probable centres of production for some of our ivories. The art in northern Syria was strongly regional, reflecting the individuality of these minor powers. For instance, the remarkable sculptures found at Tell Halaf differ markedly from those of Carchemish and Zinjirli.

The major Neo-Hittite centre of Carchemish is located at an important crossing point on the Euphrates and has yielded a fine and individual series of dated sculptures. Although many small antiquities have been found there, few reflect the art of the sculptures, though the designs on two fragmentary stone pyxides match them. The most convincing parallel between major and minor art occurs at Tell Halaf, which has a remarkable and wholly unique style, carved on sculptures of two periods – an early provincial series and a later more sophisticated one. This style can be precisely matched both on a few fragments of gold and ivory found at the site, and on one of the major groups of North Syrian ivories found at Nimrud, the 'flame and frond' group. Matches can also be made between 'round-cheeked and ringletted' ivories from Nimrud and column bases found at Zinjirli, and there are other parallels between the ivories and material from that site. A third major group is the 'Classic SW7', which consists of sets of panels forming the backs of chairs, and has been compared to the sculptures of Sakcha Gozu, located some 20 km (13 miles) north of Zinjirli. As always, the picture is complicated, for in addition to these three groups, there are many smaller groups of North Syrian ivories, or individual ivories, which cannot even be generally located to an area.

North Syrian ivories are different in character, style and technique from both Assyrian and Phoenician ivories. Their message is compelling, some figures confronting the onlooker and filling the available surface. There are differences between pieces in the forms of winged discs, the features and dress of human figures, the musculature of animals, the use of cross-hatching, the type of inlay, the use of a specific pegged dowel and so on. While many subjects, such as sphinxes and griffins, bulls and lions, and men and trees, are common across Levantine and Assyrian ivories, the style of carving of the North Syrian ivories differs. There are also motifs that are unique to the North Syrian corpus, such as animal hunts and fights, banquets, and processions of musicians, but there is no narrative as such. Equally, there is little Egyptian influence.

'Flame and frond' ivories

'Flame and frond' is one of the easiest groups of ivories at Nimrud to recognize. It was named from the characteristic flame markings on the haunches of the animals and the 'frondy' foliage of the plants, though there are numerous other diagnostic features that define the group. It is the combination of criteria, not just one or two elements, that allows the attribution of an ivory to this group. Its most distinctive features are the markings that define the musculature of the various animals and mythical beasts, and the human physiognomy, with receding forehead, large eyes, pointed nose and small mouth. The muscle markings vary slightly from animal to animal, though some are common to all (175). Standard features include almond-shaped eyes, modelled brows, 'petal' markings on the forelegs, incised lines along the top of the back, with a series of small vertical lines ending in longer vertical lines in front of the tail, the 'flames' on the hind legs and the 'pea-pod' markings on the hocks. Although flame markings began in the second millennium BC and were relatively common in the early first (occurring, for instance, on sculptures found at Hama), what is distinctive about the 'flames' on 'flame and frond' ivories is that they grow from the front of the hind legs. Ribs are sometimes marked. Sphinxes and lions have plait markings along the belly and down the back of the hind leg, and bulls and stags have wavy lines down the necks and hook markings on the shoulders.

In addition to style, the musculature of the animals and the physiognomy of the human figures, technical features typical of the group include distinctive types of inlay and dowel. Small objects, such as pyxides or flasks, were often

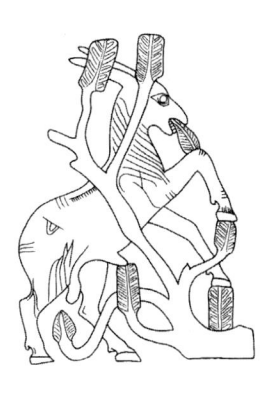

175 Drawings of the muscle stylizations on ivories of the 'flame and frond' school: TOP TO BOTTOM deer, sphinx, bull and lion. Drawn by P. Clark, reproduced from Herrmann and Laidlaw 2013, p. 96, fig. 5a.

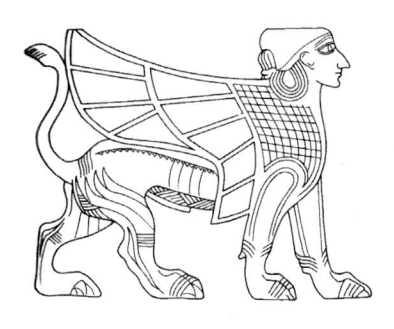

gilded and inlaid with large pieces of material, secured by means of central peg-holes to hold them in position: these are known as 'pegged inlays'. The inlays themselves survive on a few of the more or less complete pyxides found in Well AJ, but they have not been analysed. It has been suggested that they are pieces of dyed ivory. If so, this is a fundamentally different technique from the glass on frit bedding employed in Phoenician ivories. Some North Syrian dowel holes, especially those on the backs of pieces, were cut with a centred bit; this distinctive fixing consisted of a relatively wide dowel hole, with a deeper central peg-hole, and is called a 'pegged dowel'. Another unusual feature, characteristic of the group, is that the design on openwork furniture panels, is repeated on the backs, sometimes in a slightly simpler form. Cross-hatching is characteristic of most North Syrian ivories and was extensively used on 'flame and frond' pieces, especially on the bases of the wings of sphinxes or goddesses and the stems of plants. Sphinxes were a favourite motif, shown standing or recumbent. Unlike Phoenician ivories, there is little repetition in 'flame and frond' ivories.

'Flame and frond' ivories have been found in the palaces on the citadel and in Fort Shalmaneser, though the types of object differ. Only small objects were found on the citadel – lidded boxes or pyxides, fan handles, and a flask with a stopper that also served as a spoon for dispensing liquids – while furniture elements, both panels and furniture legs, were found in the Fort. There were three relatively complete pyxides in Well AJ, as well as many burnt and broken examples in the Burnt Palace. The body of a pyxis was probably cut from the base of a large tusk, with a flat section at the back. The top was hinged, with little statuettes of calves and sometimes rosettes fixed to the lid. The base was formed of a thin plate of ivory, incised with floral designs.

A beautifully preserved and relatively complete pyxis from Well AJ (IM 79514, **236**, p. 148)[2] has four calves set on the hinged lid, which is framed with a guilloche band. On the base is a pattern of incised rosettes. The sides are decorated with pairs of human-headed winged sphinxes, flanking voluted palmette plants, with a goddess on the flat back panel. Areas of gold overlay survive on hair, chests and

The Ivories of North Syria

bodies, and on some of the guilloche frames. There are large pegged cloisons on the wings and the voluted palmette tree, but no surviving inlays. The faces and musculature of the sphinxes are typically 'flame and frond'.

Another outstanding find from Well AJ is a flask, which is arguably one of the finest and most remarkable ivories ever found. It is unique and was made from most of a tusk some 36 cm (more than 14 in.) long with a maximum width of 9.5 cm (3¾ in.) (IM 79508, **237**, p. 149).[3] It was closed at the wider end by an ivory lid mounted on wood, and there was a wooden section at the narrower end, which joined the flask to a woman's head, carved from the tip of a tusk. The sides of the flask are covered with four registers of design, two with scenes of combat between lions and winged griffins and two with bulls. A central stylized tree, similar to some on the pyxides, separates the pairs of fighting beasts, while three-branched papyrus trees occupy the narrow ends of the rows of bulls. The animals carry the full range of the characteristic musculature markings. Wings, flowers and the strips of decoration that divide the registers were embellished with large pieces of pegged inlays, some of which are still *in situ*, and traces of gilding survive on the frames and on some of the animals. The woman wears a high crown, inlaid with pegged vertical strips, ringlets in front of her ears and long hair falling down her back (IM 79510, **176**).[4] Her face is finely modelled, with large eyes, straight nose and a small, pinched mouth – a type of face typical of the group, which can be matched with heads from caryatid fan handles and, on a grander scale, with the large head found by Mallowan in Well NN (ND 2549). Her collar has three strands of beads,

176 The top of a unique flask (**237**, p. 149), retrieved from Well AJ in the North West Palace, in the form of a woman's head carved in the round from the tip of a tusk. She is thin-faced, her nose is hooked, her lips pouting and her chin pointed, and her hair is dressed in ringlets and plaits; she is wearing an elaborate necklace and a high crown with inlaid panels, on top of which another feature would have been attached (12.5 × 6 × 4.7 cm; 4¹⁵⁄₁₆ × 2⅜ × 1⅞ in.). IM 79510, Baghdad, National Museum of Iraq.

177 The magnificent head of an old woman (the so-called 'Ugly Sister'), found in Well NN in the North West Palace. Her brow is low, the eyebrows prominent, the eyes large, with inlaid pupils, and the face has prominent cheekbones, a strong chin and a thin-lipped mouth; she wears a collar or necklace with pendant discs (18 × 13.7 × 5 cm; 7⅛ × 5⅜ × 2 in.). The missing tip of the nose would have been carved separately and attached to the face by means of a dowel. ND 2549, New York, Metropolitan Museum of Art.

with five large flat discs, alternately inlaid and plain. A large tenon hole is cut in the top of the crown for the attachment of another feature, now lost.

The great face ND 2549 – once a head in the round but now damaged at the back (**177**)[5] – was nicknamed 'the Ugly Sister' on discovery, so different is it from the sensuous Mona Lisa, found in the same well (**20**, p. 29; **102**, p. 89). It is carved in high relief from a vertical section of a large tusk, measures some 18 × 13.7 × 5 cm (7⅛ × 5⅜ × 2 in.) and weighs 332 grammes (c. 11¾ oz). It presumably formed part of a statuette. Her hair is parted in the middle, her face is a carefully modelled oval, with rounded cheeks and a firm chin. The eyebrows are deeply excised and the large eyes are prominent, pointed ovals, outlined by raised ribs and with inlaid pupils. The lips are thin and pursed, those of an elderly woman. She wears the usual beaded necklace with pendant ovals, some of which still contain their original gold discs.

Similar heads can be seen on another extraordinary piece from Well AJ, a massive bowl, carved from a single piece of a large tusk and measuring 15.9 × 12.4 cm (6¼ × 4⅞ in.), with a thickness of some 7.6 cm (3 in.) (IM 79511, **238**, p. 150).[6] It is decorated with the forequarters of four lions, two grasping the sides of a central bowl, and the other two, with linked paws, set between them. In front of the latter are two winged, human-headed sphinxes on either side of a stylized tree, their women's heads rising above the rim of the bowl. They have crowns, inlaid with pegged discs, their hair falls in ringlets in front of their ears and in curls on their shoulders, and they have the usual beaded necklaces with central discs. Between them, on the front of the bowl, is a Syrian version of a winged disc, with fronds above and below the disc and wings rising from volutes. The piece was richly inlaid and would also have been gilded. This ivory formed the end of what must have been an exceptionally rich flask, presumably for use in elaborate ceremonies; liquid from the flask was poured through the lions' mouths into the bowl.

Another unique ivory from the well is marked with the standard musculature but is very different, in that it is an openwork roundel (IM 79519, **178**);[7] it shows a lion grappling with a bull, which is collapsing under the strain. Once again, it shows the virtuosity of the 'flame and frond' craftsmen and illustrates that they could carve delicate openwork pieces. This is significant, as it reinforces the attribution to the 'flame and frond' group of a series of openwork furniture panels found in the Fort.

Four such panels, from Room NW15 in the Fort, form a set, despite being decorated with different subjects. They are all the same size and are framed in the same manner, with half-stylized trees on one side and papyrus and bud frames on the other. Two panels show cervids with turned heads, a stag (ND 6379, **231**, p. 146)[8] and a gazelle (ND 6314, **233**, p. 146).[9] The other pair show seated lions (ND 6349, **179**; ND 6350, **232**, p. 146),[10] wearing pectorals or collars and crowned with large sun discs set on wigs. The panels are filled with flowering, frondy foliage, and the animals are marked with the familiar musculature. An important technical feature, unique to the group, is that the designs are repeated, in a similar but simplified manner, on the backs.

Although these panels form a set, it is obvious that they were carved by more than one hand. The sensitive stag is a real masterpiece. He is delicately set in the panel, his head has a large eye, curving antlers and neat ears. The standard musculature lines round the neck, a hook marking on the shoulder, a line along the back, lines in front of the tail and flame markings on the haunch of the hind leg are well marked. The gazelle on the other hand, though in the same posture, is clumsier and more crudely worked: compare its placing within the frame, the cast of the head, the muscle markings, and even the modelling of the fronds. Such a

178 An openwork roundel of a lion attacking a bull from the 'flame and frond' group, identified by its distinctive, stylized muscle markings; the lion is mounted on the back of the bull, with its jaws sunk into the bull's haunch (8.9 × 8.8 × 1.5 cm; 3⅛ × 3⁷⁄₁₆ × ⁹⁄₁₆ in.). IM 79519, Baghdad, National Museum of Iraq. This and other discoveries from Well AJ in the North West Palace revolutionized the understanding of North Syrian art.

179 One of four 'flame and frond' openwork panels, found in a former workshop, Room NW15, in Fort Shalmaneser, which are (unusually) carved on both sides (see also **231–233**, p. 146). It shows a lion, seated in a field of lilies, with half a stylized tree on one side and a papyrus and bud column on the other; it is crowned with the sun disc and wears a heavy collar (shown frontally) (14 × 11.8 × 1.1 cm; 5½ × 4⅝ × 7/16 in.). ND 6349, London, British Museum.

pattern of more and less competent work on the panels of a single set is repeated across the ivories.

The NW15 panels form part of a large group, with examples from Rooms SW37 and SW11/12. It numbers about a hundred pieces and is one of the most original groups, characterized by a variety of subjects and a strong, individual style. The group covers the full range of production, from elaborate and richly decorated small pieces, such as pyxides, flasks and fan handles, to furniture elements, openwork panels, flat panels and legs, as well as parts of statues. Techniques include high and low relief, incision, openwork, carving in the round and inlaying and gilding.

Although relatively few 'flame and frond' ivories have been found outside Nimrud, their distribution is impressive. A number of small objects were found at Hasanlu, near Lake Urmia in western Iran, some fragments in a tomb at Tell Halaf, a few pieces at Hama and a calf statuette at Tell Afis (thought to be the site of ancient Hazrek) in central Syria. Fragments of a fan handle were discovered in the Idaean Cave in Crete. Finally, a fragment of a pottery mould was found at Zinjirli.

The ivories found at Hasanlu were, as usual, a mixed assemblage, and included the products of local craftsmen, as well as imported ivories, even some Assyrian fragments. They were found in a level of savage destruction, the date of which provides a guide to the time when the ivories were in use. Hasanlu is the largest site in the Solduz valley, with a wealthy Iron Age settlement on its citadel. An early fire led to the reconstruction of a series of buildings with columned halls; this, in turn, was the victim of a devastating attack. The date of the second destruction is unfortunately disputed. The excavators, an American team, led by Robert H. Dyson, Jr, are positive that the sack of the city was the result of an attack c. 800 BC by Menua, the king of the expanding Urartian kingdom to the west. Another theory is that Hasanlu fell to Sargon II during his famous Eighth Campaign in 714 BC. If an Urartian sack of the site is preferred, it provides a secure late ninth-century date, by which time a range of foreign as well as locally produced ivories was in circulation.

Although only a few fragments of ivory have been found at Tell Halaf, what is of real importance to ivory studies is the wealth of stone sculptures found at the site. Tell Halaf was discovered by one of the most colourful – and wealthy – archaeological figures of the early twentieth century, Baron Max von Oppenheim (1860–1946). Born into a wealthy Jewish banking family, he travelled widely in the Islamic world, spending 'whole months in Northern Arabia, Syria, and Mesopotamia with the Beduins, the free sons of the desert, in their tents'.[11] In 1899 he travelled from Damascus to Mesopotamia to prospect the best route for a railway between Aleppo and Mosul. Guided by his friend the Beduin chief Ibrahim Pasha, he discovered remarkable statues on a hill near Ras al Ain known as Tell Halaf.

Oppenheim began digging in November 1899. 'Surprises; quite undreamt of fell to my lot; it was a turning point in my life.' After only three days he was able 'to lay bare part of the great principal face of the temple-palace and, besides several large and beautiful relief slabs, I discovered the remains of some statues in the round'.[12] On his return in 1911, he brought trained archaeologists, architects and photographers. His scientific equipment, including a field railway, was carried from Aleppo to Tell Halaf by nearly a thousand camels, on a journey lasting some twenty days. He began work on 5 August 1911 but had to stop in 1913; he returned in 1929.

Oppenheim discovered an impressive temple–palace, constructed on a high, mud-brick platform, entered through an elaborate gate, which came to be called the Scorpion Gate. As inscriptions prove, the Temple–Palace was built by Kapara, probably in the tenth century BC. The back of the platform was decorated with 250 small, re-used relief slabs of basalt and red-dyed limestone, originally set up in the temple of the weather god; a further series, of later date and more sophisticated, inscribed with Kapara's name, was used on the façade of the Temple–Palace itself (**180**): these are stylistically similar to the 'flame and frond' group. The range of subjects illustrated on the sculptures, particularly the early series, is varied and lively, covering many aspects of daily life. The overwhelming impression is of a vigorous and original repertoire. The designs are in raised outline with the details incised on the surface. The most distinctive features are the muscle markings used on the various animals and mythical beasts, and the human physiognomy, both of which are the same as those on 'flame and frond' ivories.

Oppenheim found only a few ivories: a plain, circular pyxis in a male burial, and some fragments in shaft graves, sealed by sculptures of seated women. The grave goods included two fragmentary female heads, wearing compartmented crowns,[13] similar to many found in the Burnt Palace. Other ivories included the remains of an openwork stag,[14] similar to some from Rooms NE59 and

180 Bas-relief carved on a slab of basalt from the façade of the Temple–Palace of Kapara at Guzana (now Tell Halaf), showing a bull hunted by an archer, 10th century (?); both the musculature of the bull and the features of the hunter are typical of the 'flame and frond' group of ivories (140 × 200 cm; 55 × 79 in.). Tell Halaf, Palace of Kapara, inv. no. Ba 1. Reproduced from Oppenheim n.d. [1933].

126 Ancient Ivory

NW21 in Fort Shalmaneser,[15] an ape and the base of a couchant lion.[16]

It seems a reasonable possibility that 'flame and frond' ivories were made at Guzana (Tell Halaf), the capital of Bit Bahiani, and were the minor art that matched the major art of the remarkable and unique sculptures found on the site. The ivories may have been commissioned by Kapara, though this is disputed. Guzana was absorbed into the Assyrian empire during the ninth century BC, so the probable time of production for the ivories and the *floruit* of the city itself is probably the tenth and early ninth centuries.

'Round-cheeked and ringletted' ivories

The ivories of the 'round-cheeked and ringletted' group can be compared to sculptures and small objects found at Zinjirli (ancient Sam'al), in north-west Syria. They are called 'round-cheeked and ringletted' because of their chubby faces and hairstyles, as can be seen on a panel depicting a human-headed sphinx (ND 10447, **181**).[17] Most of these panels were found in Room SW37 in the Fort, and are remarkable for their lack of uniformity in size and subject; there are no sets and only a few pairs. The subjects on these relatively naive panels fill the entire surface: there are no frames. They depict humans, both male (ND 7788, **182**)[18] and female, usually represented frontally and wearing a variety of headgear, hairstyles and clothing. The faces of both humans and sphinxes are round and fleshy with arching eyebrows, long, rimmed eyes with drilled pupils, and wide noses. Their hair falls in ringlets in front of their ears. Some males have spade-shaped beards. Bodies are rounded with an absence of musculature.

Until the remarkable discoveries of the ivories in Well AJ, this group was known only by some two dozen of these rather crude panels, but, even with only these, similarities with the sculptures and column bases at Zinjirli were recognized. Zinjirli lies at the foot of the eastern flank of the Amanus range of mountains in Turkey, just north of the Syrian border, on an ancient trade route, which maintained contact between Neo-Hittite, Syrian and Phoenician centres. Its position is reflected by the mixed assemblage of ivories

ABOVE **181** Panel showing a 'round-cheeked and ringletted' human-headed sphinx couchant, which stares out impassively at the onlooker; the hair is bound by a double fillet and arranged in waves, curls and ringlets, framing the full, round face, and the chest is decorated with a criss-cross design (4.7 × 7.9 × 1.2 cm; 1⅞ × 3⅛ × ½ in.). ND 1047, London, British Museum.

BELOW **182** Two popular designs for the busy panels belonging to the 'round-cheeked and ringletted' group were sphinxes (**181**, above), and standing human figures. This bearded male, who wears a long garment, open from the thigh, and holds voluted flowers in his hands, is represented frontally (except for the legs); his hair is parted centrally and falls in ringlets framing the face, the beard is spade-shaped and curled (14.9 × 4.2 × 1.1 cm; 5⅞ × 1⅝ × 7/16 in.). ND 7788, Toronto, Royal Ontario Museum. (For another example see **296**, p. 186.)

183 Cosmetic dish – an ivory worker's tour de force – found among the well-preserved ivories in Well AJ; made from a huge slab of tusk and elaborately carved on every surface with an interlocking tangle of beasts, birds, lions, bulls, sphinxes, sheep and caprids, both real and mythological, it has separate carved flowers that fit into the outer slots of the dish (9.5 × 24 × 11.5 cm; 3¾ × 9⁷⁄₁₆ × 4½ in.). ABOVE Reverse side; BELOW dish (dia. 5 cm; 2 in.) in its surround. This astonishing and complex piece revolutionized our understanding of the output of the 'round-cheeked and ringletted' group. IM 79501–79503, Baghdad, National Museum of Iraq.

found there. Sam'al (also known as Bit Gabbari) was a small city-state, probably originally Neo-Hittite but Aramaized during the tenth century. It was excavated by Felix von Luschan and others of the Deutsches Archäologisches Institut in the late nineteenth and early twentieth centuries. The ivories were found in Palace J, built by King Kilamuwa (r. c. 840–830 BC), and in Palace K, built by King Bar-Rakib (later eighth century). Similarities between the sculptures and some of the SW37 panels depicting men are close: in addition to their general proportions and style, they share pointed, threefold hats, corkscrew curls, fat, fleshy faces and shawled garments. The sphinxes on column bases are also similar to those on the panels.

While the panels from Room SW37 are fairly basic, the ivories recovered from Well AJ are in a different league, notably an extraordinary cosmetic palette, a richly carved piece with a small central bowl, which was clearly a vessel prepared for ritual or ceremonial use. This revolutionized scholarly understanding of the group. It is carved from the length of a large tusk, and follows its natural curvature. Two separate flowers were inserted into slots at either end, presumably forming the handles of tools required to distribute the precious liquid contained in the central bowl. This massive and heavy piece is some 24 cm long and 11.5 cm deep (7⁷⁄₁₆ × 4¹⁄₂ in.). (IM 79501–79503, **183**),¹⁹ while the shallow bowl is only 5 cm across and 4.7 cm high (2 × 1⅞ in.). The whole surface is covered with a medley of birds and animals, with no space left vacant. The dominant feature is a pair of eagles, perched on either side of the central bowl, which they grasp with their claws. Beside the bowl are pairs of crossing cervids and other animals, as well as the slots to contain tools. The great eagles are flanked by pairs of winged, human-headed sphinxes with fleshy features and ringletted hair, similar to the heads on the SW37 panels. The base is filled with an interwoven mass of struggling animals, griffins, lions, bulls and cervids. Rams, back to back, occupy the ends. The vessel is competently carved, elaborate and dynamic, with a superb series of animals, mythological, fantastic, wild and domestic. It is a real masterpiece.

184 A silhouette plaque, showing a bird, its wings spread, grasping in its talons a goat that is being devoured by a pair of vultures; the fleshy face, ringlets and high collar identify the piece as another product of a 'round-cheeked and ringletted' workshop (9.8 × 15 cm; 3⅞ × 5⅞ in.). IM 79525, Baghdad, National Museum of Iraq.

A second unique piece from Well AJ is an openwork silhouette, showing a human-headed bird, grasping an unfortunate goat in its talons, with a pair of vultures devouring the goat on either side (IM 79525, **184**).[20] Although the subject is excitingly different, the features are, once again, typically 'round-cheeked and ringletted'. This plaque was fastened to its backing by a dowel cut with a centred bit – that is, a wide, shallow dowel with a central hole. This type of fixing also occurs on the SW37 panels but otherwise only on 'flame and frond' pieces, and serves as a valuable diagnostic for these two North Syrian style-groups.

Another probable 'round-cheeked and ringletted' piece is an openwork panel with a rather portly goat from SW37 (ND 10321, **185**).[21] The goat is rampant, and is supported by an unusual plant with twisted stems. The plant is similar to one at Arslan Tash (ancient Hadatu), a site with a fine collection of furniture panels as well as the frame of an actual bed (see chapter 6).[22]

A number of panels of the 'woman at the window' design were found in Room S10 of the queen's residence in the Fort and can be assigned to the three different regional traditions, the Phoenician, Syro-Phoenician and

LEFT **185** An openwork panel, showing a plump, bearded goat reaching up to browse on the entwined branches of a plant, which once also grew up behind it, thus framing its body (traces remain on the right); the absence of musculature, and the animal's rotund shape suggest that the panel may belong to the 'round-cheeked and ringletted' group (15.8 × 7.5 × 1.3 cm; 6¼ × 2¹⁵⁄₁₆ × ½ in.). ND 10321, Metropolitan Museum of Art, New York

BELOW **186** A burnt fragment of an unusual and 'heavy' version of the 'woman at the window' motif, probably another example of 'round-cheeked and ringletted' work; the fleshy face, adorned with phylactery and trilobate earrings, looks over a balustrade supported on five columns (10.8 × 11.6 cm; 4¼ × 4⁹⁄₁₆ in.). ND 7800, Baghdad, National Museum of Iraq.

130 Ancient Ivory

North Syrian. The North Syrian example (ND 7800, **186**)[23] has the usual round, fleshy face of the 'round-cheeked and ringletted' workshop, but, unlike other versions, her face is squashed into the window, which has fewer reveals and more columns to the balustrade than are found on the panels of the elegant Phoenician set (**88–89**, p. 80). She has a phylactery on her hair and heavy trilobate earrings.

'Round-cheeked and ringletted' ivories were carved in an individual and easily recognizable style. Although some of the panels found in Room SW37 are relatively provincial, the imagination of the craftsmen was carried to new heights in the cosmetic palette. Not only is the design complex and fantastic, but also there is considerable variety in the representation of detail. The plump ram in a thicket repeats a motif known from the Royal Cemetery at Ur, two millennia earlier, and appears also in the episode of the Sacrifice of Isaac in the Bible. It has long been recognized that the 'round-cheeked and ringletted' style-group belongs to the North Syrian tradition. Dirk Wicke of the Goethe University at Frankfurt convincingly proposes that this group was carved at Zinjirli and dates to between the early and mid-eighth century.[24]

The chair-backs from Room SW7

The third major group of ivories assigned to North Syria were found in Room SW7 in the Fort. These ivories are among the most unusual found at Nimrud, for they consist of a remarkable collection of curved screens, which were found stacked in rows. They formed the backs of chairs, and so are more properly discussed in the context of furniture (see chapter 6). The majority of these panels were decorated with a bearded man, wearing a long open coat and plucking fruits from a sinuous plant, as in the elegant ND 6374 (**187**).[25] Sometimes he is winged, or he may be shown standing below a Syrian version of the winged disc – that is, one with pendant volutes rather than *uraei*.

As usual with the ivories found at Nimrud, the same motif may be carved in a variety of styles. The most sophisticated versions of the bearded man, such as ND 6374, have been assigned to the Classic SW7 group. They can be

187 Panel from a curved chair-back, one of the finest found in Room SW7 of Fort Shalmaneser, belonging to the Classic SW7 group. It is a sophisticated version of the design that decorates most of the panels – a man wearing a cutaway coat over a short tunic, and grasping a sinuous plant growing up in front of him (25.2 × 11.5 cm; 9¹⁵⁄₁₆ × 4½ in.). ND 6374. Baghdad, National Museum of Iraq Museum.

The Ivories of North Syria 131

compared to a carved orthostat (stone slab) found at the site of Sakcha Gozu, 20 km (13 miles) from Zinjirli at the foot of the Qurt Dagh mountain range. This royal fortress was partly excavated by John Garstang and others in the early twentieth century, and consists of an enclosure 65 × 50 metres (215 × 165 ft), with a gate and a Hilani palace (a building with a columned portico). The Sakcha Gozu relief shows a pair of deities in similar cut-away coats, flanking a stylized tree and holding up fruit to touch the winged disc above, while another depicts a lion hunt with two hunters in a chariot. This can be compared to a panel on one of the chair-backs, as well as to a fine openwork fragment of a chariot scene (ND 10316, **10316**).[26] Originally there would have been two horses and probably four men in the cab, but only the driver and the kilt of a figure leaning out of the back survive. The pattern on their clothing – rectangles with central circles – can be seen on the sculptures of Tiglath-pileser III (r. 745–727 BC) and may suggest a late eighth-century date for these ivories. Fragments of similar openwork horses and chariots were found at Zinjirli.[27]

While the carving of the Classic SW7 group of panels is sophisticated, the same motif is also represented in various styles on other sets of panels, from competent to thoroughly provincial, and sometimes so misunderstood that the men and women are shown standing on a winged disc, representative of the sun, with vegetation growing from it (**228**, p. 145). Phoenician pieces were also discovered in Room SW7, so once again the assemblage from the room is a mixed range of material from a variety of traditions.

Other North Syrian ivories

The Assyrians conquered a vast area of territory in south-west Iran and south-east Turkey and along the present Syrian border, which at the time would have been occupied by a number of minor competing powers, as well as by the major power of Urartu. A standard feature of Assyrian conquest was the removal of the 'treasures of his palace' from whatever state they conquered. What we see at Nimrud, smashed and stripped of their valuable overlays and thrown into storage, is the remains of this eclectic assemblage of booty. But, needless to say, there are no labels!

Many ivories can be generally attributed to the North Syrian tradition, but not yet to any specific group. For instance, a scene of ferociously battling animals is a typically North Syrian motif, as can be seen in a long strip from Room NE1 at the Fort (ND 9396, **189**).[28] One of a pair, this piece originally measured about a metre (a little more than 3 ft) in length, and shows a continuous combat in which bulls are attacked by lions, the lions are attacked by winged griffins, and the griffins, in turn, are gored by the bulls. The animals' bodies are beautifully modelled. This trio of animals occurs quite frequently on combat friezes, as in the intertwining animals of ND 10320 (**190**),[29] where the bulls, struggling to the right, are attacked by a lion and a griffin, both of which are impaled on the long curving horns. There is no frame on this panel, but there are some faint muscle markings on the necks, ribs and haunches, though the last is part of a zigzag rather than a flame marking. Different versions of these combat scenes also occur on the 'flame and frond' flask from

OPPOSITE, ABOVE **188** Fragment of an openwork panel, showing a dynamic chariot scene, with parts of two charioteers, one leaning forward and driving the horse (probably one of a pair), the other leaning out of the cab at the back (only his hips survive); the charioteer wears a wig and a short skirt, the horse is equipped with an elaborate bridle with chest strap and fringed disc, and a protective cover over its back, and the chariot has a yoke pole, a cab closed with a shield, a quiver and arrows on the side and a wheel with eight(?) spokes (6.1 × 11.2 × 1.2 cm; 2⅜ × 4⅜ × ½ in.). ND 10316, London, British Museum.

OPPOSITE, CENTRE AND BELOW **189–190** A popular motif with North Syrian carvers was a continuous battle between animals, usually lions, bulls and griffins. CENTRE Part of a framed panel with a relatively spacious design of two lions attacking a bull, which, though brought to its knees, retaliates by piercing the leading lion with its horn (as restored 8.5 × 20 × 0.7 cm; 3⁵⁄₁₆ × 7⅞ × ¼ in.). ND 9396, Baghdad, National Museum of Iraq. BELOW An unframed and crowded design showing a ferocious contest, with animals tumbling over each other, clawing, biting and piercing with their horns (4.8 × 21.8 × 1.3 cm; 1⅞ × 8⁹⁄₁₆ × ½ in.). ND 10320, Baghdad, National Museum of Iraq.

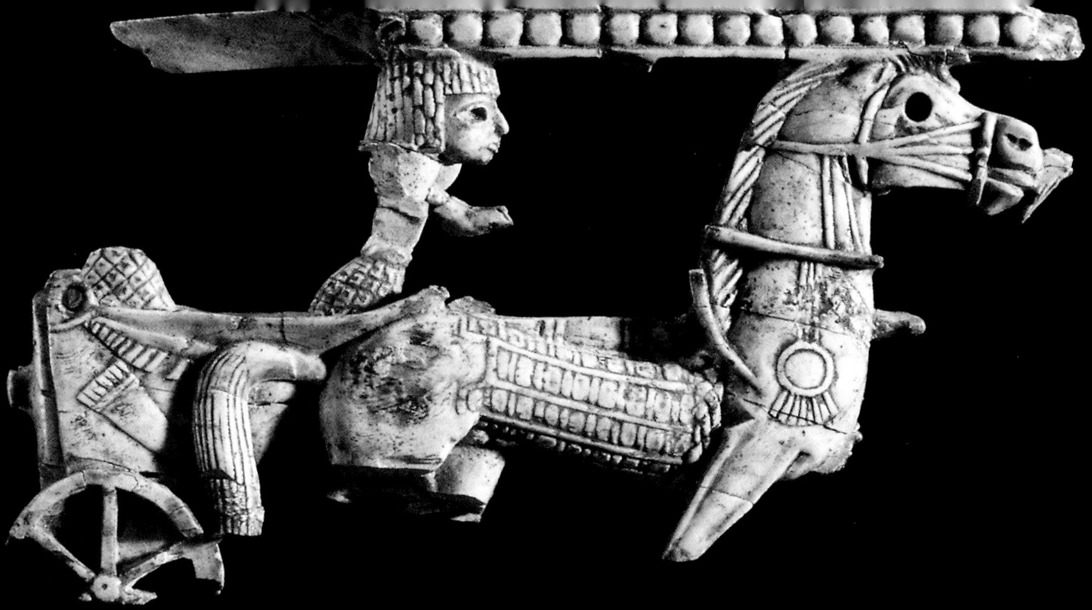

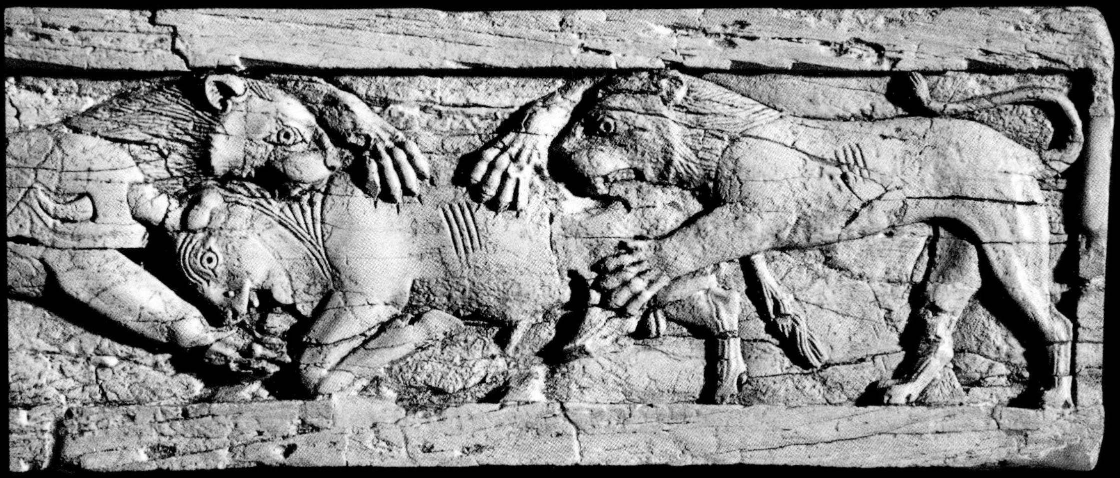

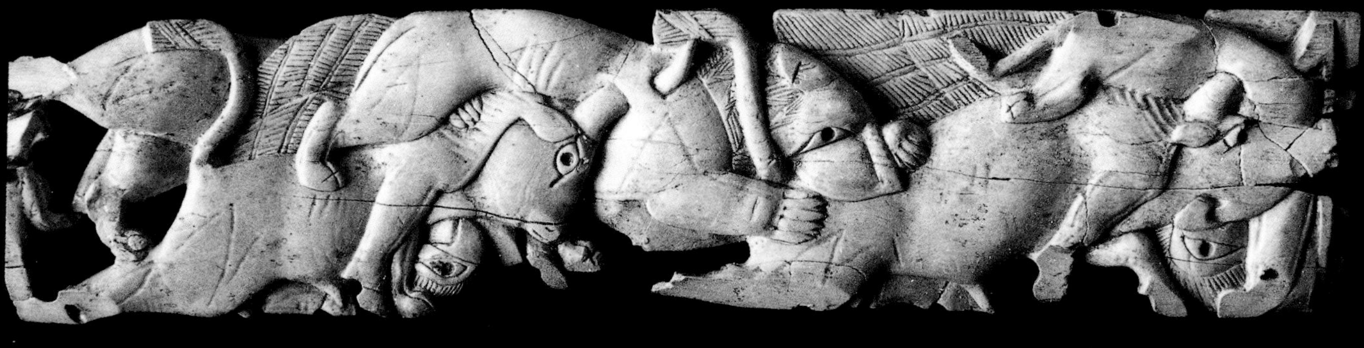

Well AJ (**237**, p. 149) and a furniture leg from SW12 (ND 12042, **234**, p. 147).

Another familiar North Syrian motif, also common across the Levant, was a procession with cattle. The animals tend to be stocky and associated with plants with frondy leaves: indeed, it is a feature of the various North Syrian versions that all are associated with plants. The bull of ND 9638 and the cow and calf of ND 10677 (**191–192**)[30] can both be attributed to the North Syrian tradition and would have been used in sets in a frieze.

Unusual ivories

Some pieces seem more outlandish, but may, nevertheless, have originated somewhere along the Syro-Turkish border or in Iran. These form a salutary reminder of the complexity

191–192 Two North Syrian versions of familiar motifs of cattle. ABOVE A massive browsing bull lowers its head to touch the fronds of a twisty plant growing up in front of it (6.1 × 11.2 × 1 cm; 2⅜ × 4⅜ × ⅜ in.). ND 9638, formerly Mosul Museum of History. Photograph Mick Sharp. BELOW A cow turns away from a similar plant to watch her calf suckling vigorously (5 × 11.5 cm; 2 × 4½ in.). ND 10677, Nasariyah, Iraq Museum.

OPPOSITE **193–195** Three pieces from a set of panels found in Room SW37, showing a mixture of unrelated images. LEFT A man reaching out to touch a plant is reminiscent of some of the panels belonging to the chair-backs from Room SW7 (**187**, p. 131), though the style, depth of carving and fixing with a crude dowel are markedly different (10.3 × 4 x. 0.9 cm; 4½6 × 1⅝6 × ⅜6 in.). ND 9085, Baghdad, National Museum of Iraq. RIGHT, ABOVE Two heroes subdue a horned central figure, gripping his crossed arms and bracing his widely splayed feet with their legs, which are awkwardly twisted so that their toes touch his (5.5 × 8.5 × 0.9 cm; 2½6 × 3⅜ × ⅜6 in.). ND 10326, Oxford, Ashmolean Museum. RIGHT, BELOW One of a series of enigmatic fragments with versions of the same design, a winged, ram-headed deity plucking fruits, accompanied by a variety of creatures – in this case an outsized locust and a dog (5 × 6.6 × 0.9 cm; 2 × 2⅝ × ⅜6 in.). ND 9084, New York, Metropolitan Museum of Art.

of ivory studies. One of these problem sets, found in Room SW37, has an extraordinary mixture of images. A fragment of a vertical side panel, showing a winged man wearing a ram's-head mask and a long open coat, is reminiscent of some of the panels from Room SW7, both in form and subject (ND 9085, **193**).[31] However, the rest of the set is dramatically different, the images varying from a battle between two men in long coats fighting a horned, central figure with crossed arms (ND 10326, **194**)[32] to a procession of bizarre figures (ND 9084, **195**):[33] a pair of opposed winged and horned men, one again in a ram's-head mask, have between them a 'locust' and some form of canine. There are no known parallels for this set.

The most unusual assemblage of ivories found at Nimrud was in Room T10, which served as the store-room for the Throne Room block of the Fort. Unhappily, it has not so far proved possible to record more than a few of these, though it has to be hoped that this work will one day be able to continue. This remarkable collection again illustrates the rich variety of ivory to be found at Nimrud. One unique set of about a dozen pieces shows a row of dumpy people with large, kohl-rimmed eyes, consisting of male and female winged deities, as well as warriors and musicians. The figures on these rather cramped panels were presumably lined up to form a procession. Some of the deities are associated with plants or with what appears to be an incense burner or altar. This unique feature consists of a column formed of rows of hanging palm leaves below a moulding topped by what appears to be a rank of wavy 'flames' (ND 12187, **196**).[34] Could this be an early version of a 'fire-altar'?

ABOVE 196 A burnt panel, part of a large set (see also 29, p. 37), showing a winged goddess standing before an incense burner or altar, consisting of a column set on a convex base, with three rows of hanging palm leaves and wavy 'flames' on a moulded feature above; the goddess, who wears a long, sleeved garment and bracelets on her wrists, has her hair dressed in a style reminiscent of a tripartite wig, and deeply excised, kohl-rimmed eyes (8 × 6.3 × 1 cm; 3⅛ × 2½ × ⅜ in.). ND 12187, Baghdad, National Museum of Iraq.

BELOW 197 One of a series of burnt fragments of an unusual design that has no known parallels. A 'winged disc' is set on an abbreviated version of a stylized tree, consisting of a pair of ribbed volutes rising from mouldings decorated with beads and scales; the central circle of the disc would have been inlaid, and is set within a crescent, framed by wings and tail (5.5 × 4.5 cm; 2³⁄₁₆ × 1¾ in.). ND 14593, Baghdad, National Museum of Iraq.

Another panel shows the 'altar' on its own. Some of the warriors hold up a stick and have a jug in the other hand, perhaps a residual memory of the Phoenician design of pharaoh figures with sceptre and jug.

Another design depicts a winged disc, set on an abbreviated tree.[35] While there are some Urartian parallels to the form of the disc in ND 14593 (**197**),[36] there are none for the 'tree'. The carving on these panels is more elegant than on those of the dumpy people with kohl-rimmed eyes.

Different again is a tall, fragmentary and heavily burnt cylinder or tube (ND 14749, **198**),[37] measuring some 32 cm (12⅝ in.) in height, carved from a large tusk. This is decorated with three registers of rampant ibex, their forelegs resting on the branches of stylized trees or frondy plants. Two animal heads, carved separately, were attached to the sides of the cylinder. The ivory was on display in the Mosul Museum but was looted in 2003. Fragments of similar pieces have been found in the Burnt Palace. It seems reasonable to assume that these were made in a North Syrian workshop.

The varied groups of ivories assigned to the North Syrian tradition show the strong regionalism of the area. While those of the 'flame and frond' group may have been carved in north-east Syria, the chubby faces of the 'round-cheeked and ringletted' group can be matched in the north-west of the country. Except that they are recognizably North Syrian, it is not possible even to suggest origins for the many other groups of ivories attributed to the tradition. However, they all share a characteristic range of subjects and types of object. There is remarkably little repetition, but considerable dynamism. It is the energy and individuality of these ivories that marks them out, as well as links to the sculptures carved along the Syro-Turkish border.

OPPOSITE 198 A tall cylinder carved from a tusk, carefully reconstructed, by Nan Shaw Reade in the 1960s, from a mass of burnt fragments: three registers show rampant ibexes, with long curving horns and beards; a row of pendant pomegranates runs along the top of the cylinder, triple frames divide the registers, and a band of guilloche decorates the foot; attached to the sides of the top register are animal heads, represented frontally (H 32 cm, dia. 11–12.5 cm; H 12⅝, dia. 4⁵⁄₁₆–4¹⁵⁄₁₆ in.). ND 14749, formerly Mosul History Museum.

137

ABOVE 199 An openwork panel showing an elegant, falcon-headed, Phoenician sphinx, wearing an Egyptian double crown set on the *nemes* headcloth, and an apron; the sphinx walks on voluted palmette flowers growing from a central plant (the flower below left probably grew from a stylized tree on the adjacent panel, not preserved), to which he raises a paw in salutation (10.9 × 8.6 cm; 4⁵⁄₁₆ × 3⅜ in.). ND 12033, Baghdad, National Museum of Iraq.

200-201 Two fragments from Room T10 in Fort Shalmaneser, which contained fragments of Assyrian ivories and a varied assemblage of Levantine ivories. LEFT A beautiful queen wearing a tall crown with lotus frieze, and a finely pleated garment, resembling fabric found in the royal tombs of the Assyrian queens (17.3 × 5.2 × 0.8 cm; 6¹³⁄₁₆ × 2¹⁄₁₆ × ⁵⁄₁₆ in.). ND 14590, Baghdad, National Museum of Iraq. RIGHT A superb winged sphinx, one of the 'Finely Carved' ivories; the wings are delicately cross-hatched at the base and chevroned ribs run along the backs; tassels adorn the wings, the haunch and the apron (9 × 15.1 × 0.5–3.3 cm; 3⁹⁄₁₆ × 5¹⁵⁄₁₆ × ¹⁄₁₆–1⁵⁄₁₆ in.). ND 14500, Baghdad, National Museum of Iraq.

ABOVE 202 Phoenician panel showing the popular motif of cows with their calves in a field of papyrus and buds; it recalls the original Egyptian depiction, for the cows are striding forwards rather than turning their heads to tend their suckling calves (5.4 × 7.9 × 0.5 cm; 2⅛ × 3⅛ × 3/16 in.). ND 12225, London, British Museum.

LEFT 203 Plaque belonging to the Phoenician Ornate Group, showing a graceful kneeling pharaoh figure wearing the Egyptian double crown (8.3 × 4.4 × 0.6 cm; 3¼ × 1¾ × ¼ in.). Baghdad, National Museum of Iraq.

RIGHT 204 An Ornate Group panel with a modelled rendering of the 'George and dragon' motif, showing the winged hero grasping a griffin by its comb and plunging his weapon into its mouth; the hieroglyphs in the plaque by the left wing can be read as 'enduring/abiding one; lord of radiance' (13.1 × 7.8 × 0.8 cm; 5⅛ × 3 1/16 × 5/16 in.). ND 11036, Baghdad, National Museum of Iraq.

BELOW 205 A broken panel, framed top and bottom, depicting addorsed, winged, ram-headed sphinxes couchant, their forelegs shown as human arms, raised in salutation to a stylized tree; they wear versions of the Egyptian double crown, and lily flowers grow above their wings (4.6 × 15 × 0.6 cm; 1 13/16 × 5⅞ × ¼ in.). ND 9603, New York, Metropolitan Museum of Art.

ABOVE LEFT 206 One of a set of Phoenician panels carved in high relief, depicting a pharaoh with sceptre and jug; they carry lightly scratched makers' marks on the reverse. Here, the pharaoh figures, wearing Egyptian double crowns and artificial beards, salute a stylized tree with ram-headed sceptres; above them, a winged disc and a row of *uraei* represent a shrine (12.3 × 7.6 × 1.1 cm; 4⅞ × 3 × ⁷⁄₁₆ in.). ND 11035, Baghdad, National Museum of Iraq. Photograph Mick Sharp.

ABOVE RIGHT 207 Phoenician trapezoidal panel, one of a set from a different workshop, having large, deeply incised makers' marks on the backs. The proportions differ from 206; the pharaohs wear plain garments, and the one on the right carries an *ankh*, not a jug (9.5 × 5.6 × 1 cm; 3¾ × 2³⁄₁₆ × ⅜ in.). ND 11098, Oxford, Ashmolean Museum. Photograph Mick Sharp.

BELOW LEFT 208 One of a set of three Phoenician panels showing youths flanking a central column of bound papyrus stalks; they grasp papyrus flowers on curving stems, rest one foot on a large flower, and more flowers adorn their wigs (8 × 6.5 × 1.3 cm; 3⅛ × 2⁹⁄₁₆ × ½ in.). ND 11015, Baghdad, National Museum of Iraq. The scene derives from an Egyptian design of two Nile gods binding together the stems of the lily of Upper Egypt and the papyrus of the delta. Photograph Mick Sharp.

BELOW RIGHT 209 In a field of voluted palmette flowers, winged gods flank an *aegis* of the goddess Bastet (a lion's head on a palmette column), their hands grasping voluted palmette flowers; the one on the left wears the Egyptian double crown, and an overskirt with decorated borders (11 × 8.8 × 1.2 cm; 4⁵⁄₁₆ × 3½ × ½ in.). ND 11102, Baghdad, National Museum of Iraq. Photograph Mick Sharp.

OPPOSITE 210 This magnificent, boldly carved openwork piece, set in a frame, shows a winged, human-headed sphinx, with tightly curled tail, stepping through voluted palmette flowers; the face is subtly modelled, and the eyes deeply excised for inlay; the sphinx wears a (misinterpreted) version of the Egyptian double crown with plumes at the sides, and has a crowned *uraeus* suspended from the chest (18.5 × 15.1 × 2.3–3.6 cm; 7¼ × 5¹⁵⁄₁₆ × ⅞–1⁷⁄₁₆ in.). ND 7559, Baghdad, National Museum of Iraq. Image © DEA/G. Dagli Orti/Getty Images.

141

ABOVE LEFT 211 A trapezoidal curved plaque, showing a woman standing with her arms extended to hold the palmette columns that frame the piece on either side; she wears a tripartite wig and a long, loose, full gown with sleeves (6.7 × 4.1 × 0.5 cm, dia. at base c. 14 cm; 2⅝ × 1⅝ × 1/16 in., dia. at base c. 5½ in.). ND 10445, Cambridge, Fitzwilliam Museum. Photograph Mick Sharp.

ABOVE RIGHT 212 A tenoned panel with a winged deity, wearing the sun disc and *uraei* crown on a tripartite wig and holding flowers in his outstretched hands; between the wings is the figure of the goddess Ma'at, crowned with a sun disc (8.8 × 4.2 cm; 3½ × 1⅝ in.). ND 8150, Baghdad, National Museum of Iraq. Photograph Mick Sharp.

BELOW 213–214 Similar designs were employed across the range of ivory pieces: these two Phoenician women, in tripartite wigs, wearing long pleated dresses and holding an *ankh*, are versions of the motif in 211. LEFT ND 13605 (11 × 5.7 × 1.2 cm; 4⅜ × 2¼ × ½ in.), Baghdad, National Museum of Iraq. RIGHT ND 13604 (9 × 4.1 × 1.2 cm; 3 9/16 × 1⅝ × ½ in.), Baghdad, National Museum of Iraq. Photograph Mick Sharp.

LEFT 215 A Syro-Phoenician 'crown and scale' openwork panel found in Well AJ (hence its colour). A winged, human-headed sphinx advances through papyrus flowers, wearing a crown with a sun disc flanked by *uraei* (a misunderstood version of an Egyptian crown); suspended from the chest is a crowned *uraeus* (21.2 × 7 × 1.2 cm; 8⅜ × 2¾ × ½ in.). IM 79528, Baghdad, National Museum of Iraq.

ABOVE RIGHT 216 This openwork 'crown and scale' panel shows a sphinx, wearing a flattened version of the Egyptian double crown, advancing towards a stylized tree in a field of papyrus flowers (6.8 × 7.7 × 0.8 cm; 2¹¹⁄₁₆ × 3 × ⁵⁄₁₆ in.). ND 12132, London, British Museum.

CENTRE RIGHT 217 Fragment of a Syro-Phoenician human-headed sphinx, crowned with a sun disc and *uraei* crown; here, the head is integral, but in other cases it was attached separately (see 220–221) (5.5 × 8.1 cm; 2⅛ × 3³⁄₁₆ in.). ND 14534, Baghdad, National Museum of Iraq.

BELOW LEFT 218–219 Two 'crown and scale' plaques of a hero slaying a griffin. Each hero wears a flattened Egyptian double crown and grasps a griffin by its comb, bracing himself with one foot against its body and thrusting a weapon into its beak. LEFT ND 10314 (10.2 × 5.1 × 1.3 cm; 4 × 2 × ½ in.), Birmingham Museum and Art Gallery. RIGHT ND 7563 (10.9 × 6 cm; 4⁵⁄₁₆ × 2⅜ in.), Baghdad, National Museum of Iraq.

BELOW RIGHT 220–221 Two 'crown and scale' sphinxes, lacking their separate heads. In the openwork panel (LEFT), the sphinx wears collar and apron, and has an *uraeus* suspended from the chest (9.7 × 6.8 × 0.9 cm; 3¹³⁄₁₆ × 2¹¹⁄₁₆ × ⅜ in.). ND 10555, London, British Museum. The forward-facing sphinx (RIGHT) wears a sun disc and *uraei* crown, collar, and apron, all rather coarsely inlaid, and has a crowned *uraeus* suspended from the chest (8.5 × 3.4 × 0.7 cm; 3⅜ × 1⅜ × ¼ in.). ND 10522, London, British Museum.

ABOVE LEFT 222 Panel with one curving side (presumably the end piece of a series of panels), showing a winged boy, kneeling, with his arms resting along the edges of his outspread wings; he holds voluted palmettes and papyrus flowers (12.3 × 6.9 cm; 4⅞ × 2¾ in.). ND 9530, Baghdad, National Museum of Iraq. Photograph Mick Sharp.

ABOVE RIGHT 223 One of a pair of openwork, tenoned panels, consisting of stylized trees, with four upward-curving, voluted branches; fronds grow from the volute ends and papyrus flowers from the central trunk (10 × 4.9 cm; 4 × 1¹⁵⁄₁₆ in.). ND 10353, Oxford, Ashmolean Museum. Photograph Mick Sharp.

BELOW LEFT 224 An openwork, tenoned panel with a winged griffin stretching up to nibble a lily; the ground is filled with lily and voluted palmette flowers (10.7 × 7.4 cm; 4¼ × 2¹⁵⁄₁₆ in.). ND 9465, Brussels, Musées Royaux d'Art et d'Histoire.

BELOW RIGHT 225 A tenoned panel showing a winged griffin, its beak raised to nibble the top of the plant growing on the edge of the panel; the ground is filled with lily, papyrus and voluted palmette flowers (9 × 6.6 cm; 3⁹⁄₁₆ × 2⅝ in.). ND 11099, Birmingham, City Museum and Art Gallery. Photograph Mick Sharp.

TOP 226 The central sections of some chair-backs had a top panel decorated with a winged disc, such as this splendid Phoenician example (8.1 × 55.7 × 0.5 cm; 3³⁄₁₆ × 21¹⁵⁄₁₆ × ³⁄₁₆ in.). ND 7949, London, British Museum.

ABOVE LEFT 227 One of four panels that decorated a chair-back, each framed in plain veneer: two show the standard subject of men grasping sinuous plants, but the central pair show seated women, offering a ring to the winged disc above (21.5 × 10.6 cm; 8½ × 4³⁄₁₆ in.). ND 7909, Baghdad, National Museum of Iraq.

RIGHT 230 Panels 1–3 of an unusual chair-back with five panels: the central panel (right) represents a male seated on a throne; to either side are winged men with griffin heads (middle) and youths carrying caprids on their shoulders (left) (25 × 10.5 cm; 9⅞ × 4⅛ in.). ND 7905, Baghdad, National Museum of Iraq.

ABOVE CENTRE 228 Two adjacent panels of six that belonged to a chair-back, four show men (right) and two women (left); besides variations in their dress and accessories, the six figures are remarkable because they stand on a version of a winged disc, symbol of the sun, which the craftsman misunderstood, turning it into vegetation sprouting fronds (21.2 × 7.4 cm; 8⅜ × 2⅞ in.). ND 7918, Baghdad, National Museum of Iraq.

ABOVE 229 One of a stylistically coherent set of tall, thin panels, each of three registers: here, the central figure wears an unusual hat, his hair and beard are arranged in curls, and he grips a flowering plant; in the upper register is a winged disc, surmounted by a female head, with arms resting along the tops of the wings, and in the lower register is a lion couchant (in others of the set, a sphinx) (28.8 × 6.7 × 0.5 cm; 11⅜ × 2⅝ × ³⁄₁₆ in.). ND 7925, New York, Metropolitan Museum of Art.

ABOVE 231 The front (LEFT) and back (RIGHT) of an openwork panel belonging to the North Syrian 'flame and frond' group, with a sensitive representation of a stag, its head turned to browse on a frond growing from a stylized tree (12.8 × 11.5 × 1.5 cm; 5¹⁄₁₆ × 4½ × ⅝ in.). ND 6379, Baghdad, National Museum of Iraq. It is one of a set of four panels, found in Room NW15 in Fort Shalmaneser, all framed in the same way and similar in size; this stag was carved by a master, but not all the panels in the set come from the same hand (see **233**). The design on all the panels is repeated in a simplified form on the reverse – an unusual feature. Photograph Mick Sharp.

BELOW LEFT 232 An openwork panel of the 'flame and frond' group, showing a lion seated in a field of lily flowers and facing a stylized tree; the lion is crowned with the sun disc, has pointed, dog-like ears and wears a tripartite wig and *usekh* collar, represented frontally (12.4 × 9.2 cm; 4⅞ × 3⅝ in.). ND 6350, Baghdad, National Museum of Iraq. Photograph Mick Sharp.

BELOW RIGHT 233 An openwork panel of the 'flame and frond' group, showing a browsing gazelle; it belongs to the same set as the panel shown above (**231**), but the relatively crude carving contrasts markedly with that of the companion piece, which is one of the finest ivories found in the Fort (12.8 × 11.8 × 1.1 cm; 5¹⁄₁₆ × 4⅝ × ⁷⁄₁₆ in.). ND 6314, New York, Metropolitan Museum of Art.

OPPOSITE 234 Part of a massive curved furniture leg, a unique piece found in Room SW12 at the Fort, consisting of two registers of design below a moulded element. In the upper register, two superbly carved bulls advance dramatically, the one in the rear overlapping the one in the lead, whose tail and hind legs can be seen in the background; the lower register shows a ferocious and evenly matched battle between a lion that springs down from above, with head and chest twisted, and a winged griffin, which retaliates viciously (22.2 × 14 cm; 8¾ × 5½ in.). ND 12042, Baghdad, National Museum of Iraq.

147

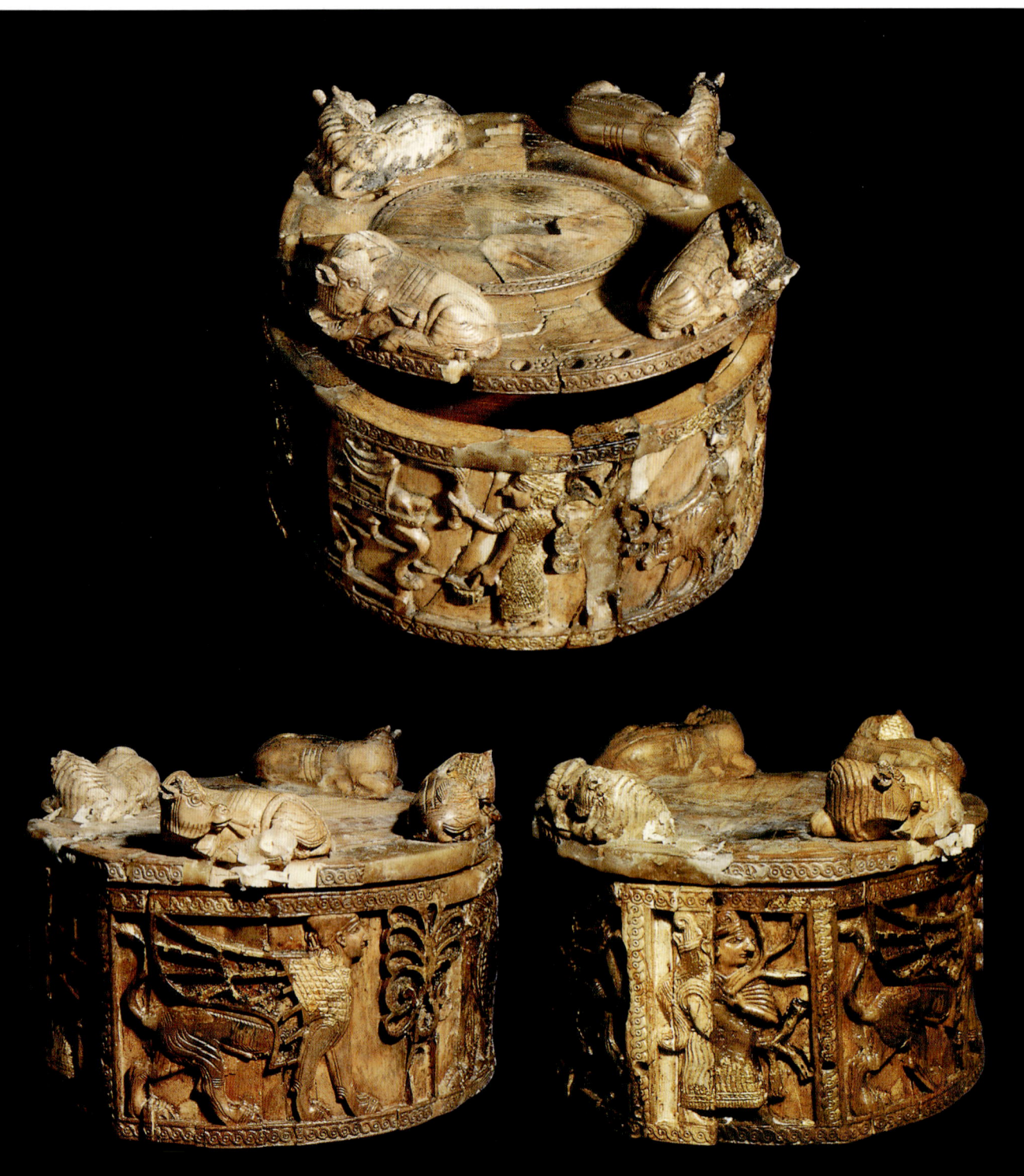

ABOVE 235 A superb oval pyxis from Well AJ in the North West Palace, complete with its lid surmounted by calves, as well as some fragments of the base: the scenes around the sides are unique, and consist of an enthroned king with table and attendant, and a sacrificial scene with a bull; as in IM 79514 (BELOW), a goddess appears on the panel at the back (6.4 × 12.8–13.9 × 0.9 cm; 2½ × 5¹/₁₆–5½ × ⅜ in.). IM 79513, Baghdad, National Museum of Iraq.

BELOW 236 A nearly complete oval pyxis from Well AJ, with its lid, which rotates on a pin, and its base, decorated with an incised design, intact: the four calves attached to the top of the lid are carved in the round, and the sides of the box are decorated with pairs of sphinxes flanking stylized trees, overlaid with gold and highlighted with inlays held in position by pegs; a flatter panel at the back shows a goddess (7 × 13.4–14.7 × 1.4 cm; 2¾ × 5¼–5¾ × ⁹/₁₆ in.). IM 79514, Baghdad, National Museum of Iraq. Numerous examples of small calves, carved like these in the round, were found by Loftus in the 19th century, but their purpose was not understood until whole pyxides of this design were found.

237 A unique discovery in the depths of Well AJ in the North West Palace was this splendid flask, highlighted with gold overlays and coloured inlays, consisting of four pieces: the main section, 35.7 cm (14 1/16 in.) long, is made from a single tusk (the thickness varies between 1.55 and 1.95 cm, 5/8 and 3/4 in.), the larger end being 9.4 × 7.4 cm (3 11/16 × 2 15/16 in.), and the smaller 6.5 × 5.4 cm (2 9/16 × 2 1/8 in.); an ivory disc mounted on wood forms a stopper at the wider end, and a wooden section joins the flask to a carved female head, cut from the tip of a tusk (**176**, p. 122). The flask is carved in four registers, two showing browsing bulls interspersed with papyrus plants, and the others battles between lions and griffins, the contests separated by stylized trees. IM 79508, Baghdad, National Museum of Iraq.

238 A magnificent double lion bowl, belonging to the North Syrian 'flame and frond' group, carved from a single piece of tusk and gilded and inlaid; it would have been attached to a flask for the dispensation of precious fluids. The bowl is held by four lions (represented only by their forequarters), two on the top, two on the bottom; the principal scene on the base shows, on either side of a stylized tree, a pair of winged sphinxes (which resemble both the woman tip from the flask and the 'Ugly Sister'; **176–177**, pp. 122–23), their heads looking out beside the bowl, with a winged disc between them (7.6 × 15.9 × 12.4 cm; 3 × 6¼ × 4⅞ in.). IM 79511, Baghdad, National Museum of Iraq.

239 The bottom half of a Phoenician hinged frontlet, showing a god with the sun disc and *uraei* crown on a tripartite wig; on his outstretched hands are goddesses seated in baskets, who hold papyrus sceptres, and to either side of him papyrus flowers support cartouches, each inscribed with three hieroglyphs and crowned with discs and feathers; above is a row of crowned *uraei* (21.6 × 10 cm; 8½ × 3¹⁵⁄₁₆ in.). IM 79583, Baghdad, National Museum of Iraq.

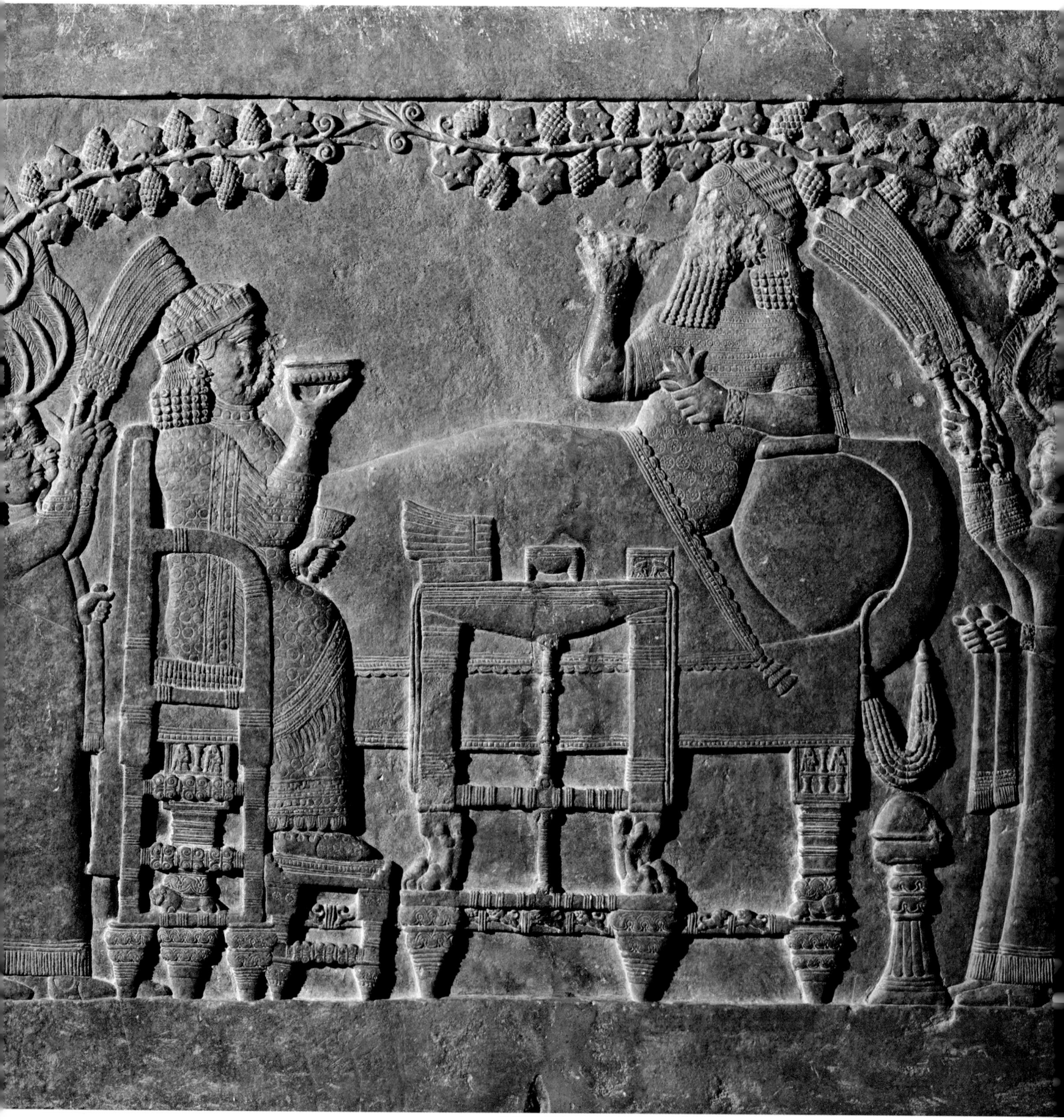

Chapter 6

The Influence of Regionalism on Furniture and the Minor Arts

[Solomon] made a great throne of ivory, and overlaid it with pure gold.*

Although the differences in style between ivories from different areas – Phoenician and North Syrian ivories, for example – are obvious and generally recognized, the immense importance of the regionalism reflected in these differences is perhaps less well understood. It affected many aspects of daily life and can be recognized both in the different kinds of furniture used across the Near East, and in the varied types of small finds, some of which were area-specific. This chapter looks at the history of furniture in the early first millennium BC, together with surviving ivories, and then at a range of small finds.

Furniture

Furniture was highly valued in the ancient world. Deities or kings sat on thrones, attendants stood. When a city was captured, the images of gods on their thrones and the furniture were carried away, thus removing the protection of the people's deities and the attributes of royalty from the defeated. Furniture was esteemed as a diplomatic gift, and some rulers and members of the nobility went to their graves accompanied by suites of furniture. The grave goods that accompanied the ruler of the city of Salamis in Cyprus included chariots and horses, chairs and beds, while the Phrygian king at Gordion was equipped with a funeral bier, tables and stands. It is notable, however, that these were male burials: significantly, the lavishly equipped tombs of the Assyrian queens had no furniture, not even a tray on which to serve food.

In the climate and soils of the Near East it is rare for pieces of furniture to have survived, but information is provided pictorially. The most complete sculptural record comes from Assyria, which has its own distinct tradition of furniture, with upright chairs, footstools, beds and tables, recorded on reliefs from the ninth to the seventh centuries BC. Late Assyrian furniture is shown in the famous Garden Scene found at Nineveh and now in the British Museum, where Ashurbanipal is celebrating his victory over the Elamites. The king is seen relaxing on a couch, raising a bowl to his lips; beside him is a table and in front of him

240 A fine depiction of Assyrian furniture on the famous relief of the Garden Scene, from the North Palace of Ashurbanipal at Nineveh, c. 645–635 BC (58.42 × 139.7 × 15.24 cm; 23 × 55 × 6 in.); this detail shows the king relaxing on a couch after his victory over the Elamite king Teumman, accompanied by his wife, who is seated on an upright chair. London, British Museum, inv. no. 124920.

his queen, seated on an upright chair, her feet resting on a footstool (**240**). The couch has a great C-shaped head enclosing a bolster, massive decorated legs and a long frieze with leaping lions. The table has leonine paws. The form and style of all the furniture are Assyrian.

The remains of actual furniture found in the Levant and Mesopotamia include a footboard belonging to a bed, and a table from Late Bronze Age Ugarit. Chair-backs, a couch and numerous furniture elements were found at Nimrud, a bed-frame at Arslan Tash, and parts of furniture at Zinjirli, all from the early first millennium BC. Thrones and a bed from a tomb at Salamis, dating to the late eighth century, are thought to have been of Phoenician manufacture, but nothing has been found in Phoenician centres. An entirely different furniture tradition flourished at Phrygian Gordion, based on an elaborate use of coloured woods, rather than ivory, as inlays, and employing a complex, geometric decorative programme. This falls outside our frame of reference.

IVORY FURNITURE FROM ROOM SW7

Stelae from North Syria show men and women at funerary banquets, seated on chairs with sloping backs, more comfortable than those favoured in Assyria. Ivory panels from such chairs formed part of one of the most remarkable discoveries in the Fort at Nimrud. This consisted of a series of relatively complete curved screens, which once formed the backs of chairs of both North Syrian and Phoenician manufacture. They had been stacked in rows at the southern end of Room SW7, behind a mass of armour. It is worth quoting the description of their discovery by their excavator, David Oates:

> From the surface of the ground to the floor, a depth of over two metres [6 ft 6 in.], fragments and plaques of ivory carved in relief were tightly packed among the debris of the fallen walls and roof, and their removal and treatment occupied us for a period of more than two months. . . . The plaques had been attached in

241 Two ivory chair-backs (ND 7904 and ND 7906) as they were first exposed, stacked upside down, in the soil in Room SW7 of Fort Shalmaneser; their wooden backings had deteriorated, leaving the fragile ivory panels in a vulnerable state. Reproduced from Mallowan and Herrmann 1974, pl. cxi.

rows of four or five to the concave surface of a curved screen, between two side-posts, which projected some distance above and below the screen and were also veneered with sheets of ivory, some carved with the same figure motifs...The screens were set upright in four rows 80 cm. to 1.00 m. [31½ in. to 3 ft 3 in.] apart across the width of the room...The ivories were fastened to their backing with dowels, some of which remain in position, but no trace survives of the material to which they were attached. It was almost certainly wood and must have been of very solid construction to survive the collapse of the building...Some parts of the ivory decoration had originally been covered with gold leaf, of which minute traces remain, but the orderly arrangement of the panels indicates that the gold had been removed before they were stacked in the positions in which we found them.[1]

A contemporary photograph shows ND 7904, which was found upside-down in the third row, next to ND 7906, as they were first exposed in the soil (**241**).

The form of many of the screens is standard: they consist of a pair of tall side-posts framing a curving central section. Typical of the group is the curved shape of the top of the side-post, which can be clearly seen on a late eighth-century relief of a noblewoman from Zinjirli, now in the Vorderasiatisches Museum in Berlin. When they were discovered, the screens were thought to have decorated bed-heads – an assumption based on European traditions of furniture. However, comparisons with chairs illustrated on North Syrian sculptures, and with relatively complete chairs found at Salamis, combined with the absence of any proof that first millennium beds had headboards, prove that they formed the backs of chairs or thrones.

The majority of the screens and loose panels are remarkably homogeneous in form, subject and style of carving, and have been attributed to a single North Syrian group, the Classic SW7 group. At least four complete examples were discovered, together with loose panels that might have been parts of another five or six. The finest and most richly decorated chair-back was raised in one piece from the third row (ND 7904, **242–244**).[2] The panels on the side-posts and the central section depict men in cut-away coats with a winged goddess in the centre. The men have shoulder-length, curly hair and spade-shaped beards, and grasp the sinuous trunks of flowering plants. The goddess has long hair, arranged in curls over the forehead and ringlets in front of the ear, and wears a long, belted dress. They all stand below a Syrian version of the winged disc, which consists of a central disc with pendant volutes and a fan of tail feathers. (This contrasts with the Phoenician version, where a pair of *uraei* or cobras flank the disc.) The outspread wings of a long version of the winged disc frames the central section at the top. The panel is decorated along

242 The long panel from the bottom of a curved chair-back (**243**, p. 156), depicting four men in a chariot hunting wild bulls (8 × 55 cm; 3⅛ × 21⅝ in.). ND 7904, panel 9, Baghdad, National Museum of Iraq.

The Influence of Regionalism on Furniture and the Minor Arts

ABOVE 243 A superb Classic SW7 chair-back, consisting of a pair of side-posts supporting a curved central section formed (originally) of five panels: on two remaining panels (right), male figures, wearing long coats with sleeves over short skirts, are shown walking under winged discs, holding up a fruit in their raised hand and grasping a sinuous plant; the central one shows a winged goddess in a long garment, holding flowers; the top panel depicts a full-size winged disc, and that at the bottom a dynamic bull hunt (**242**, p. 155) (c. 60 × 76 cm; c. 23½ × 30 in.). ND 7904, Baghdad, National Museum of Iraq.

BELOW 244 Chair-back ND 7904, before restoration.

the bottom with a lively scene of charioteers hunting bulls. The chariot holds four men, one spearing a bull behind, the other three facing forward (**242**). The principal figure, wearing an archer's protective armguard, fires an arrow at two huge bulls fleeing before the chariot at a gallop over flowering plants. The restored chair-back measures some 60 cm (23½ in.) in height and 76 cm (30 in.) in width (**243**). This luxurious and commodious throne must have conferred considerable status on its owner. The Classic SW7 chair-backs form a stylistically coherent set, which were probably produced at a single North Syrian centre and must have constituted a major constituent of tribute or booty.

Nearly all the screens and loose panels found in Room SW7 were decorated with the theme of men or women with flowering plants, but a number differ significantly from Classic SW7 examples – in the form of the chair-backs,

the sizes of the individual panels and the styles of carving. For example, it is the different form of the rather smaller chair-back that marks out ND 7909 (**245**).[3] First, there are no side-posts: instead the whole chair-back is curved. The four decorated panels of the central section are considerably smaller than the Classic SW7 panels – 18.4 × 8.2 cm (7¼ × 3¼ in.) instead of 24.5 × 10.5 cm (9⅝ × 4⅛ in.) – and the frames are of plain veneer; the dress and plants are different and the style of carving is relatively crude and provincial.

There is no indication of the shape of the chair-back to which the panels of ND 7918 (**228**, p. 145)[4] once belonged, although they are again a different size (21.2 × 7.4 cm; 8⅜ × 2⅞ in.). The men are wearing short, kilted skirts, belted at the waist, with a double tassel pendant, and hold a club over their shoulders, while the women wear long dresses, with trailing hems and an elaborate double girdle, and hold a short curved staff. However, the most unusual aspect of this set is that the winged disc has been transformed from a sun motif into a symbol of vegetation, and the figures trample it underfoot; the centre is filled with a flower, and leafy fronds grow from the disc and the volute ends. Such blasphemy would be incomprehensible in a traditional North Syrian workshop.

245 A number of the chair-backs found in Room SW7 differ significantly from the Classic SW7 group. This example lacks side-posts, is decorated on only four panels, and is carved in a more provincial style than ND 7904, though the subject is essentially the same; here, male figures holding sinuous plants are associated with women seated on backless chairs beneath winged discs, who raise a disc in one hand and hold a plant in the other (42.6 × 72.7 (top strip), 61.5 (lower strip); 16¾ × 28⅝ (top strip), 24¼ (lower strip) in.). ND 7909, Baghdad, National Museum of Iraq.

The Influence of Regionalism on Furniture and the Minor Arts

While many of the screens found in Room SW7 come from various North Syrian centres, there are some that belong to the Phoenician tradition. These differ markedly in form, size, design and style. Six short panels,[5] only some 10 cm (4 in.) high, show men seated on typically Egyptian low-backed chairs, their feet resting on footstools with voluted supports (ND 6352, **246**). Still adhering to the common subject of men and plants, the men raise one hand in salutation and hold the stalk of a large lily flower in the other. Also belonging to the Phoenician tradition is an entirely different example: it has plain side-posts and a curved central section 54.5 cm (21⁷⁄₁₆ in.) wide, and is decorated with elegant openwork spirals (ND 7910, **247**).[6] The three panels are framed by strips of plain veneer outlined with star-spangled margins, and can be compared both to one of the chairs found in the Salamis tomb and to Homer's description of the throne of Penelope:

and by the fire where she was wont to sit they placed a chair inlaid with spirals of ivory and silver, which of old the craftsman Ikmalios had made, and beneath it a footstool that was part of the chair, and upon it a great fleece was laid.[7]

The use of furniture is very much a social and a regional identifier. The upright form of throne employed by the Assyrian kings differs from the more comfortable North Syrian chairs. Equally, Bar-Rakib, king of Sam'al, illustrated his support for Assyria by sitting on an Assyrian-style backless chair,[8] which may well have been given him by Tiglath-pileser III (r. 745–727 BC). This again emphasizes the importance and significance of furniture. Although seemingly unconnected with the ancient Near East, a pioneering study of English chairs is perhaps relevant here: the furniture historian Bernard Cotton recorded the apparently spontaneous development in the eighteenth century of chair styles that differ in appearance and methods of construction from area to area. He noted that the distribution

ABOVE **246** One of a set of six small panels, all of the same size, showing men seated on typical Egyptian-style chairs and holding lilies with long stalks; the subject is common, but in the case of this set it is carved on much smaller panels (10 × 7.5 × 0.5 cm; 3¹⁵⁄₁₆ × 2¹⁵⁄₁₆ × ⅛ in.). ND 6352, Baghdad, National Museum of Iraq.

BELOW **247** A delicately carved, curved, openwork chair-back from Room SW7, originally supported by a pair of side-posts and surmounted by a railing of half-cylinders; it is decorated with spirals of ivory, between panels bordered with stars (33.3 × 54.5 × 0.3 cm, radius of curve *c.* 10 cm; 13⅛ × 21⁷⁄₁₆ × ⅛ in., radius of curve *c.* 4 in.). ND 7910, New York, Metropolitan Museum of Art. (See also **107**, p. 93.)

158   Ancient Ivory

of the different types of chair was similar to that of local dialects and described the furniture as embodying a 'common language with dialects'.[9] In this age of convenient travel and globalization, it is easy to fail to appreciate the strength of regionalism. Laying hedges, for instance, is an old British craft, doubtless soon to be lost to the slashing tractor, and it still has strong regional characteristics. The custom in Devon and Somerset of growing beech hedges on the tops of banks is entirely different from the way hedges are laid in east Wales, and both differ from the hedges of the Midlands. A similar regionalism is evident in the differing sculptural styles found in North Syrian centres such as Zinjirli, Carchemish and Tell Halaf. Style constituted a 'trademark' or 'visual language', applied both to major and minor arts, and served to identify a particular centre or state. There were probably a number of palace- or temple-based workshops in the Levant producing furniture. These would have been royal workshops, for no other would have had the necessary resources to make such costly pieces: ivory was a rare and expensive material.

THE EGYPTIAN RECORD

The record of Egyptian furniture is outstanding from early times. The belief in life after death resulted in the placing of worldly goods in tombs for use in the afterlife, and these were preserved, thanks to the dry desert climate. Actual pieces survive, as well as illustrations in paintings on the walls of tombs and elsewhere. The oldest wooden furniture dates from about 3100 BC, and superb examples were found in the Old Kingdom tomb of Queen Hetepheres (d. 2613 BC). Although the wood had decayed to powder, its covering of gold sheeting survived, and from this it was possible to restore both her bed and her throne. The queen's bed has a pronounced slope from the head down towards the decorated footboard; the legs are in the form of stylized lion's legs (**248**).[10] The throne is low, with a wide, deep seat, and supports in the form of the forelegs and hind legs of a lion, resting on a beaded drum. In the side panels are three boldly carved papyrus flowers.[11] Phoenician furniture followed Egyptian traditions.

BEDS

Two principal types of bed are known in the first millennium BC. One is the Egyptian bed with a raised head and a footboard – the latter required to stop the bed coverings sliding off the bed. The other is the Assyrian bed, initially with a raised sloping head, which developed into a C-shaped head containing a bolster, of the same design as the back of Ashurbanipal's couch in the Garden Scene (**240**, p. 152).

There are numerous examples of the traditional Egyptian bed from the period of the New Kingdom, both superb ones, such as that discovered in the tomb of Tutankhamun, and more ordinary ones from less grand tombs. They vary between 170 and 180 cm (67 and 71 in.) in length, and are 68–90 cm (26¾–35½ in.) wide. They were constructed in the usual manner of the time, with curving side-rails and carved legs of leonine design. The footboards were of separate framed construction, added above the bed-frame, and lavishly decorated and secured by curved braces.[12]

The rectangular footboard found at Late Bronze Age Ugarit is decorated with sixteen carved ivory panels, each 24 cm (9½ in.) high, forming a unit 82.5 cm (32½ in.) wide. They are carved in low relief with a variety of scenes in a quasi-Egyptian style, and were fitted together to form two

248 The state of preservation of Egyptian furniture is remarkable: this elegant bed, of a type that continued in use for centuries, belonged to Queen Hetepheres (d. 2613 BC); the frame was raised at the head, and the foot was fitted with a board to prevent the bedding from sliding off. Boston, Museum of Fine Arts, inv. no. 29.1858. Image © Scala.

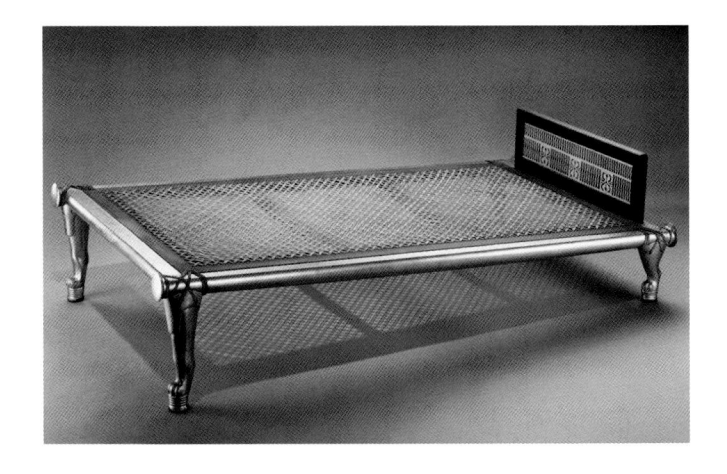

series, back to back, those facing outwards showing more public subjects, those facing inwards more intimate ones.[13]

Ivory panels and furniture elements found at Arslan Tash include the remains of a bed-frame, measuring 196 × 96 cm (77 3/16 × 37 3/4 in). Some of the ivories found at the site may well have been used to decorate the footboard. A fragmentary Aramaic inscription on an undecorated label reads '...to our lord Hazael...': Hazael (r. c. 843–803 BC) was a king of Damascus, and it has been suggested that some of these ivories may represent booty from that city – perhaps booty donated to the Assyrian governor.[14] The frame of a large, poorly preserved bed (189 × 111 cm; 74 3/8 × 43 3/4 in.) in the Salamis tomb is made of wood veneered with ivory. Found nearby were some ivory plaques and a rectangular frame (49 × 615 cm; 19 5/8 in. × 20 ft 2 in.) which had been 'thrown on a pile with bronzes, etc., in the north west corner of the dromos'.[15] The plaques were reassembled as the headboard of the bed, based on the sizes of the various pieces, 'together with imagination and analysis on the part of the Cyprus Museum technicians and [Vassos Karageorghis]'.[16] The result is an attractive, museum-worthy object, but, following Egyptian parallels, such a type of bed is extremely improbable: it is reasonably certain that the bed would have been equipped with a footboard.

LION-LEGGED CHAIRS

Furniture with leonine or bovid legs was known as early as the third millennium BC, both in Egypt and in Mesopotamia. As usual, Levantine furniture followed Egyptian design. Chairs with a high back and leonine legs can be seen on an Egyptianizing pectoral of a king of Byblos from the early eighteenth century, where two deities or kings sit either side of a winged bird below a winged sun disc.[17] The lion-legged chair became popular in Eighteenth Dynasty Egypt; perhaps its most famous example is the golden throne of Tutankhamun (**250**). Geoffrey Killen, the historian of Egyptian furniture, describes this as

> one of the most beautiful pieces of furniture ever made....The legs of the throne are fashioned in the

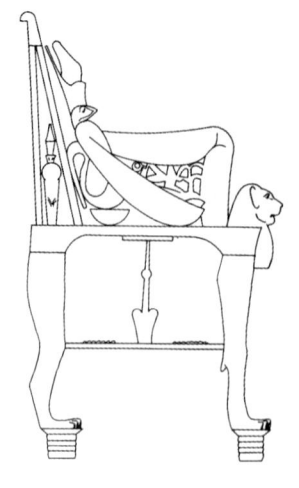

ABOVE 249 A leonine head, carved in the round, though the left side is missing; it was probably part of the arm of a chair (there is a tenon slot in the neck for fixing it) and it matches the head on the throne of Tutankhamun (250 below) (5.3 × 6.8 cm; 2 1/16 × 2 11/16 in.). ND 12053, formerly Mosul Museum of History.

LEFT 250 Drawing of the golden throne of Tutankhamun, with lion legs and capitals; there are many examples of such elements among the Nimrud ivories. Reproduced from Killen 1980, pp. 62–63.

form of the front and rear legs of a lion, the claws inlaid with glass the colour of turquoise....Both front legs have capitals in the form of lion heads, a prominent design on 18th dynasty thrones.[18]

Lion-legged chairs and their associated footstools are also shown on stelae found on the citadel near the temple quarter of Ugarit, showing the god El.[19]

Numerous leonine heads and legs, which probably formed parts of such chairs, were found among the Nimrud corpus. The head ND 12053 (**249**)[20] may well have been set above a leonine foreleg, as on Tutankhamun's throne. Traces of blue remain in the hollowed out eyes, and the mane is carved with vertical fluting, forming a ruff around the head. There are the remains of a large tenon slot in the neck.

The Nimrud lion heads are of varied sizes and styles, and some may have formed parts of statuettes rather than capitals. Another fine example, with both mane and eyes inlaid, was found in Well NN (ND 2219, **251**).[21] The ears were

160 Ancient Ivory

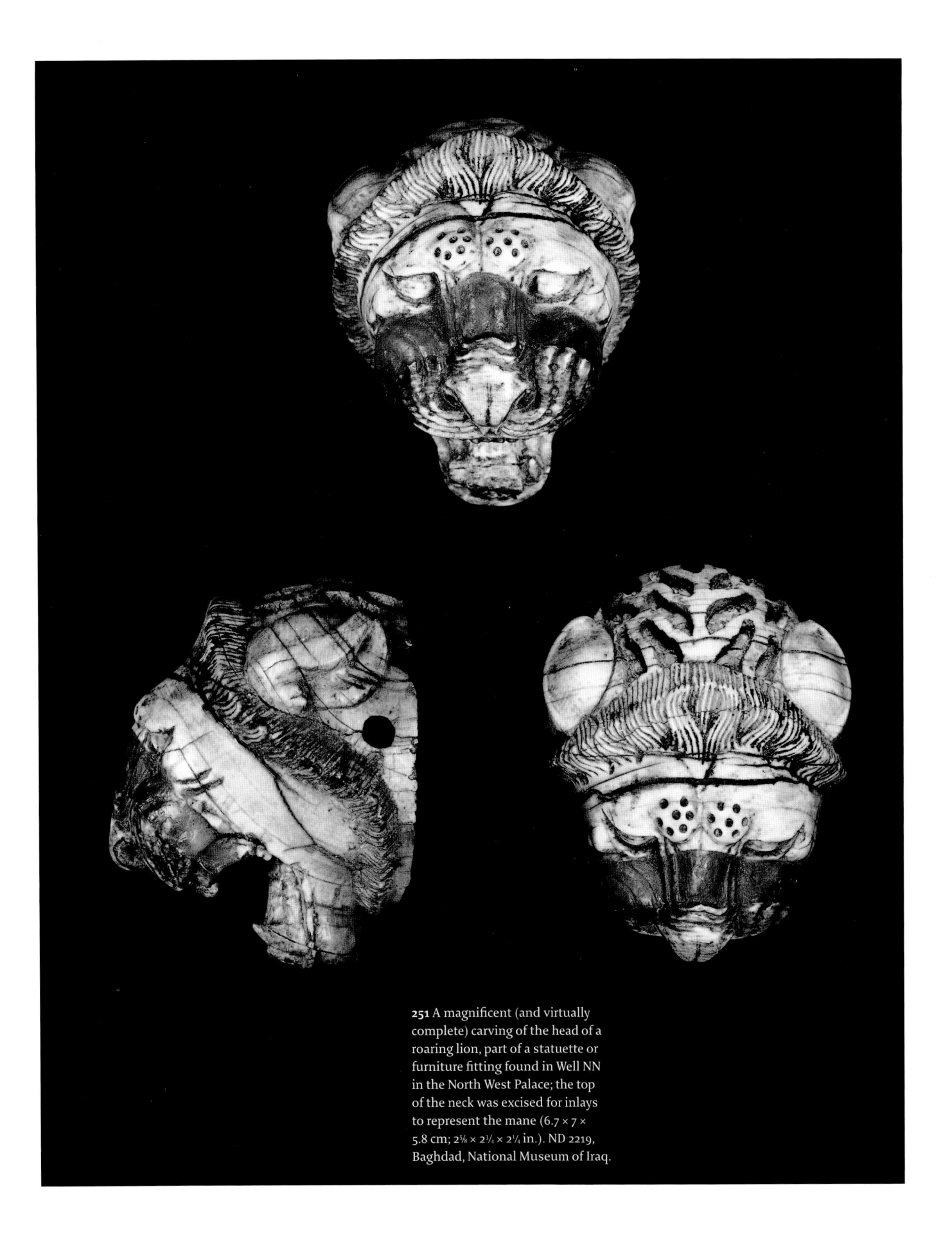

251 A magnificent (and virtually complete) carving of the head of a roaring lion, part of a statuette or furniture fitting found in Well NN in the North West Palace; the top of the neck was excised for inlays to represent the mane (6.7 × 7 × 5.8 cm; 2⅝ × 2¾ × 2¼ in.). ND 2219, Baghdad, National Museum of Iraq.

LEFT 252 A lion's head, facing forwards and carved in the round but with a flat back, for use as a furniture fitment; it wears a sun disc and *uraei* crown, the eyes are deeply excised for inlay and the mane forms a ruff around the cheeks and jaws (10.4 × 8 × 7 cm; 4¼ × 3⅛ × 2¾ in.). ND 7562, London, British Museum.

OPPOSITE 253 A beautifully modelled right hind leg of a large standing lion or sphinx; the paw is set on a plain pedestal and has three carefully carved claws (24 × 7.5 × 4.7 cm; 9⁷⁄₁₆ × 2¹⁵⁄₁₆ × 1⅞ in.). ND 11116, New York, Metropolitan Museum of Art.

carved separately and lie flat on the neck beside the mane, which rises to form a ruff. There are warts on the forehead and ribbed wrinkles, with chisel marks extending over the nose to the triangle-shaped eyes. The mouth is wide open, the jaws in a V shape, and the sharp teeth and tongue have rows of chisel marks. The back is, as usual, flat with a rectangular tenon slot.

An unusual example, unfortunately burnt and poorly preserved, was found in Room SE1 of the *rab ekalli*'s suite in the Fort (ND 7562, **252**).[22] This is rather larger than the examples discussed so far, as the lion mask is surmounted by the remains of a sun disc and *uraei* crown. The oval eyes are excised for inlays, the mouth is closed, the whiskers are incised and there are holes for the bristles.

An example of a finely modelled hind leg was found in Room SW12 and probably formed part of a Phoenician lion-legged or sphinx throne (ND 11116, **253**).[23] The paw is standing on a plain, narrow pedestal; only three claws survive, with the nails carefully represented. At a height of some 24 cm (9⁷⁄₁₆ in.), this is the tallest of a number of examples of the hindquarters of felines.

Although lion paws were ubiquitous across the area, lion heads or masks on lion-legged chairs were definitely a Levantine feature: they are not known on Assyrian chairs. On Assyrian furniture, leonine paws were used only on footstools and tables, not on thrones.[24] What we do see, on the great couch of Ashurbanipal in the Garden Scene, is statuettes of lions forming a section of the massive legs just above the long frieze of leaping lions (**240**, p. 152).[25] These suggest the purpose of such pieces as ND 11118 (**254**),[26] a roaring, couchant lion carved fully in the round and pierced vertically by a tenon slot. The carving of the head is vigorous and detailed, and the wrinkles around the gaping mouth and over the nose are strongly modelled, as are the eyes and eyelids. The mane forms a ruff around the face and extends in an oval around the foreleg and along the belly. The tail folds round the right hind leg. There are many examples of such lion statuettes, either lying or crouching (ND 12038,

162 Ancient Ivory

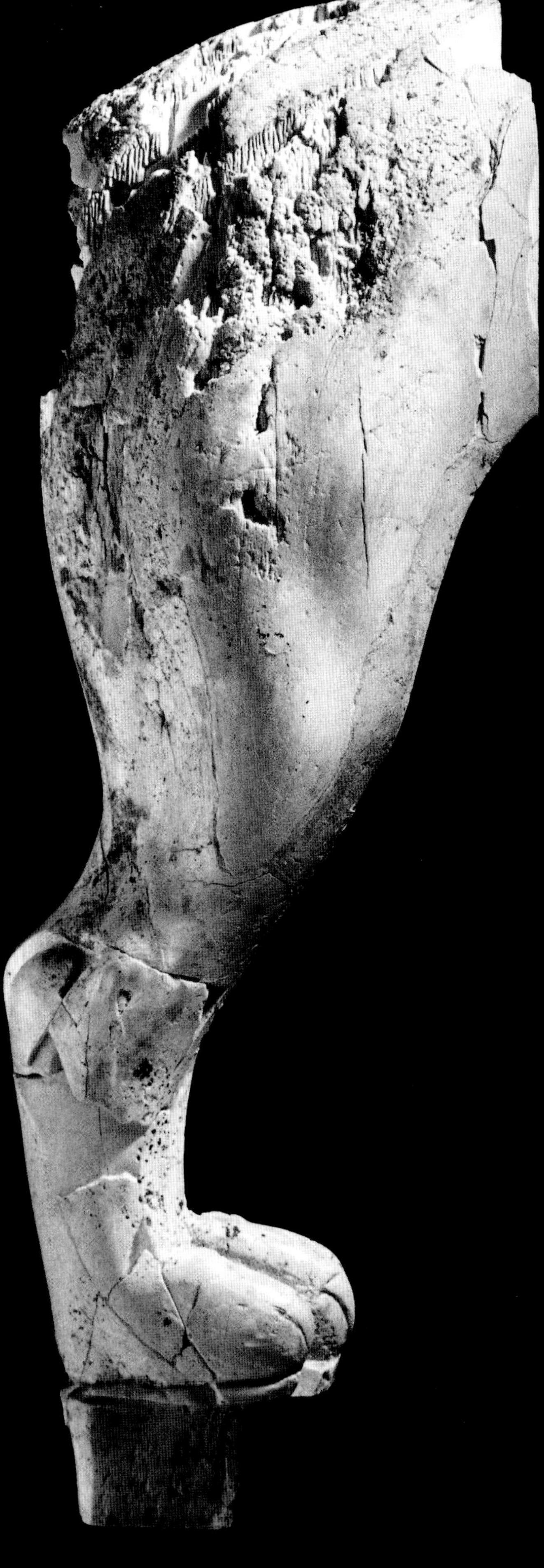

254–255 Two lions couchant, shown roaring; they are carved in the round, with tenon slots for vertical fixing, and originally formed part of the leg of a couch or other piece of furniture. The better preserved of the two (above) is more finely worked, especially on the face and mane (5 × 13.5 × 4.2 cm; 2 × 5⁵⁄₁₆ × 1⅝ in.). ND 11118, Baghdad, National Musem of Iraq. The other (below), though carved in less detail, is slightly larger, and also more naturalistic (6.6 × 13.5 × 5.8 cm; 2⅝ × 5⁵⁄₁₆ × 2¼ in.). ND 12038, Erbil Civilization Museum.

255),[27] as well as leonine heads and paws. Similar crouching lions have been found at Zinjirli, Samaria and Thasos.[28]

Lion paws and the lion-legged chair, sometimes with a mask, have a long history. They continued through Hellenistic and Roman periods into medieval and later Europe. As the furniture historian Ralph Edwards wrote in 1964:

> Between 1720 and 1735 [English] furniture with the lion mask represented the latest development of fashionable design, and during these years the head, legs and hair of the animal constituted the most important ornamental features on chairs and other furniture.[29]

THE SPHINX THRONE

Perhaps the most famous type of Phoenician chair is the 'sphinx throne'. The idea of such a chair was, as usual, of Egyptian inspiration, though adapted in Phoenicia. One of the earliest representations is on an ivory strip found at Megiddo (northern Israel) and dated to *c.* 1250–1150 BC.[30] This was part of a collection of ivories of varied character, found scattered about in an outer room.[31] The strip shows a victory celebration, with the king seated on a sphinx throne and his queen and musicians standing in front of him (**256**). The ceremonial chair consists of a seat with a high, slightly outward-slanting back and a solid flank, the upper frame of which curves downwards to the front. The solid side is covered by a winged, human-headed sphinx.

An excellent depiction of a sphinx throne can be seen on the side of a stone sarcophagus found in a tomb at Byblos (**257**). Despite an inscription (*c.* 1000 BC) by the son of Ahiram dedicating it to the dead king, it is variously dated from the thirteenth to the tenth centuries. The king, his feet resting on a footstool, has a table in front of him and is attended by a servant. The chair is similar to that on the Megiddo ivory, with a high, sloping back, covered by a cushion, and the side in the form of a winged, human-headed sphinx, the tail held upright in an S shape. The footstool rests

BELOW **256** Plaque found at Megiddo, incised with a scene depicting tribute bearers and captives before a prince seated on a sphinx throne; his queen, wearing a high crown and accompanied by a musician, stands in front of him (26.3 × 5.7 × 0.15 cm; 10⅜ × 2¼ × 1/16 in.). Jerusalem, Rockefeller Museum, inv. no. 38.780.

RIGHT **257** Detail from one side of a limestone sarcophagus found in the Royal Necropolis at Byblos, showing a dead king seated on a sphinx throne with a Phoenician tripod table in front of him, attended by a servant. National Museum of Beirut. Image © DEA/G. Dagli Orti/Getty Images. (See also **60**, p. 58.)

The Influence of Regionalism on Furniture and the Minor Arts 165

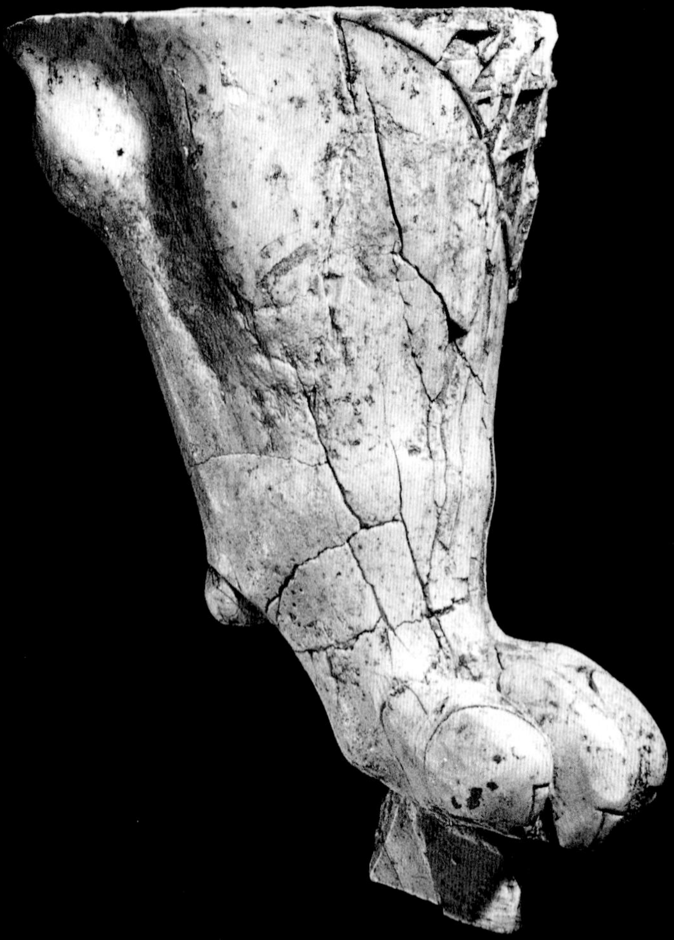

LEFT 258 The hind leg of a sphinx, carved in the round and probably originally part of a chair; the musculature around the hock identifies this as part of the 'flame and frond' group, and suggests that the chair resembled those seen on the pyxis decorated with a banqueting scene (**264**, p. 169) (21.8 × 10 × 3.6 cm; 8 9/16 × 3 15/16 × 1 7/16 in.). ND 9175, Baghdad, National Museum of Iraq.

ABOVE 259 The right foreleg of a lion of the Ornate Group, probably part of a footstool; the piece is superbly modelled, and remains of red and blue inlays survive in the collar (13 × 4.1 × 8.4 cm; 5 1/8 × 1 5/8 × 3 5/16). ND 10529, Philadelphia, University of Pennsylvania Museum of Archaeology and Anthropology.

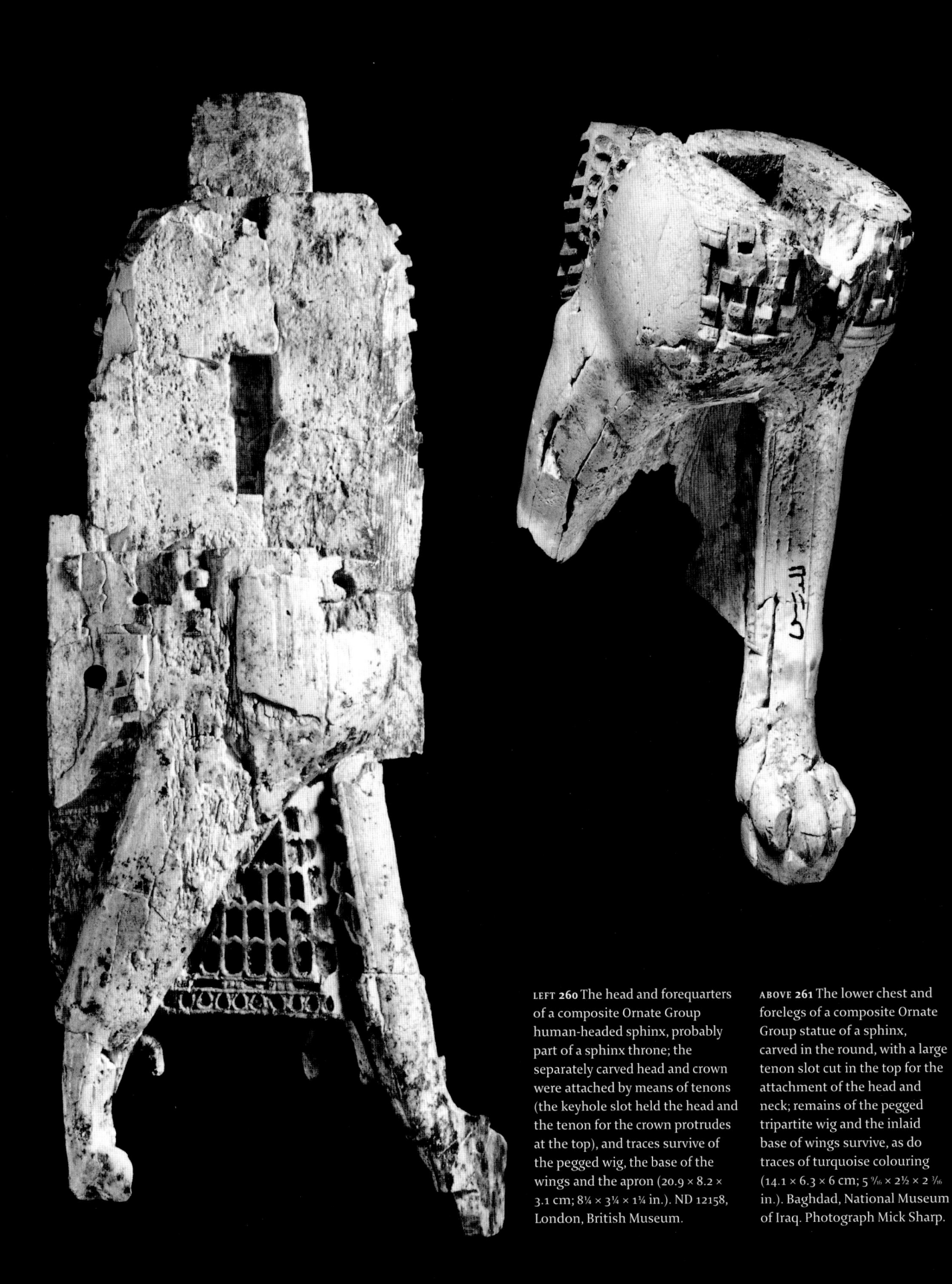

LEFT 260 The head and forequarters of a composite Ornate Group human-headed sphinx, probably part of a sphinx throne; the separately carved head and crown were attached by means of tenons (the keyhole slot held the head and the tenon for the crown protrudes at the top), and traces survive of the pegged wig, the base of the wings and the apron (20.9 × 8.2 × 3.1 cm; 8¼ × 3¼ × 1¼ in.). ND 12158, London, British Museum.

ABOVE 261 The lower chest and forelegs of a composite Ornate Group statue of a sphinx, carved in the round, with a large tenon slot cut in the top for the attachment of the head and neck; remains of the pegged tripartite wig and the inlaid base of wings survive, as do traces of turquoise colouring (14.1 × 6.3 × 6 cm; 5 9/16 × 2½ × 2 3/16 in.). Baghdad, National Museum of Iraq. Photograph Mick Sharp.

167

on voluted supports. In front of the king is a tripod table, with zoomorphic legs resting on a pedestal – a familiar Phoenician type.[32]

The same scene, carved at a very different scale and in a very different style, can be seen on a North Syrian 'flame and frond' pyxis, found in Well AJ (IM 79513, **264**).[33] It is a miniature version of that on the Ahiram sarcophagus, even sharing the same types of Phoenician furniture. One difference between the two pieces, apart from scale, material and style, is that the lotus held by the Byblos ruler hangs down, indicating that he is dead, while that on the pyxis is upright, showing that the king is alive. The furniture is identical, with a sphinx chair, footstool and table. Some of the gold overlays and inlays for the pyxis remain in place, suggesting just how rich and rare this remarkable piece must have been. That such furniture was actually made in a North Syrian centre is shown by two legs of ivory found in Room SW37.[34] They consist of a fragmentary foreleg and a hind leg with 'flame and frond' markings (ND 9175, **258**). The hind leg is still preserved to a height of nearly 22 cm (more than 8½ in.); it has the distinctive pea-pod markings on the hock.

Some inlaid Phoenician furniture elements include a rather short right foreleg, only 13 cm (5⅛ in.) high, as well as parts of sphinx figures. The leonine paw of ND 10529 (**259**)[35] is modelled and the claws incised. The sphinx side panels of a throne would have been composite, made up from numerous pieces of both ivory and wood, and subsequently overlaid in gold. A poorly preserved Ornate Group sphinx has its head turned to the front: it survives to a height of some 21 cm (8¼ in.) (ND 12158, **260**).[36] A better-preserved example, consisting only of the lower chest and legs of a sphinx, is 14 cm (5½ in.) high (ND 13929, **261**).[37] There is a large rectangular tenon slot in the top for the attachment of the upper section of the sphinx. The ends of the pegged wig can be seen on the front of the chest.

From Iron Age II (*c.* 800 BC) onwards, the sphinx throne was reserved for deities. Numerous examples have been found in the region of Tyre, as well as elsewhere, among them the throne of Astarte in the Louvre, from the 2nd century BC.[38] The design travelled to the Phoenician west,

262 The popularity of the Phoenician-style sphinx chair has continued through the millennia: such chairs are known from ancient Greece and Rome, medieval and Renaissance Europe, and from more recent times, including this 19th-century example, seen in a Swiss hotel.

and in Greece in the Hellenistic period the solid sides of some thrones incorporated animals or monsters. These Greek seats are

> among the most important creations of the Hellenistic age in the field of furniture, not only for their intrinsic beauty and stateliness, but because of their influence on the thrones of later times – the Roman, the mediaeval and the Renaissance.[39]

The sphinx chair has maintained its popularity through 3,000 years and is still in use today, as can be seen in **262**, a chair photographed in a Swiss hotel in the 1990s.

TABLES

The table set in front of the king on the Ahiram sarcophagus is a tripod table, with curved legs terminating in lion's pads and placed on low vertical supports. The table's three legs are interconnected by a horizontal stretcher, linked to the blade of the table by a vertical prop.[40] Examples of such legs were found in Room SW6 in the Fort at Nimrud (ND 6383, **263**)[41] and in the Salamis tomb. The table leg from the Fort was originally thought to belong to a chair, but in fact formed part of a typical Phoenician tripod table; it ends in a leonine paw set on a guilloche band, and is 47.6 cm (18¾ in.) high. The Salamis example is more strongly curved and slightly shorter. A similar leg can be seen on an incised ivory found in the Idaean Cave.[42] While the tripod table is

ABOVE 263 The curved leg of a typical Phoenician tripod table, ending in a lion's paw (the small fragments are the claws) set on a pedestal; it was found in the wine store, Room SW6 (47.6 × 6.5 × 4 cm; 18¾ × 2⁹⁄₁₆ × 1⁹⁄₁₆ in.). ND 6383, London, British Museum.

ABOVE RIGHT 264 Detail from the side of an oval pyxis from Well AJ in the North West Palace (235, p. 148); this scene depicts a banquet, with the king seated on a sphinx chair before a tripod table. IM 79513, Baghdad, National Museum of Iraq.

RIGHT 265 A fragmentary rectangular panel from the room with chair-backs, Room SW7, showing an elegant lady seated on a backless chair before a table loaded with food, which is balanced on the branches of a lily tree and on the lady's foot; her hair is arranged in a curled fringe and long ringlets, and she wears a full-length belted garment (25 × 14.5 cm; 9⅞ × 5¹¹⁄₁₆). ND 6369, Baghdad, National Museum of Iraq.

based on Egyptian prototypes, in the Levant it is associated with funerary meals, banquets and drinking scenes; it was adopted by the Greeks and Romans, probably via Cyprus.

As usual, the Assyrian table is different. It is illustrated on reliefs from the time of Ashurnasirpal II, and has lions' paws resting on a bar supported by bulbous feet, and a vertical rod with a palmette capital in the centre. Also shown on Assyrian reliefs are cross-legged tables with feet in the form of bull's hooves: these are principally seen in camp scenes, where they are used for preparing food,[43] and were probably collapsible. Similar cross-legged tables can be seen on some ivories from Room SW7 showing seated ladies. On ND 6369 the lady sits on a backless chair with a winged sphinx below, and rests her feet on a footstool (265);[44] her right hand stretches out to the cross-legged table in front of her, which is balanced on her foot and a flower.

The Influence of Regionalism on Furniture and the Minor Arts   169

DECORATED FURNITURE ELEMENTS
FOUND AT NIMRUD

A pair of Ornate Group furniture posts, not particularly well preserved, were found in Rooms SW37 and SW11/12.[45] They were decorated on three sides: a youth holding a lotus plant occupied the central panel, with goddesses with flails over their shoulders on the sides. The fourth side contained slots for fixing. It is not known how these pieces were used – whether they formed part of a chair or bed – but there would have been additional panels attached above and below. This pair represent a specific type of fitting, with the same assemblage of figures repeated in different sizes and styles. All of them essentially belong to the Phoenician tradition.

A smaller version, found in Room FF of the North West Palace, is closer in style to its probably Egyptian model (ND 768, **266**).[46] The goddesses on the side panels are well preserved. One wears the crown of the goddess Hathor, set on a tripartite wig, inlaid with a single piece of glass, the other the sun disc and *uraeus* crown. The sides are perforated with dowel holes.

No fewer than three of these furniture elements were found at Zinjirli (**267**). They show the central youth holding a bird-headed sceptre in one hand and a voluted palmette flower over his shoulder. His short, Egyptian-style wig is tied with an *uraeus*. His eyes are elongated, and he wears a collar and a short-sleeved tunic with apron and trailing skirt. The goddesses have tripartite wigs and long dresses, and hold *wedjat* eyes in one hand and birds in the other. These versions of a common type of fitting with a standard decorative scheme are yet another illustration of the different ways in which an object serving a particular purpose varies from workshop to workshop or area to area.

While the posts belong to the Phoenician tradition, a massive furniture leg, carved from a large tusk, forms part of the North Syrian 'flame and frond' group (ND 12042, **234**, p. 147).[47] The sides of this magnificent piece are broken off, but it still measures about 14 cm (5½ in.) in width and is 22.2 cm (8¾ in.) high. It is decorated with two registers of design: one consists of a series of overlapping bulls with their horns lowered, advancing to the left, and the other is a

ABOVE **266** A poorly preserved Phoenician furniture fitting or post, decorated on the front and sides and inlaid: on the central panel there survive only traces of a figure standing on a pedestal, with raised arm and hand holding a lotus blossom; on the sides are goddesses wearing long belted garments and holding flowers, one with the sun disc and *uraeus* crown, the other (shown here) with the Hathor crown, set on tripartite wigs (7 × 3.8 × 2.6 cm; 2¾ × 1½ × 1 in.). ND 768, London, British Museum.

BELOW **267** Drawings of one of the three Phoenician furniture fittings or posts found at Zinjirli of the same form as those from Nimrud; they have a similar range of motifs to the Nimrud examples – a central youth flanked by a pair of goddesses – but, though close in function and design, are different in style. Reproduced from Andrae 1943, pl. 65.

170   Ancient Ivory

version of the familiar North Syrian animal combat, a violent conflict between a winged griffin and a lion, the outcome of which is uncertain, as the two creatures tear at each other. The boldly marked musculature suggests attribution to the 'flame and frond' group. The registers are separated by guilloche bands, and the plain top section is curved.

Bulls were a favourite motif for decorating furniture fittings. Some circular furniture legs were decorated with rows of bulls, in separate bands, presumably set one above the other. They were either openwork, as in IM 79518 from Well AJ (**268**),[48] or consisted of sets of curved solid plaques, such as the massive bull with a small head of ND 10499 (**269**).[49] Once again, a standard motif for decorating furniture legs is carved in various ways.

PLAIN FURNITURE ELEMENTS

While decorated furniture elements can often be attributed to various regional traditions, the numerous examples of plainer fittings tend to be common across the area. A throne on a reconstructed stela from Zinjirli (**270**) illustrates how two of these elements, the palmette and the palm capital, were employed.[50] There are many versions of the palmette

LEFT **268** An openwork circular furniture fitting, with five rather slim bulls, carved in high relief, on a circular base decorated with a guilloche pattern; there was probably a matching frame above (dia. 12.2 cm; 4 13/16 in.). IM 79518, Baghdad, National Museum of Iraq.

RIGHT **269** A fine, curved plaque, one of a set that originally formed part of a circular furniture element, some 12 cm (4 3/4 in.) in diameter; it depicts a massive bull, advancing to the right, with his small head lowered (5.5 × 7.3 × 1 cm; 2 3/16 × 2 7/8 × 3/8 in.). ND 10499, Baghdad, National Museum of Iraq.

BELOW **270** Drawing of fragments of sculpture found at Zinjirli, reconstructed to show a banquet scene; a king, accompanied by attendants, is seated on an elaborate throne, incorporating friezes of running palmettes and hemi-cylindrical palm capitals, of which there are surviving ivory examples. Reproduced from Voos 1985, fig. 14.

LEFT 274 A tall and elegant palmette, with festoons and hanging branches, outlined with raised ribs. (14.4 × 5.5 × 1.3 cm; 5¹¹⁄₁₆ × 2³⁄₁₆ × ½ in.). ND 11089, Bristol City Museum and Art Gallery. A common furniture element, used in sets to form rails and friezes, examples are found across the area in various sizes and styles and in solid or openwork form.

CENTRE 272 A hemi-cylindrical palm capital – another common element – used (sideways on) as part of the stretcher on a chair or throne; here, stylized palm leaves are set between ribbed mouldings (9.9 × 5.9 × 2 cm; 3⅞ × 2⁵⁄₁₆ × ¾ in.). ND 9173, London, British Museum.

RIGHT 273 A larger, freestanding, furniture element, consisting of hemi-cylindrical, stylized palm leaves, between a series of mouldings; it would have been used vertically (14 × 11 × 3.9 cm; 5½ × 4⁵⁄₁₆ × 1½ in.). ND 10324, Baghdad, National Museum of Iraq.

(ND 11089, **271**)[51] with numerous minor variations both in decoration and in height; the pieces vary between c. 10 and 16.5 cm (4 and 6½ in.) high. Another standard fitting is a hemi-cylindrical palm capital (ND 9173, **272**).[52] Both these types have been found in abundance, not only at Nimrud but also elsewhere across the Levant – at Khorsabad, Arslan Tash, Carchemish, Zinjirli and Samaria. As can be seen on the reconstruction of the stela, the palm capitals were used to form the ends of a cross-rail on the throne and the footstool.

By the eighth century BC tusks must have been relatively plentiful, and many were found at Nimrud. They were used not only to make a variety of large furniture elements, such as a hemi-cylindrical element with stylized leaves (ND 10324, **273**)[53] and a circular fitting in the form of palm capitals with hanging leaves (IM 79546, **55**, p. 52),[54] but even to make interior fittings. The circular fitting is one of a pair of ivory examples, of which Layard found bronze and stone versions in the Room of the Bronzes in the North West Palace.[55]

Phoenician Unusually Shaped Ivories

The purpose of a distinctive group of ivories belonging to the Ornate Group, unimaginatively called 'Unusually Shaped Ivories', is unknown. It is not even known whether they formed parts of pieces of furniture, or chariot fittings, or had some other purpose. All are worked on concave plaques, with the convex back left rough, and they were fixed at the top and bottom, not at the sides. Most are beautifully inlaid. They are varied in shape, size and subject, but they are united because nearly all the designs are enclosed within the swelling branches of a stylized tree. The majority are decorated with pairs of griffins, back to back, framed by the curving branches of a tree, the form of which changes from one ivory to another. The tree of the tall ND 7615 has tiers of branches below the outward-curving pair at the top, and the ground is filled with flowers (**274**),[56] while the tree associated with the seated winged sphinx of ND 11042 is shorter (**275**).[57] Whatever their purpose, these Phoenician ivories are real little jewels.

ABOVE 274 An unusually tall example of an enigmatic group of concave decorative elements, beautifully carved and inlaid, and belonging to the Ornate Group; a pair of rampant griffins, back to back within the swelling branches of an elaborate, stylized tree, reach up to browse on fronds growing from the upper volutes (14.5 × 10.1 × 1.9 cm; 5¹¹⁄₁₆ × 4 × ¾ in.). ND 7615, Baghdad, National Museum of Iraq.

RIGHT 275 A unique, if fragmentary, example of one of the Unusually Shaped group of curved decorative elements, showing an elegant sphinx seated within the expanded branches of a stylized tree (12.2 × 8.9 cm; 4¹³⁄₁₆ × 3½ in.). ND 11042, Baghdad, National Museum of Iraq. The rich flora of this and the preceding piece is typical of the Phoenician Ornate Group.

Small finds

The finest small objects were recovered in 1975 from Well AJ of the North West Palace by the Iraqi State Board of Antiquities and Heritage, though the first examples had been found more than a century earlier by William Kennett Loftus. Digging in the ruins of the Long (or Throne) Room of the Burnt Palace, he found 'an immense collection of ivories',[58] consisting of a mass of badly burnt fragments. These were essentially forgotten until 1932, when Richard Barnett began the unenviable task of sorting, conserving and publishing them.[59] Working in essentially virgin territory, as so few parallels were known, Barnett reassembled a variety of pieces, all essentially small finds, which included parts of pyxides, bowls, flasks, fan handles and small statuettes of calves. The assemblage was, as always, mixed, and belonged to various Levantine groups: there were no Assyrian pieces. Max Mallowan found more fragments in the same room in the 1950s. However, it was the discoveries in Well AJ that shone a dramatic new light on these broken ivories. Among the magnificent finds from the well were relatively complete pyxides, with the small calf statuettes still in place on the lids, as well as flasks still equipped with their spoon-stoppers, bridle harness, statuettes and a range of other previously unknown material.

THE NORTH SYRIAN PYXIS

Perhaps the most immediately identifiable small find is the pyxis, an oval box cut from the base of a tusk, often with a flat back decorated with a goddess. The lid swings sideways on a peg fixed in the centre of the back panel, and is decorated with small calf statuettes. The thin oval of ivory forming the base is decorated with an incised floral design (IM 79513, **235**, p. 148).[60] Three more or less complete examples were retrieved from Well AJ, and many fragmentary examples of sides, lids and bases, and dozens of calf figures were found in the Burnt Palace. The pyxides from the well and most of the pieces found in the Burnt Palace all belong to the North Syrian 'flame and frond' group. The humans and animals all share the familiar physiognomy and musculature, and common technical features such as pegged inlays. Most of the designs carved on the sides of the pyxides are unique: there is very little repetition. Fragments of similar pyxides have been found at Hasanlu in north-west Iran.

Although no interior fitments have been preserved in the Nimrud examples, pyxides were usually divided into compartments. These survive in a plain example found in a tomb at Tell Halaf, which lay partly under a terrace built by Kapara, probably in the tenth century BC. The tomb's male occupant lay on his back, his mouth and breast covered with gold plates. Beside him was an ivory pyxis (**276**), plain except for guilloche bands, overlaid with gold, and a similarly decorated lid with a central rosette. The interior was divided into five compartments with the remains of rouge in one. Nearby was a silver spatula. This is a rare instance of a pyxis found in its original context. It suggests both that men used cosmetics and that pyxides formed part of standard male equipment. Ashurbanipal has just such a pyxis, suitably

276 Drawings of an ivory pyxis found in a prestigious 10th-century male burial at Tell Halaf; decorated on the outside with guilloche bands overlaid with gold foil, the pyxis had the remains of cosmetics in one of its five interior compartments, and was accompanied by a silver spatula (H 11.5, dia. 9.0 cm; H 4½, dia. 3 9/16 in.). Reproduced from Oppenheim n.d. [1933], pp. 221–22.

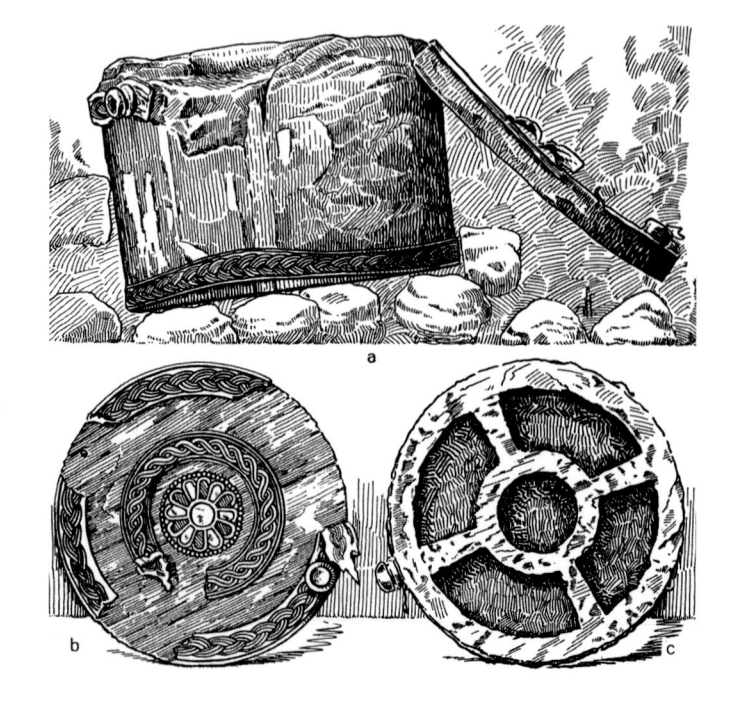

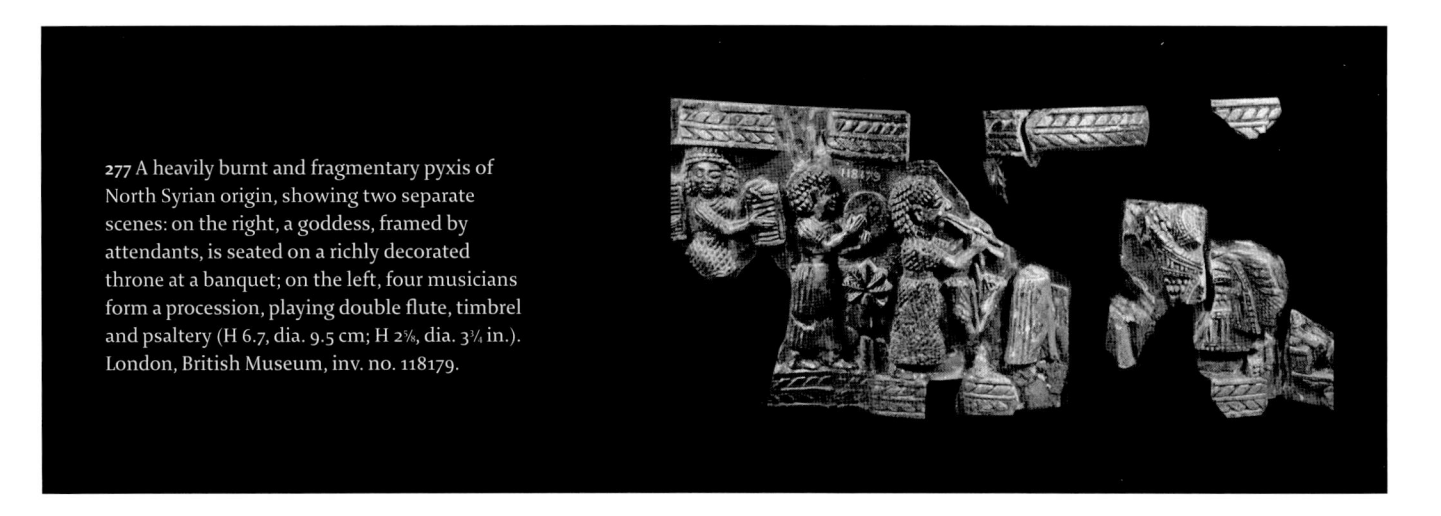

277 A heavily burnt and fragmentary pyxis of North Syrian origin, showing two separate scenes: on the right, a goddess, framed by attendants, is seated on a richly decorated throne at a banquet; on the left, four musicians form a procession, playing double flute, timbrel and psaltery (H 6.7, dia. 9.5 cm; H 2⅝, dia. 3¾ in.). London, British Museum, inv. no. 118179.

decorated with Assyrian winged, human-headed bulls, on the table beside him in the relief of the Garden Scene (**240**, p. 152). Further evidence for the use of cosmetic pyxides by men rather than women would be welcome, but the absence of pyxides, or indeed any small ivory object, from the queens' tombs is significant.

A fragmentary pyxis found by Loftus in the Burnt Palace (BM 118179, **277**) belongs to a different North Syrian group. It shows a goddess seated in an elaborate throne with a procession of musicians behind her, two of whom are represented frontally. The remains of an inscription on the pyxis, needless to say damaged, can be interpreted tentatively as 'lXXXX+ [b]yt [g]š' ('For XXXX+ of Bit Agusi').[61] Bit Agusi (with its capital, Arpad), is in the Aleppo region and was one of the early first millennium Aramaean states. The inscription, even if the reading is correct, need not mean that the pyxis was made in Bit Agusi, or necessarily that it belonged to a man of Bit Agusi. However, it differs in both subject and style from 'flame and frond' pyxides and was probably made at a different centre.

Only fragments of pyxides, carved in steatite (soapstone) or chlorite, were found at the principal North Syrian city, Carchemish, but, significantly, they too are carved in a different style from the others, and one that matches the well-documented tenth- to ninth-century reliefs from the site. As Winter comments: 'these parallels…strongly suggest that they all belong to a local tradition of carving which included soft stone for small objects as well as harder stone for architectural reliefs'. She expands this comparison by stating that 'fixed monuments such as major sculptures and architectural reliefs are most likely to have been carved locally, by local craftsmen, to exemplify the taste of the local population to which the monuments would be directed'.[62] Pyxides seem to be an essentially North Syrian product, probably dating to the tenth and ninth centuries, with regional variations reflecting the work of different centres of production.

FAN HANDLES

Another typically North Syrian production was the fan handle, examples of which were found by both Loftus and Mallowan in the Burnt Palace. They consist of a number of separate elements, the most distinctive part being the central section, which is decorated with human figures – single, double or quadruple. They have palmette capitals on their heads, surmounted by lotus blossoms, and stand on pedestal bases, also sometimes in the form of a palmette. These are then fixed to a staff with a knob at the end. The height of the fan handle – that is, without the whisk, feathers or fronds – is in the region of 40 cm (15¾ in.). Mallowan found one in the centre of the Throne Room of the Burnt Palace (ND 1095, **278**). Two naked women are set back to back, their hands by their sides. They are wearing tall crowns, still showing traces of the gold foil that once covered them. Their hair is parted centrally and falls in twisted ringlets onto their shoulders. The pupils of their eyes are drilled, and their faces are of the usual North Syrian type. They have bangles on their wrists.

The Influence of Regionalism on Furniture and the Minor Arts 175

FAR LEFT 278 A fine North Syrian fan handle, formed from a pair of naked women, carved back to back; they would have been standing on a pedestal, once fixed to a staff, with a palmette capital and lotus blossom decoration (16.6 × 5.8 cm; 6½ × 2¼ in.). ND 1095, Baghdad, National Museum of Iraq.

LEFT 279 Syro-Phoenician fan handle in the form of four youths, facing outwards from a stylized tree; each holds a stem that develops into feathery palm leaves above (H 13.2 cm; 5¹⁄₁₆ in.). There were holes in the top for the attachment of feathers or fronds, and the handle would presumably have been mounted on a staff. London, British Museum, inv. no. 118196.

ABOVE 280 Syro-Phoenician fan handle in the form of two naked women and two men, holding the stems of palmettes on which squat four monkeys; the men wear long pleated garments, open from the knee, and the women wear heavy anklets, and have their hair falling in ringlets (H 12.2 cm; 4¹³⁄₁₆ in.). London, British Museum, inv. no. 118253.

Also found in the Burnt Palace are similar Syro-Phoenician versions. While the general design is the same, the Syro-Phoenician men and women have more rounded features, the men are clothed, and the figures are topped by elaborate foliate capitals and stand on complex pedestals. BM 118196 has four men, back to back, wearing short wigs and long garments, revealing, in each case, one of their lower legs (**279**), while BM 118253 shows two nude females and two youths standing on an elaborate palm capital (**118253**).[63] Elena Scigliuzzo attributes these fan handles to the 'wig and wing' workshop.[64]

Although they vary in detail and were worked in different centres, the two groups of fan handles are alike in placing human figures above the part of the handle held by the attendant. These pieces must have been heavy and unwieldy, and were presumably used on ceremonial occasions. Once more, they demonstrate the pattern of a similar type of object or motif being used across the area but worked in individual ways.

The Assyrian fan handle was much more practical. The handle fits the attendant's hand and the long whisk of horsehair or fan of feathers or fronds extends from it. Ninth-century fan handles terminate in a ram's head, but by the seventh century they are a little more complicated. On the Garden relief of Ashurbanipal (**240**, p. 152) the bottom ends of the fan handles are concealed in the attendants' hands, while at the top there is an abbreviated, stylized tree with three volutes, possibly with another decorative feature above. Mallowan found an example of one of these in Well NN (ND 2218, **117**, p. 96).[65] Two figures kneel on either side of a stylized tree above the triple volutes; it is not certain if they are male or female. It seems possible that the use of a fan, like that of a parasol, may have been confined to the king, except, occasionally (as in the Garden relief), when the queen also benefited from this privilege.

281 A superb and unique 'bird's nest' bowl, found in the Queen's Treasury (Room S10 in Fort Shalmaneser); birds' heads peep over the rim of the bowl and, on the rectangular handle, a winged sphinx salutes a stylized tree (11.2 × 5 cm; 4⅜ × 2 in.). ND 7648, Sydney, Nicholson Museum.

The Influence of Regionalism on Furniture and the Minor Arts 177

282 A Phoenician flask and bowl in three parts, still bearing traces of gold overlay; it was found in Well AJ in the North West Palace. The flask itself (left), cut from the tusk of a small elephant, is in the form of a stylized woman wearing a tall wig and cupping her breasts in her hands; a 'lion-bowl' (below) is fitted on top by means of a tenon, and a lid closes the wider end (flask: H 28–31, W 7.4–14.5 cm; 11–11$^{13}/_{16}$ × 2$^{15}/_{16}$–5$^{11}/_{16}$ in.; bowl: 7.8 × 7.5 cm; 3$^{1}/_{16}$ × 2$^{15}/_{16}$ in.; lid: 9 × 7.4 × 0.3 cm; 3$^{9}/_{16}$ × 2$^{15}/_{16}$ × $^{1}/_{8}$ in.). IM 79505–79507, Baghdad, National Museum of Iraq.

BOWLS AND FLASKS

Bowls were a standard piece of equipment across the region, and there are numerous different types and versions, made in a variety of materials, the finest in ivory. An elegant Phoenician example from Room S10 (ND 7648, **281**)[66] has a sphinx sitting on the handle, saluting a stylized tree, while a pair of birds' heads peer over the edge of the bowl – a 'bird's nest' bowl. Also popular was an Egyptian type, common in the New Kingdom, in which the bowls were held in the extended arms of swimming maidens. Another common type has a human hand holding the bowl. Some of these bowls were attached by a tube to a flask; the bowl was filled through the tube with precious fluid from the flask, which was then poured out in a ritual act. As usual, there are marked regional differences in the types of flask and bowl.

Once again, it was the sludge at the bottom of Well AJ that preserved outstanding and relatively complete versions of both North Syrian and Phoenician flasks, together with their associated fittings and bowls. The North Syrian flask is a unique, richly carved 'flame and frond' example, with a woman-head stopper (IM 79508–79510; **176**, p. 122; **237**, p. 149). A superb lion bowl (IM 79511), with no fewer than four leonine heads, was found nearby (**238**, p. 150).

The Phoenician version, although it too consists of separate parts – flask, lid and lion bowl – is considerably simpler. The flask was carved from a relatively small tusk, with the tip cut off; the upper end was formed into the head and torso of a woman. Her hair, or Egyptian-style tripartite wig, is arranged in long tresses, delineated with cross chisel marks; the fall of the hair exposes her large, pierced ears. Her eyebrows are arched, her eyes almond shaped with drilled pupils, her nose fine and her mouth small. She has a double-stranded necklace, armlets and bracelets, and her hands, with elongated fingers, cup her small breasts. Many fragments of the wigs and elongated fingers of such flasks were found by Loftus in the Burnt Palace, as well as slightly different, plainer versions. The lion bowl was found in the well at the same level as the flask and is formed of the foreparts of a single lion, which grasps the bowl with its forepaws. The mane forms a point between the ears, which are laid flat on the head. Liquids from the flask could pass through a tube into the bowl and then be poured out as a libation (IM 79505–79507, **282**).[67] Also found was a lid to close the wider open end of the flask.

BRIDLE HARNESS

Chariots were standard equipment across the Near East from the mid-second millennium BC onwards, and were essential equipment for all armies. Because of their cultural and practical importance, they were sometimes included as grave goods in the tombs of royal and noble subjects. Like pyxides, fan handles, flasks and bowls, equestrian bridle-harness ornaments were used by the different military forces, and varied in form and style according to their area of production. They consisted of pairs of blinkers and frontlets – face-piece ornaments, fixed to the brow-band of the bridle. Although the finest pieces were found in Wells AJ and NN in the North West Palace, the majority were found in Room SW37 in Fort Shalmaneser.

Typically Levantine are spade-shaped blinkers and tall, hinged frontlets. Bronze examples of this type were found *in situ* on the bridles of the chariot horses found in the entrance to Tomb 79 at Salamis. Mounted on leather, these blinkers and the accompanying frontlets were clearly in use. Whether it was practical to use some of the relatively heavy ivory examples in battle, or whether they were employed only on ceremonial occasions remains uncertain.

Two sets of the most elaborate spade-shaped blinkers and hinged frontlets, both belonging to the Phoenician tradition, were found in Wells AJ and NN. One group has an obvious and strong debt to the art of Egypt, while the other is a less sophisticated Phoenician version. The sphinx ND 2244 (**283**)[68] belongs to the first group: it is framed by its wings and sits elegantly in the spade of the blinker. It is crowned with a sun disc and *uraeus* set on the *nemes* headcloth, and has an *usekh* collar and apron. Suspended from its chest is a crowned and winged *uraeus*. In the handle is a cartouche set on a papyrus plant and topped by sun disc and *atef* feathers; similar cartouches occupy the lower section of the hinged frontlet. The hieroglyphs in the cartouches

ABOVE 283 A classic Phoenician spade-shaped blinker (left side of the bridle), one of four found in Well NN and Well AJ in the North West Palace; a superbly balanced, crowned and winged, human-headed sphinx occupies the blinker, and a cartouche with hieroglyphs the handle (10.3 × 18.5 × 1.5 cm; 4¹/₁₆ × 7¼ × ⅝ in.). ND 2244, New York, Metropolitan Museum of Art.

BELOW 284 A less elegant Phoenician spade-shaped blinker (right side of the bridle), one of five from Well AJ in the North West Palace; the crowded design – a falcon-headed sphinx striding over the prostrate body of an Asiatic wearing a decorated helmet – occupies the entire surface (9.7 × 17.1 × 1.3 cm; 3¹³/₁₆ × 6¾ × ½ in.). IM 79565, Baghdad, National Museum of Iraq.

285 A frontlet consisting of two hinged pieces, with the figure of the Egyptian god Bes below (left, IM 79580) and a helmeted, bearded warrior or god above (right, IM 79577): the figure of Bes has a leonine head with two horns, gaping mouth and drooping moustache, wears a sleeved and belted garment, and clenches his fists across his chest; the warrior/god wears a tall, pointed helmet and is armed with a sword and a strung bow, with a quiver supported on a strap crossing his shoulder (lower section 18.8 × 6.8 × 2.1 cm; 7⅜ × 2¹¹⁄₁₆ × ¹³⁄₁₆; upper section 20.8 × 6.8 × 1.9 cm; 8³⁄₁₆ × 2¹¹⁄₁₆ × ¾ in.). IM 79577, 27980, Baghdad, National Museum of Iraq.

are, as usual, corrupted but can be read as: 'Words spoken "I give to you. . .".'[69] A blinker from the second group, IM 79565, is generally similar in form but different in spirit. The shape of the blinker itself is less elegant, with a thicker handle and less sweeping curves, and it lacks a frame. The scene, showing a falcon-headed sphinx striding over a fallen Asiatic, crowds the surface of the panel (**284**).[70]

There are similar differences between the hinged frontlets of the two sets. The finer group shows goddesses in the upper section and gods in the lower.[71] The winged goddess of IM 79584 has a Hathor crown on a tripartite wig and an *usekh* collar. Her wings fan out beside her, her arms resting on the wings and her hands holding tall, plumed feathers. She is wearing a long dress that follows her curves.[72] The hinges of the frontlets are framed by bands of *uraei*, and there are voluted palmette flowers at the tops and bottoms. The frontlets of the second group[73] are shorter and narrower and lack the bands of *uraei* (IM 79577, 79580, **285**).[74] The upper frontlet is occupied by a helmeted warrior or god, while a rather clumsy clothed version of the popular fertility god Bes can be seen on the lower; the two thus lack the cohesion of the motifs of the first set.

These two sets echo the division between the very finest Phoenician products, made at a single centre, and those that, while still obviously Phoenician in style, differ significantly in detail, suggesting production at a different centre. Such

The Influence of Regionalism on Furniture and the Minor Arts 181

286 A shield-shaped blinker, decorated with a *wedjat* eye that rests on a basket, and a human arm, the hand of which is (unusually) clenched (8.9 × 8.9 × 1 cm; 3½ × 3½ × ⅜ in.). ND 10332, Baghdad, National Museum of Iraq.

'mistress of animals' motif, and blinkers decorated with sphinxes. The triangular frontlet ND 10518 shows a nude woman, represented frontally and holding lotus flowers and the hind legs of a pair of lions. Her hair is arranged in ringlets, and she wears a phylactery or rectangular jewel with pendants on her forehead, trilobate earrings, a beaded necklace and heavy anklets. She is standing on a lotus flower below a Phoenician version of a winged disc (**288**).[77] The human-headed sphinx of ND 10399 has its head turned to the front and wings outspread. The hair is parted centrally and falls in ringlets onto the large decorated collar (**289**).[78] Parts of the wings and collar were painted.

A frontlet with just such a naked woman and a blinker with a sphinx, which resemble Syro-Phoenician examples, can be seen on a sculpture of a horse's head found at Zinjirli (**287**). Similar frontlets and blinkers, made in bronze, are known across and beyond the area, in the sanctuary at Samos and even in Etruria.

variation is common and can also be seen, for instance, in the panels with pairs of pharaoh figures equipped with sceptre and jug (**206–207**, p. 140).

No example of the Well type of bridle harness was found in Room SW37, though more than 120 pieces were excavated there; these reflect the usual assemblage of a variety of shapes, subjects and styles. There were more than sixty of the simplest form of blinker,[75] which is shield-shaped, is based on Egyptian originals and was light enough to have been used on a regular basis, though bronze examples were probably more practical. The most popular decorative motif was the *wedjat* eye, which was worked in a variety of ways, modelled, incised and painted or stained (ND 10332, **286**).[76] Other motifs on the blinkers include the scarab beetle and stylized trees.

Many of the remaining blinkers are simpler, smaller, lighter, spade-shaped examples, decorated with simple bosses, sphinxes or rather clumsy seated youths, while the frontlets are sub-triangular, decorated with floral motifs or frontal examples of the 'mistress of animals' design below winged discs. Elena Scigliuzzo has attributed some of these to the 'wig and wing' group, including frontlets with the

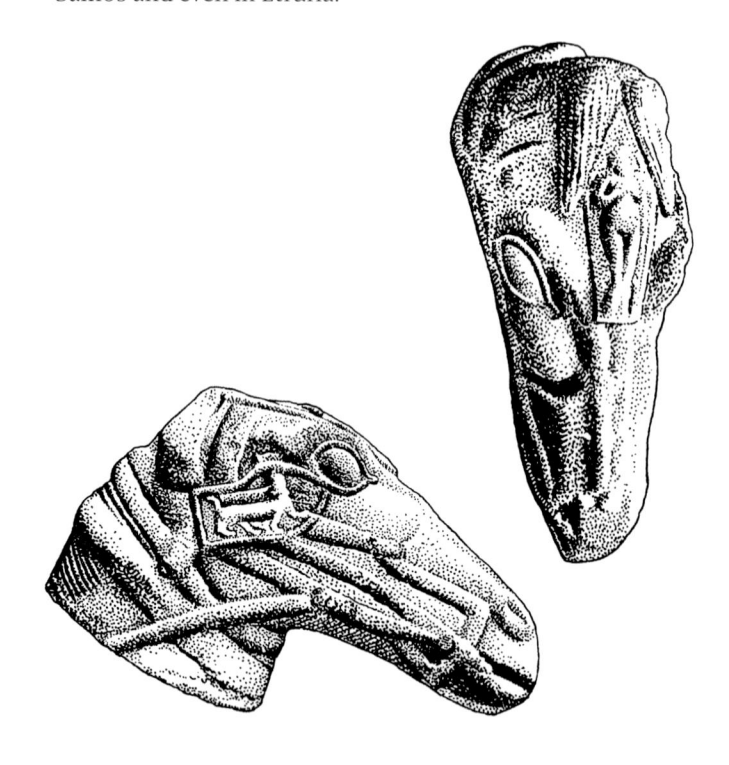

287 Drawings of a stone sculpture of a horse's head found in the Iron Age citadel of Zinjirli and now in the Staatliche Museen in Berlin; they show a spade-shaped blinker with a striding sphinx and a triangular frontlet with a naked maiden, as employed on the bridle. Reproduced from Luschan 1911, pp. 336–37, figs 248–49.

182 Ancient Ivory

RIGHT 288 A triangular frontlet, with a design of a naked maiden, standing on a lotus flower and holding lotus flowers and the hind legs and tails of two lions; she is richly bejewelled, wearing a rectangular frontlet with pendants, earrings, a beaded collar and bangles on her ankles, and her hair falls in ringlets; above is a winged sun disc flanked by *uraei* (16.1 × 7 × 2.6 cm; 6⅜ × 2¾ × 1 in.). ND 10518, New York, Metropolitan Museum of Art.

BELOW 289 A spade-shaped blinker, framed by a guilloche band, showing a human-headed sphinx advancing to the left, with the head represented frontally and framed by the wings and a large collar below; there are traces of colour on the wings, hair and collar (13 × 7.3 × 2 cm; 5⅛ × 2⅞ × ¾ in.). ND 10495, Baghdad, National Museum of Iraq

PHOENICIAN STANDS

Another type of object concentrated in Room SW37 was a small trapezoidal plaque found in sets of six to ten matching pieces, which once made up stands. These plaques are wider at the base than the top, and either curved or flat; the curved examples were made up into circular stands with a probable diameter of 12–15 cm (4¾–6 in.), and the flat pieces into faceted, hexagonal or octagonal stands (**290**). Their striated backs indicate that they would have been mounted on wooden forms. There is no evidence of bases or lids. As an elegant and stable unit, they may have been used as stands to support shallow libation bowls. About 250 plaques were found in Room SW37, and another two dozen elsewhere in the Fort. This suggests that they may have formed part of a specific consignment of booty, probably from a Phoenician centre.

(ND 10644 and 10649, **291–292**),[79] often in pairs of popular motifs include sphinxes or griffins flanking stylized trees. The sphinxes are usually crowned with the Egyptian double crown on a headcloth and wear an *usekh* collar and apron. Some stride over fallen youths, both Asiatics with long hair and 'Egyptians' with short wigs. The falcon-headed sphinx of ND 10644 walks over a youth in a short Egyptian wig; the feather of Maat (representing truth or justice) rises from the paw. The hieroglyphs in the upper register are mainly unrelated signs, which can be read as 'bring...Beloved of Seth'. The griffin of ND 10469 raises a paw to the floral column or stylized tree in front of it, while on ND 9584 a griffin is shown being slain by a winged hero (**293**).[80] Other human figures include pharaohs, winged goddesses holding winged and crowned *uraei* (ND 10521, **294**)[81] and rows of women. Various versions of the stylized tree also appear (ND 7997, **295**).[82]

AN EGYPTIANIZING CYLINDRICAL CONTAINER

The treasures found in Well AJ include a remarkable and entirely different type of object (IM 79516, **125**, p. 99).[83] This magnificent Egyptianizing ivory shows a triumph scene, based on a very common Egyptian convention of victory: the king slays kneeling foes with a mace or *khopesh*-sword, lifted above his head, ready to deliver the death-blow. Here, curiously, the mace or a *khopesh* has been replaced by an angled feather-fan.[84] The pharaoh, in his blue war crown, wears the heavy *usekh* collar and a short skirt with elaborate apron and long, open overskirt. He is holding a bow and arrows in his left hand. The second figure, with the short wig and bearded face of a Levantine (or Asiatic), is carrying a captured foreign chief over his arm. He too has a collar, short skirt, apron and open overskirt, and holds a very un-Egyptian sceptre with circular disc at the top. A dog walks beside him. Framing the scene are two winged goddesses, 'which are of Egyptian inspiration and show intriguing deviations from Egyptian usage'.[85] The piece is beautifully gilded and inlaid, with large, shaped pieces of inlay, as well as sections of alternate inlay in the garment borders and stalks: both characteristics are typical of Egyptianizing and Ornate Group ivories.

In this brief survey it has been possible to comment on no more than a few of the varied types of object that the ivories found at Nimrud might have decorated. The variety, both of object and design, reflects the strong regionalism of the Levant, with the finest Phoenician works following, but adapting, Egyptian motifs and designs, while those belonging to the many North Syrian polities were influenced by a different, Syro-Turkish world. And Assyria, of course, followed its own distinctive way, though the evidence of this from Nimrud is scant.

290 Drawings by Jean Williamson of sets of trapezoidal plaques, which, when assembled, would have formed faceted (above) and truncated conical (below) pieces; the striated backs of the plaques indicate that they were mounted on a wooden core. As there is no evidence of lids or bases, they were probably used as elegant and stable stands for cups or bowls. Reproduced from Herrmann 1986, no. 8.

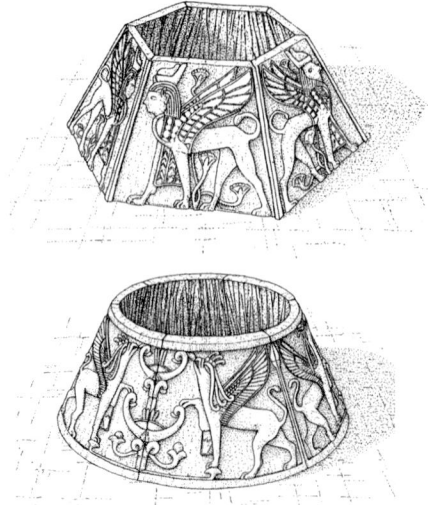

Examples of Phoenician flat and curved trapezoidal plaques, sets of which formed faceted or truncated conical stands.

TOP LEFT 291 One of a set of three flat plaques in two registers; the upper register contains a row of hieroglyphs (mainly miswritten) and the lower a falcon-headed sphinx striding over a prostrate human figure (8 × 7.4 × 0.7 cm; 3⅛ × 2¹⁵⁄₁₆ × ¼ in.). ND 10644, Baghdad, National Museum of Iraq. Photograph Mick Sharp.

TOP RIGHT 292 One of a set of three curved plaques, showing a rampant griffin, browsing on the foliage of a stylized tree (6.5 × 8.3 × 0.7 cm, dia. at base c. 17 cm; 2⁹⁄₁₆ × 3¼ × ¼ in., dia. at base c. 6¾ in.). ND 10469, Baghdad, National Museum of Iraq. Photograph Mick Sharp.

ABOVE LEFT 293 A fragmentary curved plaque showing a winged hero, crowned with the sun disc and wearing a *shendyt* kilt, fighting a griffin, which turns its head to accept the spear; the griffin rests one paw on a voluted palmette flower (6.5 × 3.7 × 0.8 cm, dia. at base c. 14 cm; 2⁹⁄₁₆ × 1⁷⁄₁₆ × ⁵⁄₁₆, dia. at base c. 5½ in.). ND 9584, Cleveland Museum of Art.

CENTRE RIGHT 294 One of a set of three curved plaques, showing a winged goddess crowned with a sun disc, holding a lily in one hand and a winged and crowned *uraeus* in the other (6.1 × 7.1 × 0.7 cm, dia. at base c. 24 cm; 2⅜ × 2¹¹⁄₁₆ × ¼ in., dia. at base c. 9½ in.). ND 10521, Boston, Museum of Fine Arts.

BOTTOM RIGHT 295 An unusually broad curved plaque, with a stylized tree formed of voluted branches that end in fronds and papyrus flowers (4.8 × 6.6 cm; 1⅞ × 2⅝ in.). University of Melbourne, Australia.

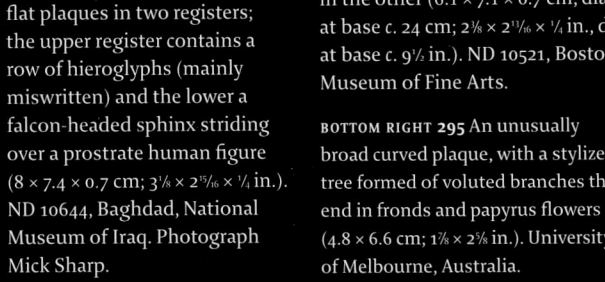

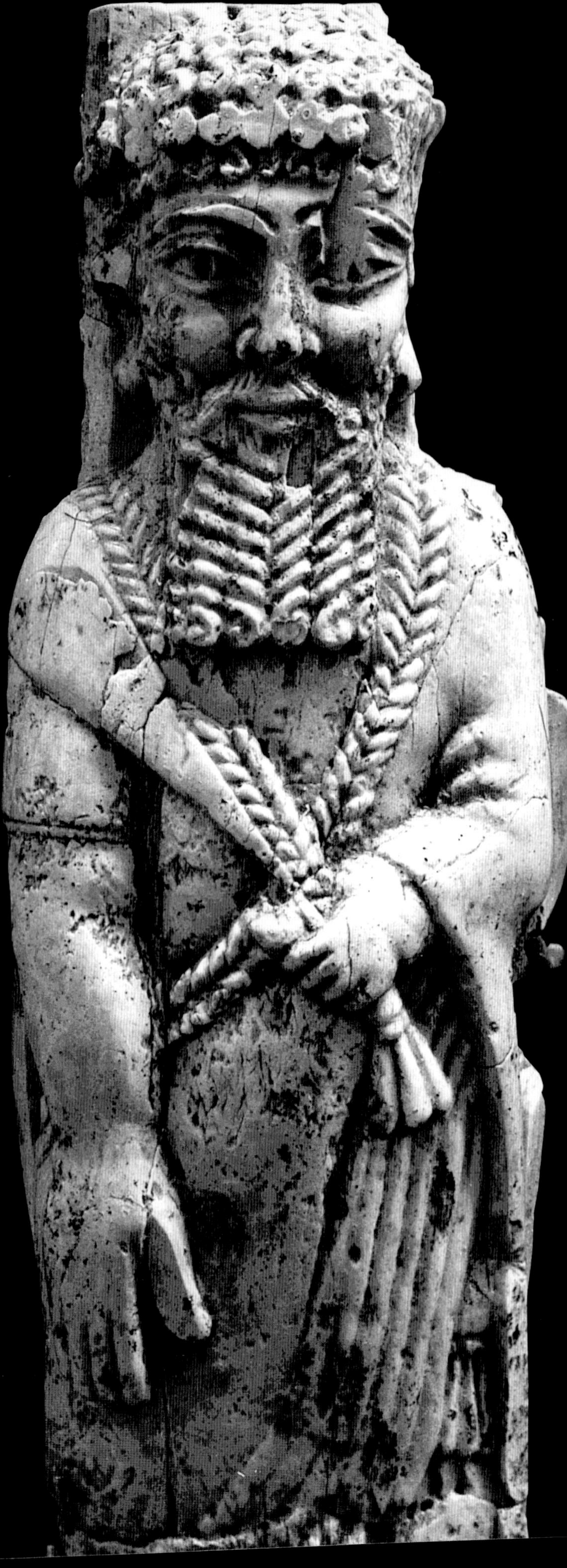

Chapter 7

The Age of Ivory

Ivory as a material has a unique and fascinating appeal by virtue of its rich warm colour and sheen. Since very early times, ivory has been synonymous with luxury, as witnessed in the Old Testament reference to Ahab's 'house of ivory', the epitome of luxurious living.*

It was the discovery of thousands of ivories at Nimrud that revealed the wealth and sophistication of the Levant in the final years of the second millennium and the early first millennium BC. For many years it had been thought that the centuries between the end of the so-called 'International Age', with its series of communicating empires, and the time of Assyrian ascendancy in the ninth century BC was a 'Dark Age'. The Hittite empire had collapsed and Rameses III (r. c. 1184–1153) had fought three great wars against a league of invaders, generally known as the 'Sea Peoples'. All along the Levantine coast, Canaanite cities, such as Ugarit, Dor and Ashkelon, were destroyed, as were cities in Cyprus and even some in inland Syria.

The resulting power vacuum led to a new political map of the area. In northern Syria the fall of the Hittites led to a resurgence of indigenous culture, manifested in the rise of the Aramaeans, while from the end of the twelfth century BC the Phoenician city-states, profiting from the decline of Egypt, went from strength to strength, stepping into the commercial void left by the fall of Ugarit. The Phoenicians traded vigorously with Cyprus and with the newly established polity of Philistia, located along the southern Levantine coast. Inland they came into contact with the developing power of Israel. This pattern of a series of independent minor powers underlies the regionalism reflected in the art of the region. And it is the art, specifically the ivories, that reveals the great wealth of these states at this time.

However, a shadow was cast over the area by the growing power of Assyria. While cities along the Mediterranean coast remained independent for much of the eighth century BC, those closer to Assyria, especially those along the River Khabur, were less fortunate. They were sited on one of the main east–west trading routes that connected the core Assyrian lands with the west, and Guzana (modern Tell Halaf) was incorporated into the Assyrian empire probably by the middle of the eighth century. Thus the probable dates for the *floruit* of ivory production along the Mediterranean coast may be between c. 1050 and 800 BC, while that in north-east Syria would have ceased fifty years earlier, the political background providing a framework into which it can be fitted.

296 The upper part of a North Syrian 'round-cheeked and ringletted' panel, showing a bearded male, carved in high relief and represented frontally; his hair is curled and his beard spade shaped, and he wears a shawl over his tunic (13.7 × 4.1 cm; 5⅜ × 1⅝ in.). ND 10697, Baghdad, National Museum of Iraq. Image © Werner Forman Archive.

Trying to date the ivories

The information provided by the archaeological context of the ivories is limited. Kalhu was founded in the early ninth century BC and the city was destroyed by the combined forces of the Medes and the Babylonians in 614 and 612 BC, so these are the earliest and latest possible dates for the deposition of the ivories. However, the majority had probably been stored there not later than the end of the eighth century – the time when Sargon II moved to his new capital city of Dur Sharrukin (Khorsabad), soon to be abandoned because of his death in 705. Thereafter, Nineveh became the capital. Although Kalhu enjoyed a second flourishing during the reign of Esarhaddon (r. 680–669 BC), most booty acquired in the seventh century would probably have been stored at Nineveh rather than Kalhu.

Another possible strand of evidence to aid grouping the ivories may be the various store-rooms in which the booty was deposited. Room SW7, for instance, has a collection of chair-backs, originally mounted on wooden frames, most of which are Syrian in style and are often dated to the eighth century BC. The huge assemblage in Room SW37 is mixed, but contains a number of specific collections, such as small Phoenician stands and bridle harness, as well as some 'champlevé' ivories, paralleled at Samaria in the kingdom of Israel. These may all have been parts of a single consignment of booty from the west, perhaps deposited towards the end of the eighth century.

Comparison of ivories with bas-reliefs and stelae is another aid to dating, which may suggest locations for some of the ivories. The most obvious group is, of course, the ivories of Assyria, which can be dated by comparison with the fine series of bas-reliefs from the various Assyrian cities: these illustrate changes in fashion from the ninth to the seventh centuries. There are also sculptures from sites along the Syro-Turkish border. The rulers of cities such as Sam'al, Carchemish and Guzana, embellished their processional ways, their palaces and temples with sculptures, both freestanding statues and bas-reliefs, and there were also funerary stelae. Typically, these vary from city to city and illustrate the differences between styles prevalent in north-east and north-west Syria. Identifying themselves was a preoccupation of these new political entities, which had to demonstrate their wealth and power – art was a key means of establishing identity.

One of the most remarkable and individual of the new North Syrian states was the Aramaean kingdom of Bit Bahiani, with its capital of Guzana. One of its rulers, Kapara, built himself the extraordinary Temple-Palace on a platform, which was entered via the Scorpion Gate. The sculptures decorating the entrance to the palace were more sophisticated versions of the re-used, earlier sculptures that lined the walls of his platform (**297**). The early series, in particular, depicts scenes of everyday life and the environment in a lively fashion. In E. D. van Buren's view: 'the sense of awe and dynamic force rendered by these sculptures is overwhelming'.[1] The distinctive style of the sculptures, with their human physiognomy and animal musculature, is repeated on 'flame and frond' ivories, the minor art reflecting the major. The 'flame and frond' repertoire is impressive, with its range of ceremonial pieces, including massive flasks and spoon-stoppers, fan handles and pyxides, and elaborate furniture, and it reflects the artistic vigour of this Aramaean city. Nearly all known 'flame and frond' ivories were found at Nimrud, but a few were found at Hasanlu, an important Mannaean city in north-west Iran (sacked *c.* 800 BC), at Tell Halaf, at Hamath (the site of Hama, destroyed by Sargon II *c.* 720 BC), at nearby Tell Afis (thought to be the site of Hazrek), and in the Idaean Cave in Crete, a shrine sacred to Zeus, at the top of Mount Ida.

Another unusual North Syrian style-group is the 'round-cheeked and ringletted' ivories, with their fat-faced sphinxes (ND 10447, **181**, p. 127).[2] Similar sphinxes can be seen on column bases found at Zinjirli, and it is generally agreed that this style-group may have been made there, probably in the eighth century. Although parallels with sculptures and some ivory furniture legs and fragments reinforce the attribution of this group to Zinjirli, once again, the ivories found there constitute a mixed assemblage, including Phoenician, North Syrian and Assyrian material, and suggest an ongoing tradition of elite exchange.

Unfortunately the sculptural sequence is much more fragmented in central Syria and Phoenician centres. A fine stela, with a winged sphinx wearing a version of the Egyptian double crown in the rather squat proportions typical of Syro-Phoenician ivories (**298**),[3] was found out of context in the Umayyad mosque in Damascus, which was built on the ruins of the great temple to Hadad. Hazael (r. c. 843–803 BC), the successful king of Damascus, was able to exploit a period of Assyrian decline. Ivory labels with his name have been found in Fort Shalmaneser at Nimrud and at Arslan Tash (ancient Hadatu), east of Carchemish, as well as on bronze bridle frontlets found in the Heraion (temple to Hera) on the island of Samos in southern Greece, and in Eretria. The Arslan Tash ivories include a number of Syro-Phoenician pieces, such as sphinxes, pharaoh figures flanking central motifs, examples of the 'woman at the window' and cattle, one of which, with a pair of ram-headed sphinxes, between stylized trees, is generally similar to the sculpture from Damascus. Many find parallels among the Nimrud corpus.

ABOVE 297 Sculpture of a lion from the right side of the façade of the Temple–Palace of the Aramaean ruler Kapara at Guzana (now Tell Halaf), showing typical North Syrian 'flame and frond' musculature (128 × 220 cm; 50⅜ × 86⅝ in.). Tell Halaf, Palace of Kapara, inv. no. Ba 4. Reproduced from Oppenheim n.d. [1933].

BELOW 298 A Syro-Phoenician basalt relief found in a secondary context in the wall of the Umayyad mosque in Damascus. A winged, human-headed sphinx wears an Egyptian double crown. Damascus, National Museum, inv. no. SO 30. Image © Erich Lessing/akg-images.

The Age of Ivory

Another important Syrian power was Hamath, Neo-Hittite until the late ninth century BC but then Aramaeized. A series of sculptures was found there, as well as a range of different ivories, including some fine 'flame and frond' pieces. Hamath controlled the neighbouring state of Luhuti (Aramaic: Lu'ash). One of a group of ivory frontlets, with a 'mistress of animals' holding lotus flowers, and lions under a Phoenician version of the winged disc,[4] has the word 'Lu'ash' inscribed on its back. She can be compared with many Syro-Phoenician 'woman at the window' panels.

In the nineteenth century some fragmentary stelae were found on the island of Arvad, an important Phoenician city-state frequently mentioned in the Assyrian annals and famous for its shipbuilding. Arvad and its equivalent on the mainland, Antaradus (modern Tartus), were northern Phoenician emporia, which traded with central and northern Syria and south-east Turkey. Their different political connections were reflected in their art, as can be seen in some undated sculptures first published by Georges Perrot and Charles Chipiez in 1885 and republished by the Belgian scholar Eric Gubel, who has dated them between 850 and 750 BC.[5] Three stelae show pairs of griffins flanking a stylized tree, and another a couchant sphinx, both below panels of linked palmettes (**299**). The designs can be paralleled by ivories from Nimrud, including a set of delicate openwork panels with similar griffins from the Fort (ND 6434, **300**).[6]

Some poorly preserved *naiskoi* or shrines, now in the Louvre, were found at Sidon. The pediments of the *naiskoi* have friezes of *uraei* above winged discs, while on the sides are figures holding ram-headed sceptres and tall-necked pitchers. Gubel drew attention to their similarity to the panels from Room SW12 that show pharaoh figures with sceptres and jugs, and dated them to *c.* 850–675 BC.[7]

299 Drawings of designs on stelae found by Ernest Renan on the island of Arvad in April 1861 (now in Paris, Musée du Louvre, inv. nos AO 4829, AO 4836). LEFT Opposed griffins on either side of a stylized tree, with a frieze of palmettes above (H of sculpture 49.5 cm; 19½ in.). RIGHT A winged sphinx couchant, beneath a frieze of rows of linked palmettes (H of sculpture 61 cm; 24 in.). Reproduced from Perrot and Chipiez 1884–85, iii, p. 131, fig. 76; p. 129, fig. 73.

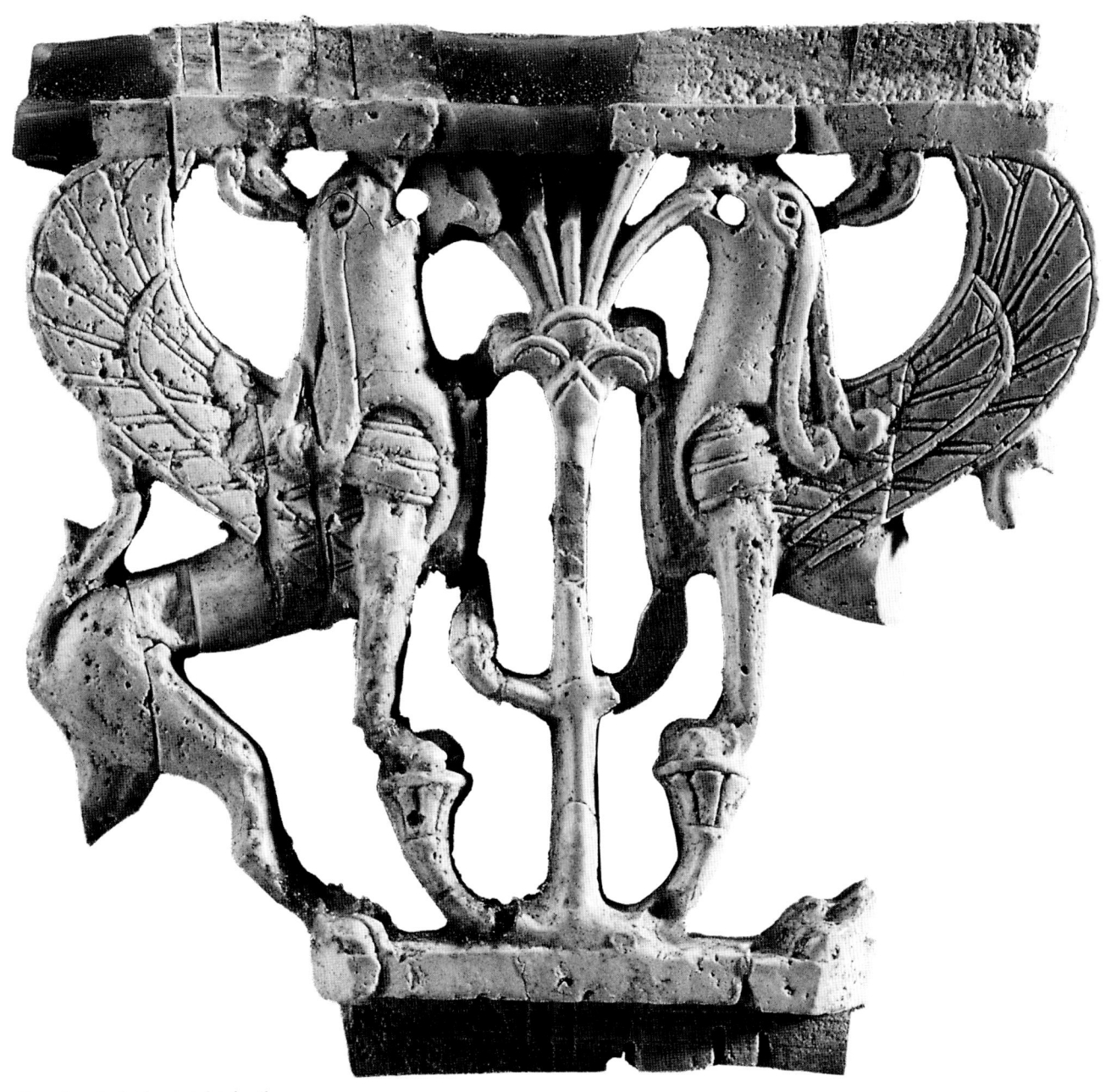

300 One of a set of at least eight, fragile, openwork panels, showing rampant griffins with upward-curving wings, confronting a central stylized tree and nibbling on its fronds (8 × 8.5 × 1.1 cm; 3⅛ × 3⅜ × 7/16 in.). ND 6434, Baghdad, National Museum of Iraq.

Evidence from ivories found elsewhere

A collection of some 300 items was found in Late Bronze Age levels at the important site of Megiddo and illustrates the use of ivory as a luxury item. The collection consisted of pieces from Syria, Anatolia and the Aegean, and the excavator, Gordon Loud, commented that this must represent the hobby of an eccentric Canaanite prince.[8] However, such an eclectic group can better be understood as an example of royal gift exchange:

> The giving of presents forms part of a network of honorific activities – it is as honourable to give as to receive – in which the use or display of treasure for its own intrinsic value becomes a symbol of prestige and status.[9]

The same mechanism probably underlies the varied character of most early first millennium assemblages, for nearly all are mixed. Smashed and burnt ivories were, for instance, found at Hasanlu and consisted of some North Syrian 'flame and frond' examples, some Iranian pieces and some Assyrian examples, as well as some made in the distinctive local style. The ivories found at Zinjirli include Phoenician furniture elements as well as fragments from a number of different Nimrud groups, and can probably be dated no later than the end of the eighth century BC. A collection from Samaria unfortunately lacks a secure context, since most pieces were found in debris in Hellenistic and Roman levels, but they again illustrate the range of material collected by, or given to, the Israelite king: there are North Syrian, Syro-Phoenician and Phoenician ivories, but, significantly, no Assyrian examples. Samaria paid tribute and would not have been honoured with royal gifts.

A few ivories have been found in tombs – in an early first millennium tomb at Tell Halaf, at Salamis in Cyprus and in the Bernardini tomb in Etruria. Vassos Karageorghis, the excavator of Salamis, thinks that the ivories found there were of Phoenician manufacture. They could have been heirlooms, before being deposited in the tomb, which is generally dated to the end of the eighth century. Fragments of delicately inlaid wings of Phoenician style have been retrieved from the grave gifts in the Bernardini tomb. Ivories have also been found in sanctuaries – the Heraion at Samos and the Idaean Cave in Crete – where quantities of bronzes and ivories of many types were found. These include parts of 'flame and frond' fan handles, Syro-Phoenician panels with sphinxes, and fragments of a Phoenician pharaoh statuette. In all these cases, external evidence, though illustrating the geographical spread of the ivories, sheds relatively little light on either their place or date of production; all that can be said is that most contexts predate the end of the eighth century BC.

Phoenician ivories

The *floruit* of Phoenician craft production, not only of ivories, but also of its better-known products – metal bowls, textiles and glass – has to be considered within the context of political and economic history in the early first millennium BC. Tyre became the pre-eminent Phoenician city during the reign of Hiram I (r. 971–939 BC): it was the richest and most famous city of the time and the most important port in the Mediterranean. Tyre continued to flourish during the ninth century, exchanging 'gifts' with, or paying a reasonable tribute to Assyria until the accession of Tiglath-pileser III (r. 745–727 BC), when Assyrian policy changed. The city's time of greatest prosperity was, therefore, from c. 1050 to 740 BC. It is probable that the finest Phoenician ivories were produced in the royal workshops there during those years. The palace was the vital axis of the Tyrian economy,[10] and such elite production would almost certainly have been controlled by the palace. Royal patronage has always stimulated luxury crafts, for it was only in the courts that the necessary resources of labour, materials, tools and workshop premises were readily available on an appropriate scale.

Until it was recognized that the majority of the ivories found at Nimrud can be attributed to the Phoenicians, knowledge of their art had been based on finds – principally their metal bowls – from the outlying regions with which they traded. These bowls were made in bronze, silver or gold, and richly decorated, often with motifs similar to those on the ivories. They have been found in shrines and tombs from

Italy to Iran. Many were found by Austen Henry Layard at Nimrud and others in Cyprus, while recently a magnificent gold example was found in a late eighth-century tomb of the Assyrian queens. It shows a series of Egyptianizing scenes, with designs similar to some on ivories (**113**, p. 94), and it is inscribed, 'Belonging to Queen Yaba, wife of Tiglath-pileser, King of Assyria'.

Like the other traditions, Phoenician ivories belong to a number of style-groups, united by a common technique. Their designs are strongly influenced by both the art of Egypt, adapted to reflect Phoenician ideology, and the Egyptians' technique of carving and decoration. Typical of the finest pieces is highlighting with delicate inlays and overlaying with gold, decoration that gives them a jewel-like appearance, although many examples were simply modelled and highlighted with gold. The finest items, including all those that are inlaid, were probably carved in the royal workshops of Tyre. Others may have been worked in one of the other independent Phoenician centres, such as Byblos or Arvad.

The volume of ivories found at Nimrud illustrates the scale of early first millennium production, while the variation in the standard of work within identical sets suggests the presence of master craftsmen and their assistants or apprentices. However, while it is easy to suggest work by more than one craftsman, it is much harder to identify the work of the same hand, especially across the series. It is unlikely that it will ever be possible to identify the 'master' of this or that ivory, in the way that the great Sir John Beazley was able to do with Greek vase-painting. He had the good fortune to have a number of signed vases, around which he could build his groups. In the case of ivories, what has been established is that craftsmen of varying standards worked as teams, preparing sets of pieces, and that they carved a range of motifs.

THE STATUS OF IVORY

While the Phoenician manufacture of bronze, glass and textiles was designed for international trade, there is a question about whether ivory objects were treated in the same way. As Maria Aubet notes, 'Both Homer and the Biblical texts are unanimous in considering carved ivory as an article of luxury and social prestige (Ezekiel 27:6) or as synonymous with ostentation, power and corruption (Od. 19:565)'.[11] The use of thrones decorated with ivory and gold, such as the one commissioned by Solomon (2 Chronicles 9), would probably have been restricted to palace and temple. Equally, many of the smaller objects, such as elaborate flasks with complicated pouring mechanisms for the dispersal of precious liquids, pyxides, such as the one seen beside Ashurbanipal in the Garden relief from Nineveh or that found in the male tomb at Tell Halaf, and fan handles, were probably reserved for the king. And some bridle equipment was so heavy that it cannot have been used on a daily basis. All these have an obvious ritual purpose, emphasized by the fact that there is a marked absence of small toilet articles or mirrors in ivory, even in the tombs of the Assyrian queens. Phoenician ivory production focused on furniture and ceremonial pieces.

THE PHOENICIAN LEGACY AND REPUTATION

It is surprising that so little is remembered of this nation of entrepreneurs, who can be considered as the ancient equivalent of the Venetians. They were in constant contact with the peoples of the Mediterranean, establishing colonies and sailing to Spain and beyond. In addition to disseminating the alphabet, they also influenced the art and furniture of the Greeks, and ultimately those of Rome and Europe. Phoenician art and its craftsmen were highly praised and prized across the area. Homer in the *Iliad* records that they were expert craftsmen in metal and luxury textiles and exceptional sailors. However, in the later *Odyssey* they are negatively described as traders and pirates: they are 'fine sailors but rogues'.[12] The ancient Greeks considered trade to be incompatible with their concept of aristocracy and ethics: the Homeric ideal assumed that goods were acquired through looting and piracy. In the Greek world the professional trader, and therefore the Phoenicians, belonged to a despised social class.

Although highly regarded in antiquity, Phoenician art has been disparaged by art historians up to the present. In 1908 the archaeologist Sir Cecil Smith questioned 'the artistic influence which such a nation of hucksters is likely to have exercised on an artistic people such as the Greeks'.[13] The scholar William Albright wrote that Phoenician art

> impresses the specialist as bastard, since it disregarded all the precise standards which the Egyptian artists had laboriously built up and preserved. Yet the Phoenicians drew accurately and gracefully; and by discarding much of the conventional conceptualism of Egyptian art, they paved the way for the Greek miracle of the fifth century B.C.[14]

Even as late as 1975, Richard Barnett, the scholar who catalogued the Layard and Loftus ivories, considered that there was a fundamental difference between the social and economic backgrounds of craftsmen in Egypt and Phoenicia:

> In Phoenicia the artisan stood much closer to the commercial class, and less close to the priest, than in Egypt. The Phoenicians made things, not for use in tombs and the future life, but for the world of the living. Their object was to please, and especially to sell to the feminine market.[15]

There is no evidence to support these extraordinary statements. Phoenician ivories were designed for temple and palace rather than for daily use. Barnett went on to suggest that Phoenician art was designed to corrupt the social order: 'Their copious supply of luxury goods' was designed to enrich the 'land-owning aristocracy at the expense of the peasants'.[16] As recently as 2001, Aubet repeated and expanded on the idea of commercial production for a foreign market:

> The Phoenician cities consisted of large centres specializing in the manufacture of luxury and prestige articles destined for international trade and to satisfy the needs of a very restricted social elite in the east for prestige, authority and dominion.[17]

This derogatory and Eurocentric view of Phoenician art was probably based on the distribution of bronzes, the bowls and bridle harness, rather than on the ivories: ivories were not traded but were booty.

The Assyrian legacy

In the mid-nineteenth century that remarkable pioneer Austen Henry Layard revealed the hitherto unknown riches of Assyria. The Assyrians' artistic legacy is magnificent and novel, from the great guardian figures flanking their doorways, to the dated sequence of bas-reliefs panelling the walls of their throne room suites, from the decoration of the principal doors and furniture with bronze plaques, to textiles, jewelry and seals. It was the art of a superpower, designed both to protect the Assyrians from the forces of evil and to safeguard their power. They developed the art of story-telling, recording dramatic scenes that showed their hunting and military exploits in detail, suggesting time and place. This was a new development, foreshadowed in the late second millennium BC, but fully developed only in the early first millennium, and then lost.

Their artistry was outstanding in the carving of soft Mosul marble and in working bronze and other metals. Their favoured decorative techniques – incision and light modelling – are seen in the details worked on the reliefs and in the bronze bands. Compared with their achievements in stone and bronze, their working of ivory was less impressive. It was clearly not a favourite medium. This may have been because of a long tradition in Assyria, for it was a land not rich in timber and other rare materials – the Assyrians were not a nation of carpenters.

Because the changes in Assyrian art from the ninth to the seventh centuries BC are well documented, most Assyrian ivories found at Nimrud can be dated to the ninth century (though one set of panels belongs to the reign of Tiglath-pileser III, r. 745–727 BC). At that period the Assyrians were using the same decorative techniques on ivory as on bronze – light incision or low modelling, neither of which really exploits the advantages of this superb material. However, later, perhaps after large quantities of ivory became available and after the arrival of foreign craftsmen who were more competent at working it, larger pieces, such as the magnificent statuette of a courtier (**53–54**, p. 51),[18] can probably be dated to the eighth century.

There are two surprising facts about Assyrian ivory; one is that so few pieces have been found, and the other relates to their distribution within the site. Those ivories decorated with narrative scenes cluster around elite royal areas – throne daises in the North West Palace, the Nabu Temple, and, in Fort Shalmaneser, around the throne dais in the Residency and the review dais in the South East Courtyard. Ivories were employed to decorate royal thrones. Pieces with animal, floral or geometric motifs were more widely distributed than those bearing scenes, but none were found in the Burnt Palace nor in the great store-rooms in the Fort. There is an obvious difference between the location of Assyrian and non-Assyrian ivories at Nimrud, and the remains there witness to the popularity in Assyrian art of bronze over ivory.

Indeed, the Assyrians seem to have had little interest in ivory. Not only are there few ivories in the characteristic Assyrian style, but it is also clear that the Assyrian kings placed little value on the ivories that they captured. The majority, stripped of their gold overlays, were simply stored, while Assyrian ivories clustered in elite royal areas. So why did the Assyrians go to the trouble of transporting Levantine ivories from the shores of the Mediterranean back to Kalhu, if they had no liking or use for them? If all they wanted was the gold overlays, these could easily have been removed on the spot, when the booty was taken.

In the ancient world, art served an important purpose: it was designed to protect deities and kings from evil. Clearly the Levantine ivories had failed to protect their original owners. However, it was Assyrian policy to empty the palaces of defeated enemies, because it was essential to remove the symbols of royalty. By so doing they unwittingly preserved an outstanding record of the art of the Levant, saving for posterity the otherwise lost art of the early first millennium, including that of the Phoenicians.

301 The upper section of a Phoenician hinged frontlet found in Well AJ, showing a winged goddess wearing the Hathor crown and holding tall plumed feathers; her arms rest along the tops of her wings and below is a frieze of *uraei* (H 22.6 cm; 8⅞ in.). IM 79584, Baghdad, National Museum of Iraq. (For the lower section of the frontlet see 239, p. 151.)

The Age of Ivory 195

THE ANCIENT NEAR EAST

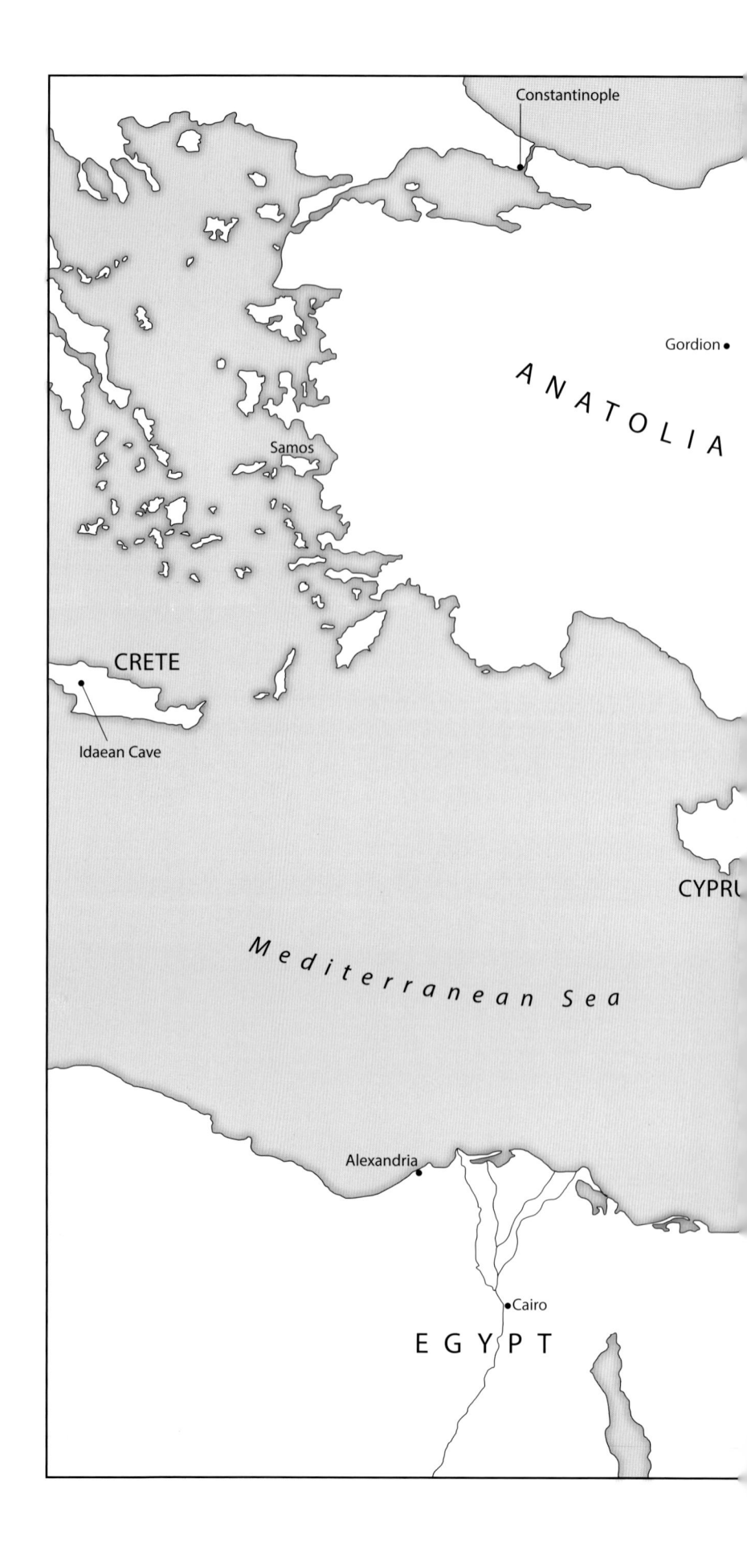

Notes

PREFACE

*Mallowan 1966, i, 32.
1. Layard 1849, ii, 8.
2. Barnett 1975, 24.
3. Herrmann 1992, no. 224.
4. Herrmann and Laidlaw n.d. [2009], no. 356a.
5. BM 127412.

INTRODUCTION

*Layard 1849, i, 2–3.
1. Herrmann and Laidlaw n.d. [2009], no. 349.
2. Spar 2008.
3. Liverani 2008, 166.
4. Baker 1966, 60.
5. Simpson 1995, 1654.
6. Margueron 2008, 238.
7. Barnett 1982, 25.
8. Gitin 1997, 101–02.
9. Herrmann and Laidlaw n.d. [2009], no. 223.
10. Herrmann 1992, no. 177.
11. Herrmann 1986, no. 904.
12. Barnett 1975, 61–62.

CHAPTER 1

*McCall 2008, 65.
1. Waterfield 1963, 13.
2. Ibid., 33.
3. Layard 1849, i, 1–2.
4. Waterfield 1963, 39.
5. Ibid., 4.
6. Ibid., 7, 9.
7. Larsen 1994, 23ff.
8. Waterfield 1963, 116.
9. Layard 1849, i, 25.
10. Ibid., 26.
11. Ibid., 29–30; Herrmann and Laidlaw n.d. [2009], no. 79.
12. Layard 1849, i, 4.
13. Reade 2008, 4.
14. Layard 1849, ii, 8.
15. Larsen 1994, 102.
16. Ibid., 104.
17. Barnett 1975, 23–24.
18. *The Athenaeum* (24 Mar. 1855), 351; see Barnett 1975, 24.
19. *The Mansell Collection of Photographs of the Principal Historical and Religious Monuments which are Exhibited in the Babylonian and Assyrian Galleries of the National Collection* (London, n.d.).
20. British Museum, *A Guide to the Babylonian and Assyrian Antiquities*, 2nd edn (London, 1908).
21. Barnett 1975, p. iii.
22. Mallowan 1966, i, 26.
23. Herrmann and Laidlaw n.d. [2009], no. 123.
24. Ibid., no. 348.
25. Christie 1977, 457.
26. Mallowan 1966, i, 163.
27. Ibid., 151–57.
28. Ibid., 148–51; Herrmann and Laidlaw n.d. [2009], no. 44.
29. Mallowan 1966, i, 150–51.
30. Mallowan 1952a, 15.
31. Herrmann and Laidlaw n.d. [2009], no. 213.
32. Ibid., no. 341.
33. IM 79529; Herrmann and Laidlaw n.d. [2009], no. 242.
34. Oates and Oates 2001, 82.
35. Herrmann and Laidlaw n.d. [2009], no. 263.
36. Mallowan 1966, ii, 369.
37. Oates and Oates 2001, 145.
38. Oates 1959, 104–06.
39. Oates 1961, 3–5.
40. Herrmann 1992, no. 110.
41. Herrmann and Laidlaw 2013, no. T1.
42. Ibid., no. T73.
43. Oates and Oates 2001, 145.
44. Layard 1849–53, i, p. vi.
45. Herrmann and Laidlaw n.d. [2009], nos 99 and 100.
46. Ibid., no. 110.
47. Reade 1965, 127.
48. Roaf 1983.
49. At the time of writing, one volume remains to be completed.

CHAPTER 2

*Isaiah 10:5–6.
1. Grayson 1991, 218–19.
2. Mallowan 1966, i, 65.
3. Herrmann and Laidlaw n.d. [2009], no. 49.
4. Oates and Oates 2001, 41.
5. Herrmann and Laidlaw n.d. [2009], no. 18.
6. Mallowan 1952a, 8–9.
7. Herrmann and Laidlaw n.d. [2009], no. 224.
8. Ibid., no. 225.
9. Mallowan and Davies 1970, no. 140.
10. Mallowan 1952a, 11.
11. Al-Qaissi 2008, 49.
12. See Herrmann and Laidlaw, n.d. [2009], no. 138.
13. Mallowan 1952a, 11; Herrmann and Laidlaw n.d. [2009], no. 56b.
14. Reade 1965, 127.
15. Herrmann and Laidlaw n.d. [2009], no. 57.
16. Mallowan 1966, i, 241.
17. Ibid., 249–50.
18. Herrmann and Laidlaw n.d. [2009], no. CP2.
19. Ibid., pls 125–32.
20. Ibid., no. CP10.
21. Barnett 1975, 224; Hermann and Laidlaw n.d. [2009], no. 43.
22. Herrmann and Laidlaw n.d. [2009], nos 203 and 204.
23. Ibid., no. 206.
24. Herrmann 1992, no. 1.
25. Ibid., nos 180 and 220.
26. Ibid., no. 321.
27. Herrmann and Laidlaw n.d. [2009], no. 230.
28. Ibid., no. 223.
29. Ibid., no. 232.
30. Layard 1853, 195.
31. Mallowan 1952a, 15.
32. Layard 1853, 198–99.

CHAPTER 3

*2 Chronicles 2:13–14.
1. Aubet 2001, 6–7.
2. Ibid., 145.
3. Grayson 1991, 147.
4. Aubet 2001, 97.
5. Markoe 2000, 80–81.

6 Aubet 2001, 356.
7 Ibid., 160.
8 Markoe 2000, 93.
9 Tubb 2008, 2014.
10 Markoe 2000, 143.
11 Grayson 1991, 218–19.
12 Mallowan 1966, i, 70.
13 Luckenbill 1927, ii, 211, para. 527.
14 Barnett 1982, 29–30.
15 Gubel 2000.
16 Herrmann and Laidlaw n.d. [2009], no. 146.
17 Layard 1849, ii, 10.
18 Herrmann 1986, no. 1003.
19 Kitchen 1986, 41.
20 Herrmann 1986, no. 991.
21 Ibid., no. 992.
22 Ibid., no. 1029.
23 Ibid., no. 255.
24 Herrmann and Laidlaw 2013, nos 95 and 96.
25 Orchard 1967, no. 42.
26 Herrmann 1992, no. 197.
27 Herrmann 1986, no. 1009.
28 Herrmann and Laidlaw 2013, no. 38.
29 Kitchen in Herrmann and Laidlaw 2013, 134–35.
30 Herrmann and Laidlaw 2013, no. 39.
31 Kitchen in Herrmann and Laidlaw n.d. [2009], 161–62.
32 Crowfoot and Crowfoot 1938, pl. I, 2.
33 Kitchen 1986, 39.
34 Ibid., 38–39.
35 Herrmann 1986, no. 996.
36 Kitchen in Herrmann 1986, 199.
37 Herrmann 1986, no. 1021.
38 Ibid., no. 1015.
39 Barag 1983.
40 Herrmann 1986, no. 1006.
41 Kitchen in Herrmann 1986, 200.
42 ND 7658 and 7659; Herrmann 1992, nos 291 and 292.
43 Crowfoot and Crowfoot 1938, pl. II, 2.
44 Karageorghis 1969, 13
45 Karageorghis 1974, 93–95.
46 Mallowan and Herrmann 1974, no. 88.
47 Kitchen in Herrmann and Laidlaw 2013, 32.
48 Herrmann 2012b.
49 Herrmann 1986, no. 1043.
50 Herrmann 1992, 35.
51 Barag 1983, 167.
52 Herrmann 1986.
53 Herrmann 1992, 36.
54 Herrmann 1986, no. 1062.
55 Ibid., no. 1082.
56 Herrmann 1992, no. 481.
57 Ibid., no. 479.
58 Herrmann 1986, no. 1096.
59 Ibid., nos 12–18.
60 Ibid., no. 12.
61 Herrmann and Laidlaw 2013, no. 167.

62 Herrmann 1992, no. 224.
63 Herrmann 1986, no. 1051.
64 Herrmann and Laidlaw 2013, no. 190.
65 Kitchen in Herrmann and Laidlaw 2013, 160.
66 Herrmann 1986, no. 1176.
67 Herrmann and Laidlaw n.d. [2009], no. 356.
68 Mallowan 1966, i, 139, 142.
69 Ibid., 140.
70 Ibid., 139; Barnett 1975, 190.
71 Herrmann 1986, no. 1258.
72 Herrmann and Laidlaw n.d. [2009], no. 262.
73 Herrmann 1992, no. 471.
74 Herrmann and Laidlaw 2013, no. 417.
75 Herrmann 1986, no. 602.
76 Ibid., no. 1107.
77 Ibid., no. 1111.
78 Ibid., no. 1112.
79 Herrmann and Laidlaw 2013, no. 558.
80 Herrmann 1986, no. 720.
81 Herrmann and Laidlaw 2013, no. 58.
82 Ibid., no. 61.
83 Ibid., no. 340.
84 Cecchini 2005, 245.
85 Herrmann and Laidlaw 2013, nos. 64–82.
86 Ibid., no. 64.
87 Gubel 2002, 82–83.
88 Herrmann and Laidlaw 2013, nos 83–93.
89 Ibid., no. 84.
90 Herrmann 1986, nos 546–548.
91 Herrmann and Laidlaw 2013, no. 302.
92 Ibid., no. 314.
93 Herrmann 1992, no. 102.
94 Ibid., no. 103.
95 Ibid., no. 107.
96 Ibid., no. 334.
97 Herrmann and Laidlaw 2013, no. 680.
98 Ibid., no. 682; Stampolidis 2014, 294, no. 162.
99 Herrmann and Laidlaw n.d. [2009], no. 260.
100 Ibid., no. 259.
101 Herrmann and Laidlaw 2013, no. 688.
102 Feldman, 2014, 29–31.
103 Herrmann and Laidlaw n.d. [2009], no. 348.
104 Herrmann and Laidlaw 2013, App. 7.
105 Herrmann 1986, no. 1292.
106 Herrmann 1992, 14.
107 Ibid., no. 300.
108 Ibid., no. 302.
109 Ibid., no. 297.
110 Layard 1853, 566–67.

CHAPTER 4

*Isaiah 8:4.
1 Winter 1981, 101; repr. 2010, 279.
2 Herrmann 1992, no. 406.
3 Scigliuzzo 2005.
4 Herrmann 1992, no. 226.

5 Scigliuzzo 2005, 583.
6 Herrmann 1992, no. 110.
7 Ibid., no. 115.
8 Ibid., no. 207.
9 Herrmann and Laidlaw 2013, no. 279.
10 Herrmann and Laidlaw 2013, no. T39.
11 Herrmann 1986, no. 490.
12 Herrmann 1986, no. 1127.
13 Herrmann and Laidlaw 2013, no. T36.
14 Herrmann 1986, no. 316.
15 Herrmann and Laidlaw n.d. [2009], 88, fig. 35, a photographic reconstruction of fragments found in the Idaean Cave.
16 Herrmann and Laidlaw 2013, no. T35.
17 Herrmann 1986, no. 527.
18 Ibid., no. 599.
19 Crowfoot and Crowfoot 1938, pl. V, 3.
20 Herrmann and Laidlaw 2013, no. 251.
21 Ibid., no. 257.
22 Cecchini 2005, 244.
23 Herrmann and Laidlaw 2013, no. 65.
24 Herrmann 1986, nos. 350 and 337; Mallowan and Herrmann 1974, no. 357.
25 Herrmann 1986, no. 357.
26 Ibid., no. 940.
27 Ibid., no. 368.
28 Herrmann 1992, no. 382.

CHAPTER 5

*Oppenheim n.d. [1833], 7–8.
1 Grayson 1991, 42.
2 Herrmann and Laidlaw n.d. [2009], no. 233.
3 Ibid., no. 236.
4 Ibid., no. 236b.
5 Ibid., no. 349.
6 Ibid., no. 237.
7 Ibid., no. 238.
8 Herrmann 1992, no. 454.
9 Ibid., no. 455.
10 Ibid., no. 456.
11 Oppenheim n.d. [1933], 1.
12 Ibid., 8.
13 Ibid., pl. lix, p. 218.
14 Ibid.
15 Herrmann 1992, nos 332, 368–378.
16 Oppenheim n.d. [1933], pl. lix.
17 Herrmann 1986, no. 906.
18 Ibid., no. 889.
19 Herrmann and Laidlaw n.d. [2009], no. 239.
20 Ibid., no. 240.
21 Herrmann 1986, no. 583.
22 Thureau-Dangin et al. 1931, pl. xxxiii, no. 43
23 Herrmann 1992, no. 109.
24 Wicke 2005.
25 Mallowan and Herrmann 1974, no. 5.
26 Herrmann 1986, no. 657.

27 Andrae 1943, pls 71, ae–ak, and 72, f, k, n, o, r.
28 Herrmann 1992, no. 308.
29 Herrmann 1986, no. 668.
30 *Ibid.*, nos 722 and 701.
31 *Ibid.*, no. 923.
32 *Ibid.*, no. 929.
33 *Ibid.*, no. 926.
34 Herrmann and Laidlaw 2013, no. T72.
35 *Ibid.*, nos T109–T118.
36 *Ibid.*, no. T111.
37 *Ibid.*, no. T129.

CHAPTER 6

2 Chronicles 9:17.
1 Oates 1959, 104–06.
2 Mallowan and Herrmann 1974, no. 1.
3 *Ibid.*, no. 46.
4 *Ibid.*, no. 65.
5 *Ibid.*, nos. 77–82.
6 *Ibid.*, no. 95.
7 Odyssey XIX:55–57.
8 Akurgal 1962, pl. 130.
9 Cotton 1990, 13.
10 Baker 1966, 39–45.
11 Killen 1980, p. 59
12 Baker 1966, 102–06.
13 Barnett 1982, 29.
14 Winter 2010, 283.
15 Karageorghis 1974, 92.
16 *Ibid.*
17 Gubel 1996, pl. 34a.
18 Killen 1980, 62–63.
19 Yon 1991, no. 10, 305–07, fig. 16a; Cecchini 2005, 244–45, fig. 2.
20 Herrmann and Laidlaw 2013, no. 726.
21 Herrmann and Laidlaw n.d. [2009], no. 353.
22 Herrmann 1992, no. 206.
23 Herrmann and Laidlaw 2013, no. 740.
24 Curtis 1996.
25 *Ibid.*, pl. 46a.
26 Herrmann and Laidlaw 2013, no. 717.
27 *Ibid.*, no. 721.
28 Winter 2010, 332.
29 Edwards 1964, 136.
30 Gubel 1987, 49–54.
31 Barnett 1982, 27.
32 *Ibid.*, 254–58.
33 Herrmann and Laidlaw n.d. [2009], no. 234.
34 Herrmann 1986, nos 1441 and 1442.
35 *Ibid.*, no. 1440.
36 Herrmann and Laidlaw 2013, no. 707.
37 *Ibid.*, no. 708.
38 Fontan et al. 2007, 117, cat. 70.
39 Richter 1966, 29.
40 Gubel 1987, 251–61.
41 Herrmann 1992, no. 486.
42 Herrmann 1996, pl. 43e.

43 Curtis 1996, 176–78.
44 Mallowan and Herrmann 1974, no. 47.
45 ND 10571, Herrmann 1986, no. 1043; ND 12152, Herrmann and Laidlaw 2013, no. 47.
46 Herrmann and Laidlaw n.d. [2009], no. 346.
47 Herrmann and Laidlaw 2013, no. 471.
48 Herrmann and Laidlaw n.d. [2009], no. 275.
49 Herrmann 1986, no. 266.
50 Voos 1985.
51 Herrmann and Laidlaw 2013, no. 660.
52 Herrmann 1986, no. 1452.
53 *Ibid.*, no. 1455.
54 Herrmann and Laidlaw n.d. [2009], no. 232.
55 Curtis 1996, pl. 48.
56 Herrmann 1986, no. 1254.
57 Herrmann and Laidlaw 2013, no. 247.
58 Barnett 1975, 23.
59 *Ibid.*, p. iii.
60 Herrmann and Laidlaw n.d. [2009], no. 233.
61 Mitchell in Herrmann (ed.) 1996, 165.
62 Winter 2010, 573.
63 Barnett 1975, nos S293 and S294.
64 Scigliuzzo 2009, 209–37.
65 Herrmann and Laidlaw n.d. [2009], no. 363.
66 Herrmann 1992, no. 140.
67 Herrmann and Laidlaw n.d. [2009], no. 286.
68 *Ibid.*, no. 359.
69 Kitchen in Herrmann and Laidlaw n.d. [2009], 196.
70 *Ibid.*, no. 248.
71 IM 79583 and 79584.
72 Herrmann and Laidlaw n.d. [2009], no. 252.
73 IM 79577, 79580.
74 Herrmann and Laidlaw n.d. [2009], no. 245.
75 Orchard 1967, nos 1–63.
76 Orchard 1967, no. 30.
77 *Ibid.*, no. 137.
78 *Ibid.*, no. 112.
79 Herrmann 1986, nos 95 and 153.
80 *Ibid.*, no. 85.
81 *Ibid.*, no. 49.
82 *Ibid.*, no. 171.
83 Herrman and Laidlaw n.d. [2009], no. 258.
84 Kitchen in Herrmann and Laidlaw n.d. [2009], 198.
85 *Ibid.*, 198–99.

CHAPTER 7

*Winter 2010, 187.
1 Van Buren in Herrmann 1989, 98.
2 Herrmann 1986, no. 906.
3 Herrmann and Laidlaw n.d. [2009], no. 86.
4 ND 10518, Orchard 1967, no. 137.
5 Perrot and Chipiez 1884–5, iii, 131, fig. 76, 129, fig. 73; Gubel 2000, 188–89.
6 Herrmann 1992, no. 460.
7 Gubel 2002, 82–83.
8 Barnett 1982, 25.

9 Aubet 2001, 134.
10 *Ibid.*, 31, 117–18
11 *Ibid.*, 47.
12 Odyssey XV:455.
13 Smith 1908, 182; see also Herrmann and Laidlaw n.d. [2009], 54.
14 Albright 1942, 13.
15 Barnett 1975, 56.
16 *Ibid.*, 60, 62.
17 Aubet 2001, 79.
18 IM 79520, Herrmann and Laidlaw n.d. [2009], no. 230.

Suggested Reading

A general introduction to the history and archaeology of the region is provided by Michael Roaf's *Cultural Atlas of Mesopotamia and the Ancient Near East* (New York, 1990). A more focused historical perspective is offered in Roger Moorey's *The Biblical Lands* (New York, 1991), which outlines the early story of the Holy Land, the Canaanites and the Phoenicians.

NIMRUD

An accessible and comprehensive overview of the site of Nimrud and the excavations there in the nineteenth and twentieth centuries is given in Joan and David Oates's *Nimrud: An Assyrian Imperial City Revealed* (London, 2001), which is strongly recommended. Max Mallowan provides a lively and readable account of his important excavations at Nimrud in *Nimrud and its Remains*, 3 vols (London, 1966), while Henrietta McCall sets his work in context in *The Life of Max Mallowan* (London, 2001).

Mohens Trolle Larsen vividly describes the early history of excavations at Nimrud in *The Conquest of Assyria: Excavations in an Antique Land, 1840–1860* (London and New York, 1994), while Gordon Waterfield focuses on the most important figure of Nimrud in his *Layard of Nineveh* (London, 1963). Fascinating reading is provided by Layard's own accounts of his work: *Nineveh and its Remains*, 2 vols (London, 1849) and *Discoveries in the Ruins of Nineveh and Babylon* (London, 1853), as well as his more popular account, *Nineveh and Babylon...Abridged* (London, 1867).

THE IVORIES

A British Museum catalogue focusing on the Assyrians, J. E. Curtis and J. E. Reade, *Art and Empire: Treasures from Assyria in the British Museum* (London, 1995), provides an essential backdrop to the study of the ivories, the majority of which have been published in a series of catalogues, *Ivories from Nimrud*, I–VII (1967–2013), by the British School of Archaeology in Iraq, now the British Institute for the Study of Iraq. (At the time of writing, one volume remains to be completed.) The volumes are available on the institute's website, http://www.bisi.ac.uk/content/ivories-nimrud.

CONTEXTUAL CATALOGUES

The catalogues of two exhibitions held at the Metropolitan Museum of Art in New York give up-to-date summaries. They are J. Aruz, K. Benzel and J. M. Evans (eds), *Beyond Babylon: Art, Trade and Diplomacy in the Second Millennium b.c.* (New Haven and London, 2008), and J. Aruz, S. B. Graff and Y. Rakic (eds), *Assyria to Iberia at the Dawn of the Classical Age* (New Haven and London, 2014).

THE PHOENICIANS

Accessible coverage of the Phoenicians may be found in Mark Woolmer's *Ancient Phoenicia: An Introduction* (London, 2011) and G. E. Markoe's *The Phoenicians* (London, 2000). The most important recent work on the Phoenicians is Maria Aubet's *The Phoenicians and the West: Politics, Colonies and Trade* (2nd edn, Cambridge, 2001), which sets the Phoenicians in their wider context as they colonized the Mediterranean and beyond.

Bibliography

Akurgal, E., 1962, *The Art of the Hittites*. London

Albright, W. F., 1942, *Archaeology and the Religion of Israel*. Baltimore

Al-Gailani Werr, L., J. E. Curtis, H. Martin, A. McMahon, J. Oates and J. Reade (eds) 2002, *Of Pots and Plans: Papers on the Archaeology and History of Mesopotamia and Syria presented to David Oates in Honour of his 75th Birthday*. London

Al-Qaissi, R., 2008, 'Restoration work at Nimrud', in Curtis et al. (eds) 2008, 49–52

Andrae, W., 1943, *Ausgrabungen in Sendschirli, v: Die Kleinfunde von Sendschirli*, Mitteilungen aus den Orientalischen Sammlungen 15. Berlin

Aruz, J., K. Benzel and J. M. Evans (eds) 2008, *Beyond Babylon: Art, Trade and Diplomacy in the Second Millennium b.c.*, exhibition catalogue, Metropolitan Museum of Art, New York. New Haven and London

Aruz, J., S. B. Graff and Y. Rakic (eds) 2014, *Assyria to Iberia at the Dawn of the Classical Age*, exhibition catalogue, Metropolitan Museum of Art, New York. New Haven and London

Aubet, M. E., 2001, *The Phoenicians and the West: Politics, Colonies and Trade*, 2nd edn. Cambridge

Baker, H. D., K. Kaniuth and A. Otto (eds) 2012, *Stories of Long Ago: Festschrift für Michael D. Roaf*. Münster

Baker, H. S., 1966, *Furniture in the Ancient World*. London

Barag, D., 1983, 'Glass inlays and the classification and dating of ivories from the ninth–eighth centuries B.C.', *Anatolian Studies* 33, 163–67

Barnett, R. D., 1935, 'The Nimrud ivories and the art of the Phoenicians', *Iraq* 2, 179–210

Barnett, R. D., 1939, 'Phoenician and Syrian ivory carving', *Palestine Exploration Quarterly*, 4–19

Barnett, R. D., 1956, 'Phoenicians and the ivory trade', *Archaeology* 9, 87–97

Barnett, R. D., 1963, 'Hamath and Nimrud: shell fragments from Hamath and the provenance of the Nimrud ivories', *Iraq* 25, 81–84

Barnett, R. D., 1975, *A Catalogue of the Nimrud Ivories in the British Museum (1957)*, 2nd rev. edn. London

Barnett, R. D., 1982, *Ancient Ivories in the Middle East*, Qedem: Monographs of the Institute of Archaeology, Hebrew University of Jerusalem 14. Jerusalem

Barnett, R. D., E. Bleibtreu and G. Turner 1998, *Sculptures from the Southwest Palace of Sennacherib at Nineveh*. London

Bruce, W. N. (ed.), 1903, *Sir A. Henry Layard …: Autobiography and Letters from his Childhood until his Appointment as H.M. Ambassador at Madrid*. London

Bunnens, G., 1997, 'Carved ivories from Til Barsib', *American Journal of Archaeology* 101, 435–50

Caubet, A., 2008, 'Ivory, shell and bone', in Aruz et al. (eds) 2008, 406–15

Cecchini, S. M., 2005, 'The "Suivant du Char royal": a case of interaction between various genres of minor art', in Suter and Uehlinger (eds) 2005, 243–64

Cecchini, S. M., 2016. 'Osservazioni sugli avori assirizzanti di Nimrud', *Rivista di Studi Fenici* 44, 51–60

Cecchini, S. M., S. Mazzoni and E. Scigliuzzo (eds) 2009, *Syrian and Phoenician Ivories of the Early First Millennium BCE: Chronology, Regional Styles and Iconographic Repertoires. Patterns of Inter-Regional Distribution*, Acts of the International Workshop, Pisa, December 9th–11th 2004. Pisa

Cholidis, N., L. Martin and J. Boehme 2011, *The Tell Halaf Adventure*. Berlin

Christie, A., 1977, *An Autobiography*. London

Cotton, B. D., 1990, *The English Regional Chair*. Woodbridge

Crowfoot, J. W., and G. M. Crowfoot 1938, *Early Ivories from Samaria*, Samaria-Sebaste 2. London

Curtis, J. E., 1996, 'Assyrian furniture: the archaeological evidence', in Herrmann (ed.) 1996, 176–80

Curtis, J. E., and J. E. Reade 1995, *Art and Empire: Treasures from Assyria in the British Museum*. London

Curtis, J. E., and G. Herrmann 1998, 'Reflections on the four-winged genie: a pottery jar and an ivory panel from Nimrud', *Iranica Antiqua* 33, 107–34

Curtis, J. E., H. McCall, D. Collon and L. al-Gailani Werr (eds) 2008, *New Light on Nimrud: Proceedings of the Nimrud Conference, 11th–13th March 2002*. London

D'Albiac, C., 1992, 'The griffin combat theme', in Fitton (ed.) 1992, 105–12

Davies, N. de G., 1943, *The Tomb of Rekh-mi-re at Thebes*. New York

Edwards, R., 1964, *The Shorter Dictionary of English Furniture*. London

Feldman, M. H., 2014, *Communities of Style: Portable Luxury Arts, Identity, and Collective Memory in the Iron Age Levant*. Chicago and London

Fitton, J. L. (ed.), 1992, *Ivory in Greece and the Eastern Mediterranean from the Bronze Age to the Hellenistic Period*, British Museum Occasional Paper 85. London

Fontan, E., N. Gillmann and H. Le Meaux (eds) 2007, *La Méditerranée des Phéniciens: de Tyr à Carthage*, exhibition catalogue, Institut du Monde Arabe. Paris

Gitin, S., 1997, 'The Neo-Assyrian empire and its western periphery: the Levant, with a focus on Philistine Ekron', in Parpola and Whiting (eds) 1997, 77–103

Grayson, A. K., 1991, *Assyrian Rulers of the Early First Millennium B.C.*, 1 (1114–859 B.C.), The Royal Inscriptions of Mesopotamia, Assyrian Periods 2. Toronto

Gubel, E., 1987, *Phoenician Furniture: A Typology Based on Iron Age Representations*, Studia Phoenicia 7. Leuven

Gubel, E., 1996, 'The influence of Egypt on western Asiatic furniture, and evidence from Phoenicia', in Herrmann (ed.) 1996, 123

Gubel, E., 2000, 'Multicultural and multimedial aspects of early Phoenician art', in Uehlinger (ed.) 2000, 185–214

Gubel, E., 2002, *Art phénicien: la sculpture de tradition phénicienne*. Paris

Gubel, E., 2005, 'Phoenician and Aramaean bridle-harness decoration', in Suter and Uehlinger (eds) 2005, 111–47

Gubel, E., 2009, 'The "Unusually Shaped Ivories" (USI) Group with stylized trees', in Cecchini et al. (eds) 2009, 187–207

Herrmann, G., 1986, *Ivories from Nimrud*, IV: *Ivories from Room SW37, Fort Shalmaneser*, pts 1–2. London

Herrmann, G., 1989, 'The Nimrud ivories, 1: The Flame and Frond School', *Iraq* 51, 85–109

Herrmann, G., 1992, *Ivories from Nimrud*, V: *The Small Collections from Fort Shalmaneser*. London

Herrmann, G. (ed.), 1996, *The Furniture of Western Asia, Ancient and Traditional*. Mainz, 153–64

Herrmann, G., 1996, 'Ivory furniture pieces from Nimrud: North Syrian evidence for a regional tradition of furniture manufacture', in Herrmann (ed.) 1996, 153–64

Herrmann, G., 2000, 'Ivory carving of first millennium workshops, traditions and diffusion', in Uehlinger (ed.) 2000, 267–82

Herrmann, G., 2002, 'The Nimrud ivories, 5: The Ornate Group', in al-Gailani Werr et al. (eds) 2002, 128–42

Herrmann, G., 2005, 'Naming, defining, explaining: a view from Nimrud', in Suter and Uehlinger (eds) 2005, 11–21

Herrmann, G., 2008, 'The ivories from Nimrud', in Curtis et al. (eds) 2008, 225–32

Herrmann, G., 2012a, 'Some Assyrianizing ivories found at Nimrud: could they be Urartian?', in Kroll et al. (eds) 2012, 339–50

Herrmann, G., 2012b. 'Some Phoenician furniture pieces', in Baker et al. (eds) 2012, 241–48

Herrmann, G., and A. Millard 2003 'Who used ivories in the early first millennium BC?', in Potts et al. (eds) 2003, 377–402

Herrmann, G., H. Coffey and S. Laidlaw 2004, *The Published Ivories from Fort Shalmaneser, Nimrud*. London

Herrmann, G., and S. Laidlaw n.d. [2009], *Ivories from Nimrud*, VI: *Ivories from the North West Palace (1845–1992)*. London

Herrmann, G., and S. Laidlaw 2013, *Ivories from Nimrud*, VII: *Ivories from Rooms SW11/12 and T10, Fort Shalmaneser*. London

Hussein, M. M., M. Altaweel and M. Gibson 2016, *Nimrud: The Queens' Tombs*. Baghdad and Chicago

Kamil, Ahmed, 1999, 'Inscriptions on objects from Yaba's tomb in Nimrud', in M. S. B. Damerji (ed.), *Gräber assyrischer Königinnen aus Nimrud*. Mainz, pp. 13–18

Karageorghis, V., 1969, *Salamis in Cyprus*. London

Karageorghis, V., 1974, *Excavations in the Necropolis of Salamis*, III, Salamis 5. Cyprus

Killen, G., 1980, *Ancient Egyptian Furniture*, I: 4000–1300 B.C. Warminster

King, L. W., 1915, *Bronze Reliefs from the Gates of Shalmaneser*. London

Kitchen, K. A., 1986, 'Egyptianizing features in the Nimrud Ivories', in Herrmann, 1986, 37–46

Kroll, S., C. Gruber, U. Hellwag, M. Roaf and P. Zimansky (eds) 2012, *Bianili-Urartu. The Proceedings of the Symposium held in Munich, 12–14 October 2007*. Leuven

Larsen, M. T., 1994, *The Conquest of Assyria: Excavations in an Antique Land, 1840–1860*. London and New York

Layard, A. H., 1849, *Nineveh and its Remains*, 2 vols. London

Layard, A. H., 1849–53, *The Monuments of Nineveh*, 2 vols. London

Layard, A. H., 1852, *A Popular Account of Discoveries at Nineveh*. London

Layard, A. H., 1853, *Discoveries in the Ruins of Nineveh and Babylon*. London

Layard, A. H., 1867, *Nineveh and Babylon: A Narrative of a Second Expedition to Assyria during the Years 1849, 1850, & 1851…Abridged by the Author*. London

Liverani, M., 2008, 'The Late Bronze Age: materials and mechanisms of trade and cultural exchange', in Aruz et al. (eds) 2008, 161–67

Loud, G., 1930, *The Megiddo Ivories*, Oriental Institute Publications 52. Chicago

Loud, G., and C. B. Altman 1938, *Khorsabad, pt 2: The Citadel and the Town*, Oriental Institute Publications 40, Chicago

Luckenbill, D. D., 1927, *Ancient Records of Assyria*, II. Chicago; repr. 1989

Luschan, F. von, 1911, *Ausgrabungen in Sendschirli*, IV, Mitteilungen aus den Orientalischen Sammlungen 14. Berlin

McCall, H., 2001, *The Life of Max Mallowan*. London

Mallowan, M. E. L., 1951, 'The excavations at Nimrud (Kalhu), 1949–1950: ivories from the North West Palace', *Iraq* 13, 1–20

Mallowan, M. E. L., 1952a, 'The excavations at Nimrud (Kalhu), 1949–1950', *Iraq* 14, 1–23

Mallowan, M. E. L., 1952b, 'The excavations at Nimrud (Kalhu), 1949–1950: ivories from the North West Palace', *Iraq* 14, 45–53

Mallowan, M. E. L., 1966, *Nimrud and its Remains*, 3 vols. London

Mallowan, M. E. L., 1978, *The Nimrud Ivories*. London

Mallowan, M. E. L., and L. G. Davies 1970, *Ivories from Nimrud (1949–1963)*, II: *Ivories in Assyrian Style*. London

Mallowan, M. E. L., and G. Herrmann 1974, *Ivories from Nimrud (1949–1963)*, III: *Furniture from SW.7, Fort Shalmaneser*. London

Margueron, J.-C., 2008, 'Ugarit: gateway to the Mediterranean', in Aruz et al. (eds) 2008, 236–50

Markoe, G. E., 1985, *Phoenician Bronze and Silver Bowls from Cyprus and the Mediterranean*, Classical Studies 26. Berkeley, Calif.

Markoe, G. E., 2000, *The Phoenicians*. London

Moorey, P. R. S., 2001, 'The mobility of artisans and opportunities for technology transfer between western Asia and Egypt in the Late Bronze Age', in Shortland (ed.) 2001, 1–14

Moortgat, A., 1955, *Tell Halaf*, III: *Die Bildwerke, unter Verwendung der Bildeschreibungen*. Berlin

Moscati, S., 1999, *The World of the Phoenicians*. London

Muscarella, O. W., 1980, *The Catalogue of Ivories from Hasanlu, Iran*, University Museum Monograph 40. Philadelphia

Oates, D., 1959, 'Fort Shalmaneser: an interim report, 1957-58', *Iraq* 21, 98–129

Oates, D., 1961, 'The excavations at Nimrud (Kalhu), 1960', *Iraq* 23, 1–14

Oates, J., and D. Oates, 2001, *Nimrud: An Assyrian Imperial City Revealed*. London

Oppenheim, Max von, n.d. [1933], *Tell Halaf: A New Culture in Oldest Mesopotamia*, trans. G. Wheeler from *Der Tell Halaf: eine neue Kultur im altesten Mesopotamien* (1931). London and New York

Orchard, J. J., 1967, *Ivories from Nimrud*, I: *Equestrian Bridle-Harness Ornaments*. London

Parpola, S., and R. M. Whiting (eds) 1997, *Assyria 95. Proceedings of the 10th Anniversary Symposium of the Neo-Assyrian Text Corpus Project, Helsinki, September 7-11, 1995*. Helsinki

Perrot, G., and C. Chipiez 1884-85, *Histoire de l'art dans l'antiquité*, II–III. Paris

Potts, T., M. Roaf and D. Stein (eds) 2003, *Culture through Objects: Ancient Near Eastern Studies in Honour of P. R. S. Moorey*. Oxford

Poulsen, F., 1912, *Der Orient und die frühgriechische Kunst*. Leipzig; repr. Rome, 1968

Reade, J. E., 1965, 'Twelve Ashurnasirpal reliefs', *Iraq* 27, 119–34

Reade, J. E., 2008, 'Nineteenth-century Nimrud: motivation, orientation, conservation', in Curtis et al. (eds) 2008, 1–21

Richter, G. M. A., 1966, *The Furniture of the Greeks, Etruscans and Romans*. London

Roaf, M. D., 1983, *Sculptures and Sculptors at Persepolis*. London [*Iran* 21, special issue]

Roaf, M., 1990, *Cultural Atlas of Mesopotamia and the Ancient Near East*. New York

Rosser-Owen, M., 1999, 'A Cordoban ivory pyxis lid in the Ashmolean Museum', *Muqarnas* 16, 16–31

Safar, Fuad, and Muyasser Sa'ied al-'Iraqi 1987, *Ivories from Nimrud*. Baghdad [in Arabic]

Sakellarakis, J., 1992, 'The Idaean Cave ivories', in Fitton (ed.) 1992, 113–40

Scigliuzzo, E., 2005, 'The "wig and wing workshop" of Iron Age ivory carving', *Ugarit Forschungen* 37, 557–607

Shortland, A. J. (ed.), 2001, *The Social Context of Technological Change: Egypt and the Near East*. Oxford

Simpson, E., 1995, 'Furniture in western Asia', in J. M. Sasson et al. (eds), *Civilizations of the Ancient Near East*, III. New York, 1647–71

Smith, C. H., 1908, 'The ivory statuettes', in D. G. Hogarth, *Excavations at Ephesus: The Archaic Artemesia*, 2 vols. London, vol. I, 155–85

Spar, I., 2008, 'The Amarna letters', in Aruz et al. (eds) 2008, 168–9

Stampolidis, N. C., 2014, 'Near Eastern imports and imagery on Crete during the Iron Age', in Aruz et al. (eds) 2014, 282–94

Suter, C. E., and C. Uehlinger (eds) 2005, *Crafts and Images in Contact: Studies on Eastern Mediterranean Art of the First Millennium BCE*, Orbis Biblicus et Orientalis 210. Fribourg

Thureau-Dangin, F., A. Barrois, G. Dossin and M. Dunand, 1931, *Arslan-Tash*. Paris

Tubb, J. N., 2008, 'Sea peoples and Philistines', in Aruz et al. (eds) 2008, 38–45

Tubb, J. N., 2014, 'Phoenicians and Aramaeans', in Aruz et al. (eds) 2014, 132–40

Uehlinger, C. (ed.), 2000, *Images as Media: Sources for the Cultural History of the Near East and the Eastern Mediterranean, 1st Millennium BCE*, Orbis Biblicus et Orientalis 175. Fribourg

Voos, J., 1985, 'Zu einigen späthethitischen Reliefs aus den Beständen des Vorderasiatischen Museums Berlin', *Altorientalische Forschungen* 12, 65–86

Wartke, R.-B., 2005, *Sam'al: ein aramäischer Stadtstaat des 10. bis 8. Jhs. v. Chr. und die Geschichte seiner Erforschung*. Berlin

Waterfield, G., 1963, *Layard of Nineveh*. London

Wicke, D., 2005, '"Roundcheeked and ringletted": gibt es einen nordwestsyrischen Regionalstil in der altorientalischen Elfenbeinschnitzkunst?', in Suter and Uehlinger (eds) 2005, 67–110

Winter, I. J., 1981, 'Is there a south Syrian style of ivory carving in the early first millennium B.C.?', *Iraq* 43, 101–30; repr. in Winter 2010

Winter, I. J., 2010, *On Art in the Ancient Near East*, I: *Of the First Millennium B.C.E.* Leiden and Boston

Yon, M., 1991, 'Stèles de pierre', in M. Yon et al. (eds), *Arts et industries de la pierre*, Ras Shamra-Ougarit 6. Paris, 273–353

Acknowledgments

The task of retrieving and recording the thousands of ivories found at Nimrud by the various expeditions, British, Iraqi and Italian, is enormous, and ranges from their initial discovery, lifting and conservation to photography and cataloguing. It is not possible to thank all those who have contributed to the work in many ways.

Over the last century, a large body of images has been built up, recording the Layard and Loftus ivories in the British Museum, as well as those recovered by the British School of Archaeology in Iraq (now the British Institute for the Study of Iraq) and the superb pieces excavated by the Iraqi State Board of Antiquities and Heritage. I have assembled the pictorial record of the ivories into an archive consisting of many thousands of photographs, taken by numerous photographers. These have been scanned to ensure preservation and simplify access. This work has depended on the generosity of the directors and staff of the many museums that hold ivories from Nimrud, who have made possible the recording and photography of their collections and whose help I gratefully acknowledge. The greatest number of pieces and the finest examples are held in the National Museum of Iraq, Baghdad, while some others were distributed to museums throughout Iraq, many of which have been lost in the recent disturbances. The next largest collection is held by the British Museum in London and consists of the ivories found by Layard and Loftus in the nineteenth century, as well as many discovered during the excavations carried out by the British School of Archaeology in Iraq. Until the 1970s expeditions working in Iraq were allowed a share of the finds, an arrangement known as the 'division'. The BSAI distributed some ivories received in this 'division' to museums in the USA, notably the Metropolitan Museum, New York, and to institutions in the UK, Belgium, Denmark, Canada, Australia and Japan.

Many photographers have helped in recording the ivories, particularly Mick Sharp, who changed the way ivories were photographed, Stuart Laidlaw and Donny George. Scanning and archiving has been undertaken by Stuart Laidlaw and Helena Coffey.

Numerous colleagues have helped me through the years. I am particularly grateful to Ken Kitchen for sharing his expertise on the Egyptianizing ivories and Alan Millard for his advice on Aramaic fitters' marks. I have greatly profited from discussions with Julian Reade, Christopher Walker and Dirk Wicke.

I am very grateful to the Institute of Archaeology, University College London, for support and help through the years, and to the Middle East Department of the British Museum. The museum has assisted me in more ways than I can describe, giving me access to the ivories and to its excellent library, and storing the paper copy of the photographic archive. Furthermore, the Keeper of the Middle East Department, Jonathan Tubb, arranged for a generous subvention by the Friends of the Ancient Near East towards the cost of publishing *Ancient Ivory*, which has made possible the copious illustration of the book.

I should also like to thank Colin Ridler, Commissioning Editor at Thames & Hudson, for his invitation to write this book and to make these wonderful objects more available. I am also indebted to project manager, Jen Moore; to Rosemary Roberts for skilful copy-editing; and to designer, Samuel Clark, and production controller, Celia Falconer, for turning a mass of material into an attractive book.

Georgina Herrmann
March 2017

Index

Ahiram, King 58, 58, 165
Albright, William 194
el Amin, Dr Mahmud 26
Arslan Tash 108, 130, 160, 172, 189
Arvad 55, 56, 190, 190, 193
Ashur 31, 42, 42, 43
Ashurbanipal 47
   Garden Scene 74, 116, 152, 153–54, 159, 162, 174–75, 177, 193
Ashurnasirpal II 20, 32
   Kalhu 9, 19, 41–42
   Nabu Temple 46, 47, 47
   North West Palace 7, 23, 28, 29, 38, 42–43, 45–46, 58
Assyrianizing panels 48, 49, 97
Ataliya, Queen 32, 33, 94
Aubet, Maria 193, 194

Baniti, Queen 94
Bar-Rakib, King 129, 158
Barag, Professor Dan 68
Barnett, Richard 26, 174, 194
bas-reliefs 45, 46, 126, 152, 188, 189, 194
Bastet 76, 77, 140
Beazley, Sir John 193
beds 130, 153, 154, 155, 159–60
Bes 63, 63, 181, 181
Bit Agusi (Tell Rifaat) 119, 175
Bit Bahiani 119, 127, 188
the Black Obelisk 18, 25
blinkers 63, 179, 180, 181, 182, 182
boat scenes 60, 61–62
Botta, Paul Émile 22
Boutcher, William 25, 47–48, 48
bowls 174, 179, 184, 194
   'bird's nest' bowl 177
   gold bowls 32, 94
   lion bowls 123–24, 150, 178, 179

   metal bowls 192–93
bridle harnesses 77, 174, 179–83, 188, 189, 193, 194, 195
British School of Archaeology in Iraq 14, 20, 26
bulls 96, 148, 149, 175
   battles with animals 70, 124, 124, 132, 133, 149
   browsing bulls 76, 76, 116, 134, 134, 147, 170
   bull hunts 12, 13, 46, 126, 154, 155, 156, 157
   bull-man 42, 42
   'flame and frond' ivories 120, 120, 122, 124, 124, 126
   furniture decoration 169, 171, 171
Buren, E. D. van 188
Burnt Palace 126, 136, 174, 177, 195
   Loftus discoveries 14, 25, 175, 179
   Long Room 174, 175
   pyxides 121, 175
Byblos 56, 58, 105, 160, 165, 193

Canning, Sir Stratford 22–23
Carchemish 119, 120, 159, 172, 175, 188
cattle 134, 148, 189
   'flame and frond' ivories 121, 125
   Mallowan's finds 28, 28
   suckling calves 68, 76, 76, 101, 116, 117, 134, 134, 139
   see also bulls
Central Palace 47–48, 48, 53
chairs 93, 153, 154
   chair-backs from Room SW7 130–32, 135, 145, 154, 154, 188
   Classic SW7 group 120, 155, 156, 157
   lion-legged chairs 160–65

   see also thrones
'champlevé' ivories 71, 188
chariots 12, 13, 132, 133, 155, 157, 179
Chipiez, Charles 190
Christie, Agatha 14, 26, 35
   'Mona Lisa' of Nimrud 28, 84–85
   Nimrud excavations 27, 29, 92, 93
Classic SW7 group 120, 130, 131–32, 137, 155, 156, 157
containers 184
Cooper, F. C. 30
cosmetics 128, 129, 174–75
Cotton, Bernard 158–59
couches 74, 116, 152, 154, 159, 162, 164
courtiers 14, 15, 50, 51, 195
'crown and scale' ivories 105, 108–11, 117, 143
cylinders 99, 101, 137

deities 88, 105, 106, 116, 153
Deutsches Archäologisches Institut 129
Dur Sharrukin (Khorsabad) 22, 106, 107, 108, 172, 188
Dyson, Robert H. Jr 126

earrings 33
Edwards, Ralph 165
Egyptianizing ivories 59–66, 67, 88, 98, 99, 99, 184
Enkomi 12, 13, 66, 70, 70
Esarhaddon 35, 37, 47, 58, 86, 188

al Fakhri, Junaid 34
fan handles 96, 125, 174, 175–77, 179, 188, 192, 193
Feldman, Marian 84
fire-altars 135–36, 136

'flame and frond' ivories 120–27, 130, 136, 192
   cattle 120, 121, 122, 123, 124, 126
   flasks 122, 132, 134, 149, 179
   furniture elements 124–25, 125, 166, 170–71
   lions 108, 120, 123–24, 125, 146, 150
   pyxides 168
   sculptures in the style of 188, 189, 190
flasks 124, 125, 174, 178, 188, 193
   'flame and frond' 122, 122, 132, 134, 149, 179
footstools 153, 158, 160, 162, 165, 168, 169
palm capitals 172
Fort Shalmaneser 20, 31, 34–37, 60, 121, 189, 195
   distribution of ivories 53
   Residency 53, 63, 63
   Room NE2 53, 85–88
   Room NE59 81, 110, 126–27
   Room NW21 106, 116, 127
   Room S10 36, 81, 107, 130–31, 179
   Room SW7 35–36, 130, 131–32, 135, 154–59, 169, 188
   Room SW11/12 35, 36, 63, 64, 77, 79, 83–84, 109, 125, 134, 162, 170, 190
   Room SW37 35, 36, 61–62, 64–65, 79, 85, 109, 110, 125, 127, 129, 135, 168, 170, 179, 182, 188
   Room T10 36–37, 53, 109, 110, 111, 135
frontlets 151, 179, 181–82, 183, 189, 195
furniture 66–67, 147, 153–72, 188, 192, 193
   see also chairs, tables, etc
furniture fittings 52, 52, 67, 102
   'flame and frond' 124–25, 125
   lion's head 162, 162
   long panels 116–17

gaming boxes 12–13, 12
Garden Scene relief 74, 116, 152, 153–54, 159, 162, 174–75, 177, 193
Garstang, John 132
genies 44, 45, 48, 49, 50
'George and dragon' motif 70–71, 139
Gitin, Seymour 13
goats 130, 130
goddess panels 66–67
griffins 73, 100, 116, 144, 191
　battles with animals 122, 132, 133, 147, 149, 171
　griffin and hero motifs 70–72, 105, 110, 110, 143, 184, 185
　stelae 190, 190
　'Unusually Shaped Ivories' 172, 173
'grooved cheek' group 79
Gubel, Eric 77, 190

Halbherr, Federico 81
Hama, Queen 32, 94
Hamilton, Robert 26
Hasanlu 125–26, 188
Hathor 67, 170, 170, 181, 195
Hazael 160, 189
Heh 66, 66
hero and griffin panels 70–72, 105, 110, 110, 143, 184, 185
Herodotus 56, 60
Hetepheres, Queen 159, 159
Hiram I 57, 192
Homer 57, 93, 158, 193
Horus 64–66, 65, 67, 99, 102
Hussein, Muzahim Mahmoud 32, 34

Idaean Cave, Crete 81, 82, 109, 111, 125, 168, 188, 192
inlays 66, 68–69, 193
　inlay figures 48, 49
　pegged inlays 120–21
　Syro-Phoenician ivories 109–10, 117
Iraqi State Board of Antiquities and Heritage 14, 20, 31–33, 38, 45, 174
Isis (goddess) 64, 65, 99

Islamic State 7, 9, 32, 92
Ithobaal 56, 56, 58, 58

Jehu of Israel 18, 25
Jones, Felix 34
jugs 114–16, 140

Kalhu 9, 14, 37, 41–46, 47, 53, 58, 188
Kapara 126, 127, 174, 188
Karageorghis, Vassos 66, 160, 192
Killen, Geoffrey 160
Kitchen, Professor Ken 60, 64

'Lady of the Well' 28, 29, 84–85, 89, 123
Laessoe, Jorgen 34
Layard, Austen Henry 20–24, 21, 28, 194
　the Black Obelisk 18, 25
　discovers first ivories 6, 14, 16, 20, 23–25, 52, 107
　Egyptianizing ivories 59–60, 64
　lions 88
　metal bowls 193
　North West Palace 23, 23, 37, 38, 45, 48, 53, 172
lions 88
　battling 116, 122, 132, 133, 147, 149, 171
　chryselephantine plaques 7, 71–72, 90, 91
　double lion bowl 150
　'flame and frond' ivories 108, 120, 123–24, 125, 146, 150
　furniture fittings 162, 162, 164
　lion-bowl 178, 179
　lion-legged chairs 160–65
　Sakcha Gozu relief 132
　sculpture 189
　statuettes 160, 161, 162, 165
Loftus, William Kennett 20, 25, 26, 148, 194
　Burnt Palace 14, 174, 175, 179
　Central Palace 47–48
long panels 116–17, 117, 155
Loud, Gordon 192

Luli, King 56, 56
Luschan, Felix von 129

Mallowan, Max 19, 20, 26–31, 32, 38, 92, 93
　Ashurnasirpal II stela 42, 43, 45
　chryselephantine plaques 71–72, 90, 91
　Fort Shalmaneser 34–35
　'Mona Lisa' of Nimrud 28, 29, 84–85, 89
　Nabu Temple 47
　small finds 174, 175, 177
　Throne Room ivories 45–46
　tusk discoveries 52
　'Ugly Sister' 122–23, 123
　Well AJ 14
Maximian, Archbishop of Ravenna 13, 13
Megiddo 12, 165, 165, 192
'mistress of animals' motif 182, 190
Mitford, Edward 21–22
'Mona Lisa' of Nimrud 28, 29, 84–85, 89, 123
al-Muslah, Saleh Mohammad 27

Nabu Temple 36, 46–47, 53, 96, 106, 195
naiskoi 77, 190
necklaces 32, 94, 95
Ninurta 43, 43
North West Palace 19, 20, 20, 42–47, 195
　construction 58
　destruction by Islamic State 7, 9, 32, 92
　distribution of ivories 53
　Egyptianizing ivories 60
　Layard 23, 23
　restoration programme 31–33
　Room of the Bronzes 30, 172
　Room V/W 16, 37–38, 81, 107, 116
　royal tombs 31–33, 94
　Throne Room 7, 35, 42, 45–46, 48
　Well AJ 14, 29, 31, 33–34, 45,

50–52, 53, 59, 72, 83, 121–22, 123–24, 127, 129–30, 132, 134, 168, 174–75, 179, 184
　Well NN 28, 71, 122, 177, 179

Oates, David 35–36, 154–55
Omri 57, 64
Oppenheim, Baron Max von 126
Ornate Group 59, 60, 61, 67–76, 85, 88
　bridles 77
　containers 184
　deities 14–15, 54, 67, 68
　footstools 166
　furniture posts 170
　plaques 70–71, 139
　portraiture 81–85
　Salamis ivories 66
　sphinxes 74–76, 78, 79, 167, 168
　'Unusually Shaped Ivories' 172, 173

palm capitals 52, 52, 172, 172, 175, 176, 177
pendants, agate eye 95
Perrot, Georges 190
pharaohs 69–72, 74, 99
　kneeling pharaoh figure 6, 7, 69, 139
　pharaoh figures with sceptres and jugs 77, 88, 114–16, 136, 140, 182, 190
　statuettes 81, 81, 82, 83–84, 85, 85, 192
　Syro-Phoenician 105
　upper body of a pharaoh 68, 101
plaques 62, 63, 139, 165, 171
　chryselephantine plaques 7, 71–72, 90, 91
　curved 96, 103, 108, 142
　North Syrian plaque 37, 37
　Phoenician stands 184, 184, 185
　silhouette 129, 130
Plenderleith, Dr J. J. 72
portraiture 81–85
Poulsen, Frederik 26, 60, 104

Preziosi, Amadeo 21
pyxides 179, 193
- 'flame and frond' 59, 120–21, 122, 125, 168, 188
- North Syrian 174–75
- oval pyxis from Well AJ 121, 148, 166, 169, 174

Raof, Michael 38
Rassam, Hormuzd 23, 24, 25, 108, 108
Rawlinson, Henry Creswicke 25, 48, 49, 97
Re 61, 62, 62, 98
Reade, Julian 38
Reade, Nan Shaw 84, 137
Rekhmire 10, 11, 38
Renan, Ernest 190
Rich, Claudius James 22
Ross, Henry 23
round, carving in the 85–88
'round-cheeked and ringletted' ivories 120, 127–31, 136, 186, 188
roundels, openwork 124, 124

Sakellarakis, Yannis 81, 82
Salamis 66, 153, 154, 158, 160, 168, 179, 192
Samaria 57, 64, 105
- ivories found at 64, 66, 71, 103, 165, 172, 188, 192
sarcophagus 58–59, 58, 165, 165, 168
Sargon II 64, 126, 188
- Nabu Temple 36, 106, 107
- palace of 22, 29
- Queen Ataliya 32, 94
- writing boards 30
scarab beetles 61, 62, 62, 63, 63, 77, 99, 182
sceptres 114–16, 140
Scigliuzzo, Elena 106–7, 177, 182
screens 155, 157–58
sculptures 120, 126, 136, 188–90
Sennacherib, King 56, 56
Shalmaneser III 18, 20, 25, 31, 32, 34, 39
Shalmaneser V 32, 94
Shamshi-ilu 31, 32, 94

Sidon 56, 57, 58, 77, 105
Smith, Sir Cecil 194
South West Palace 23, 56, 56
sphinxes 74–76, 190
- blinkers 179, 180
- borrowing from Phoenician art 111, 112, 113, 113
- 'crown and scale' 108–11
- falcon-headed 74, 75, 138, 180, 181, 184, 185
- 'Finely Carved' ivories 138
- 'flame and frond' ivories 120, 121, 122
- 'grooved cheek' group 78, 79, 81
- human-headed 8, 72, 97, 98, 100, 104, 109, 111, 127, 129, 141, 143, 165, 167, 180, 182, 183, 189
- images of on bowls 150, 177
- openwork statuettes 83, 83
- Ornate Group 74–76, 78, 79, 167, 168
- pyxis 148
- ram-headed 118, 139, 189
- 'round-cheeked and ringletted' 15, 127, 188
- sphinx throne 165–68, 169
- Syro-Phoenician 105
- 'triple flower' 111, 112, 113
- 'Unusually Shaped Ivories' 172, 173
- 'wig and wing' 104, 106, 106
stands 184, 184, 188
statuettes 40
- beardless Assyrian courtier 50, 51, 195
- calves 174
- lions 160, 161, 162, 165
- pharaohs 81, 81, 82, 83–84, 85, 85, 192
- Room NE2 85–88
stelae 42–43, 43, 160, 188, 189, 190, 190
symmetry 76–77, 79

tables 153, 154, 162, 168–69, 169
'tall crown' ivories 105, 111, 112, 113, 118
Tell Halaf (Guzana) 119, 159, 187
- ivories found at 125, 126, 127, 174, 188, 192
- pyxides 174, 174, 193
- sculptural styles 120, 126–27, 159, 188
Temple-Palace of Kapara 126, 126, 188, 189
Thoth 61, 62, 62
thrones 154, 159, 193, 195
- Classic SW7 chair-back 156, 157
- Maximian of Ravenna's throne 13, 13
- palm capitals 172
- panels from 15, 155
- plain thrones 171
- sphinx throne 162, 165–68, 169
- throne of Penelope 158
Tiglath-pileser I 58, 119
Tiglath-pileser III 58, 158, 194
- Queen Yaba 32, 94, 193
- sculptures of 48, 50, 132
tombs, royal
- grave goods 159, 179, 192
- tombs of Assyrian queens 31–33, 94, 95, 138, 153
- Salamis 66, 153, 154, 158, 160, 168, 179, 192
'triple flower' 111, 112, 113
Tubb, Jonathan 57
Tutankhamun 12, 12, 19, 61, 159, 160, 160
Tyre 55, 56, 57, 58, 64, 105, 192, 193

Ugarit (Ras Shamra) 10, 12, 58, 114, 159, 160
'Ugly Sister' 11, 122–23, 123, 150
'Unusually Shaped Ivories' 72, 72, 102, 172

Westmacott, Richard 25
Wicke, Dirk 131
'wig and wing' ivories 104, 105, 106–8, 111
- bridle harnesses 182
- fan handles 177
Winter, Irene 104, 175
'woman at the window' motif 36, 79, 80, 81
- furniture panels 16, 37, 38, 39, 130–31, 130
- Syro-Phoenician 105, 130–31, 189, 190
- 'wig and wing' ivories 106, 107, 107
Woolley, Leonard 26
writing boards 29, 30

Yaba, Queen 32, 33, 94, 193

Zinjirli (Sam'al) 129, 131, 155, 165
- column bases 120, 127, 188
- frontlets 182, 182
- furniture elements 154, 170, 170, 171–72, 192
- pottery mould 108, 125
- 'round-cheeked and ringletted' ivories 188
- sculptural styles 159